The
PIGEON TRAINER *and the*
BIRMINGHAM ROLLER

John Bender

VENDERA
PUBLISHING

Vendera Publishing

Interior Design by Naomi Middleton
www.scribefreelance.com

Cover Design: Molly Burnside
www.crosssidedesigns.com

Edited by Richard Dalglish

ISBN: 978-1-936307-53-1

Printed in the United States of America

CONTENTS

INTRODUCTION...5

PART ONE: How It All Began.....................................7

   My First Roller Pigeon.. 17

   The Library Discovery 19

   Meeting Bill Berry 21

   Dave Staebler.. 25

   Jack Shaw 29

   Berle Adams 31

   Joe Roe.. 33

   George Abner 39

   My First Flying Competition................................. 41

   Carl Hardesty 44

   Roller World Cup Trophy 50

   The Roller Video Project 51

   John "Duck" Dadosky.. 52

   Roy Thayer 55

   Building the World Cup Team 57

   1994 World Fly.. 61

   1994 World Team Bird Information 67

   1995 World Cup Competition............................... 69

PART TWO: The Ins and Outs of Roller Care.................... 72

   Preparing Your Birds for Competition (Week by Week) 77

   Preparation for Fly Day.. 87

PART THREE: Breeding Pigeons................................... 103

   Breeding a Family of Rollers written by Ken Easley........................ 124

PART FOUR: Pigeon Housing..................................... 193

PART FIVE: General Care.. 219

    Champion Performers 240

    Pondering Possible Rollers in The Future........................ 244

    A History of Pigeons 247

    On the Relationship of Pigeons and Primates:
    A Journey in Science and History written by Ben J Novak 248

    Birmingham Roller Origins written by Tom Monson...................... 269

ABOUT THE AUTHOR... 285

INTRODUCTION

Welcome to *The Pigeon Trainer & The Birmingham Roller*, a one-of-a-kind book that explains my thoughts on aspects of the art of roller pigeon flying. My name is John Bender. I held the rolling pigeon World Champion title in 1994 along with a second place in the North Central East Subregion that year. Prior to that, in 1993, I took 10th in the World Cup finals and first place in the North Central East Subregion. These were all based on 20-bird flying competitions.

I also attained second place in 1992 in the All Ohio State fly, first place for eight years in a row in local flying competitions from 1987 to 1994, and again in 1996. These wins were all in eleven-bird flying competitions.

I by no means know everything there is to know about roller pigeons. But what I would like to do is share with you as a new roller fancier the basic roller keeping principles and flying techniques that will help you enjoy and understand your birds better. My aim with this book is to save you some time in your journey towards getting a good team of rollers in the air. Plus some tips on competing if you decide to. As with most subjects pertaining to rollers there is more than one way to approach it with a favorable outcome.

The following information is my approach gathered from years of raising and flying pigeons, and it has worked out very well for me. To my advanced roller pigeon fancier friends, I hope that you will enjoy and find something useful in this book.

To this day, I've had a very enjoyable journey with roller pigeons. But my journey started many years earlier, when, as a child, a fascination with birds, specifically pigeons, consumed me.

Therefore, to give you the best possible advice on raising pigeons, I feel it best if this book begins with my own story, serving as part autobiography, so that you understand my journey from child to world champion roller pigeon flyer. I want to help you reconnect to your own story, therefore mine is very detailed. If you wish to skip ahead and get straight to the "how-to's" of roller pigeons, that is completely fine. But if you want to know how I developed my approach to pigeon training, it begins in my childhood. Read on to discover why my love for pigeons has lasted over 50 years. And so the story begins ...

PART ONE
— *How It All Began* —

I was born and raised in a little Appalachian river town by the name of Portsmouth in Southern Ohio, just a few miles from where Leonard Slye, better known as Roy Rogers, lived as a boy. While Roy Rogers is mostly known as a singing cowboy star of the 40s and 50s, he was also a pigeon fancier. The old pigeon men from our area would tell me about Roy raising pigeons "just up the road on Duck Run."

There were many pigeon fanciers to visit in my youth, and boundless racing homer and roller pigeons in the city and county side of Portsmouth. Portsmouth was a pigeon haven with many varieties. I was inquisitive and tried to visit any loft I saw. Most fanciers were very friendly to me and would show me around and answer any questions I might have.

My fascination with birds actually started at the early age of six when my father brought home a cardinal he had caught one day in the horse barn. I was so intrigued with the bird that my dad called me Red Bird for the rest of his life, which was fitting, having been blessed with a head of fire-red locks.

As much as I was fascinated by the cardinal, I was equally intrigued with the fact that my father was able to catch a bird. So my mother showed me how to make a trap to catch and observe birds. She also bought me a parakeet. From that moment on, I was all about parakeets and any wild bird I could catch.

My great adventure with pigeons began at eight when I was having a conversation with my grandfather about birds. I was explaining to him how much I enjoyed the flight of birds and how I flew my parakeets at home in the house. I mentioned to him how I would enjoy releasing them outside to fly if they would come back. His reply changed my life forever.

He said, "You know, John, there is a bird called a pigeon that you could do that very thing with."

I excitedly asked a few more questions about them and then went straight to my mother to tell her the great news. "Mom, I must see these birds. This would be the greatest thing if I could do this."

"The next time we go to the city I will show you one," she said.

We lived in the country on the outskirts of town, but we visited the city now and then. Once in the city, my mom started pointing out the common pigeons to me. There were a lot of them in the city back in those days, way more compared to what there is now, over 50 years later. We soon saw a small group of pigeons down on the ground. She pulled the car over to the side so I could get a better look. They were bigger than I had expected, and the coloring on the birds was very interesting too.

They were the common colors that I know today as that of the wild rock doves, blue check, and blue bar patterns. They were beautiful to me. Oh, how I wanted one. I was surprised at how close they would let me get to them. All other birds I had tried to approach would fly away before this point. After a few futile attempts at grabbing one, I gave up and we left.

From that moment on, I had to have one and always looked for them on our visits to the city. A few months later my parents divorced and my mom, brothers, sister and I moved to the city. We stayed with my grandmother. When you are used to the country and move to the city, it's somewhat of a culture shock. The city smells were of blacktop parking lots and old musty buildings. Gone were the smells of fresh apples clinging to the trees, freshly mowed grass, and wonderful scents of springtime.

I thought the city was horrible, and all the people were much different from "country folk." Their mannerisms made it hard to get used to living there. They were everywhere. I called them "city slickers." I probably picked that term up from one of the old men my father would introduce me to in the country.

Eventually, I grew comfortable with city life, and I started striking out on my own as my confidence grew. I would explore the alleys and streets of my new neighborhood, always looking for birds.

By now I had turned nine, and one of my greatest discoveries was the feed store a couple blocks down the street. They had baby chickens and ducks in the display window area. I'd stand outside for an eternity watching them huddle under the heat light. It reminded me of my past in the country.

I soon started going inside the feed store, and when no one was looking I would reach over the divider and pick one up to pet it a little. I would try to do this quickly and put it back, because I knew this would probably get me into trouble. As I left, I knew I would be back to this place every chance I could.

One day while at my grandmother's apartment I was gazing out the window at a tall white building across the street. The building had some pigeons on the window ledges, and to my surprise, a white self pigeon landed. Later, a black self landed. For those new to pigeons, a self is a solid colored pigeon, whether all white, all black, all red, or all blue. A self can be many colors, but one has to be that color all over to be a self.

Once the black self came in and landed on the ledge next to the white one, I thought these two were the most beautiful birds I had ever seen. I stared at them for the longest time through my grandmother's window. If only I could get my hands on them.

Next to my grandmother's apartment was the barber shop. The barber had a gravel parking lot out back for his customers. I noticed that pigeons would land there and peck around. I thought it might be possible to trap one of these birds with a box trap.

So I got a wooden box from my grandmother's back porch that she kept for saving old pop bottles. I bought some kite string that would give me plenty of distance to hide myself, and I also grabbed a ruler to prop it up with. I tied the string to the bottom for pulling to release the box to drop. I then propped the box up with the ruler to allow the pigeons to go under. Then I threw bread under the box to entice them in. But alas, no pigeons took the bait.

As the days passed, more pigeons came and more opportunities arose for me to try to capture one. After many failed attempts to catch a pigeon (mostly because the box was a little too light and wild pigeons were so quick and alert), a white pigeon with little brown and black marks over its body landed by the box. It seemed a little smaller than most that had been coming around. Looking back, it was a young light tortoise grizzle pigeon not too long out of the nest. I nervously held the string and crossed my fingers. "Come on buddy. Go for the bread."

He pecked around the box and seemed to be uninterested in the bread. I was dying from anticipation. Finally he eyed the bread and went for it. I jerked the string as fast as I could. Yes! I just caught my first pigeon!

The first thing I did was to clip its wings so it couldn't fly away. I was shown how to do this feat without hurting or injuring a bird back when I was taming one of my old parakeets. Next, I went to the feed store to ask what to feed a pigeon.

The feed store man said, "Pigeon feed," and laughed. "Come here, son, and I will show you some." He scooped up a handful and said, "How much do you want?"

"Can I get a dollar's worth?" I asked.

"Sure," he replied. "I'll fix you right up. But you will need some grit too. Pigeons gotta have it. You won't need as much as the feed. Just give them a little once in a while and they will do fine."

When I got back home, I fed my pigeon feed and water. With his wings high and pecking fast, he got his belly full. I was in awe of how he drank. This bird didn't drink like the other birds I've had. I thought he drank water like our old country horse, Smokey.

I played with my new pigeon constantly and would even take it over to the local park to watch it walk around in the grass. This little pigeon was a great friend to me. I'd forgotten all about flying this pigeon. My desire for one of these great birds was fulfilled for the moment.

A few months later my mother found us a new place to live. She found a small, white house with a very small yard on the corner of an alley. The new place was in the east end of the city. I didn't mind this move. I was glad to see us getting a new start. I looked forward to my own room and having a grassy yard area to play with my pigeon.

Exploring the alley one day I found an old dog house that was set out to be thrown away. I thought it would make a better place to keep my pigeon. He would have a lot more room compared to the orange crate he was in now.

After a little struggle, my brother Greg and I loaded it on our wagon and got it back to the house. I put in food and water, set my bird in, and propped some wire in front of the hole with a brick. Things went well with my new setup.

Every afternoon after a hard day at school I would run home and get the bird out for some holding and talking. Sometimes we would play pirates and he could be my talking parrot. He was good about staying on my shoulder. He was a pretty calm bird and didn't get too excited. We did this every day for some time. Life was good, until one day I came home and he was gone. I was devastated. I never did find out what happened to my bird. I had no choice but to move on.

Many days after my loss, I walked to the feed store to pet the baby chicks in the window. While crossing the alley I saw a beautiful black and white splash pigeon. I got as close as I could, but he flew away, right into an open storage door at the back of one of the buildings. I ran in, looked around, but couldn't tell where he went. The building was full of boxes on wooden pallets. I thought if I could climb up on some of the boxes I could spot the black and white pigeon.

I started climbing and looking all around in case I was in the wrong spot. I knew I would have to corner him to keep him from flying back out the door. Then a man yelled in a firm voice, "Hey kid, what are you doing up there?"

"Well, sir, this pigeon was in the alley and I was trying to catch it. He flew right in here. I know he is in here somewhere."

"Okay, but make it quick. You're not allowed in here and I have to close up."

I was glad but scared at the same time. Could I find the bird? Would the man get mad at me before I do and run me out? "I'm going for it," I thought. As fast as I could, I went up and down all the stacks, but never found the bird. With my head hanging low, I went back out into the alley towards the feed store.

Going into the feed store, I was glad to see the baby chicks still there. Everyone seemed busy and were not paying any attention to me. So, I quickly slipped my arm over the divider and snatched up a chick. He was a beautiful little black and yellow chick. After a while, I looked around to make sure it was okay to reach over and put him back. But for some reason I couldn't do it. I was crushed from losing my pigeon, so I did the unthinkable to ease my pain. I slipped him into my pants pocket and started towards the door while trying to act normal, wondering if anyone had seen me. Luckily, no one said anything and I made it outside.

I wanted to get him out of my pocket as soon as possible. My pants were tight and I hoped they didn't squeeze him to death before I got him out. I went into the alley and out of sight. I reached in and gently pulled him out. He was just fine. About halfway home it dawned on me what I had done. I had stolen a baby chick. I had never stolen anything before. I knew that if my mother found out she would make me bring the baby chick back plus I'd receive a whoopin'. I couldn't tell her. I decided it would have to be a secret between me and the chick.

The new chick was fun to play with. I had been feeding the chick some of my old pigeon feed and he seemed to be doing just fine. While letting him peck around in the grass after eating, he spotted a little red worm by the edge of the doghouse. He ran right up and ate it as fast as he could.

"Oh, you like worms? I never thought of that. I'll get you some more."

After the little guy had several, I noticed he wasn't acting right. The worms were killing him, and there wasn't anything I could do about it. I soon learned that he was just too small and fragile to eat live worms. I was sad to see him go, but I learned a big lesson that day. I should have never taken the chick without paying for it. I would continue to go back to the feed store, but never to steal a chick again.

Not long after that day, my mother decided to visit one of my aunts in town. I was glad to see my cousin Rodney. Rodney and I went out back to play, and I noticed that he had an 8 by 8 pigeon pen with a fight pen on the outside full of common pigeons.

Rodney had caught them all at night in some of the condemned buildings in the city.

"Oh, you have to take me with you and show me. I want to catch some too."

"Sure, we'll go tomorrow night."

The next night, I showed up about an hour before dark. Rodney was ready with a burlap feed sack and a flashlight. As we walked, he gave me instructions on what to do when we got there.

Finally we reached a giant red brick apartment building about four stories high with the windows all broken out. The front door had a white sign on it that said it was condemned and unlawful to enter. We slipped in and pushed the door closed so no one would notice. It was almost dark, but we could still see fairly well. You could tell that some of the local winos had been sleeping in the building. Old blankets and trash from food were lying everywhere. The building smelled musty and damp, which reminded me of the smell of the city when we first moved here. The smell of lots of old condemned buildings in town had a huge impact on me. Now I knew why the city smelled so bad.

The birds we were after were on the top two floors, which were dangerous floors. The ceiling leaked water that trickled down through the floors, causing them to rot away. Rodney told me to stay close to the walls, away from the center of the floors, in order to stay safe. After climbing a few flights of stairs, I understood why. The center of the floors were just big holes. You could see down through them to the lower floors.

Some pigeons flew out broken windows when they heard us coming, so he reminded me to stay quiet. I could see feathers, eggshells, and a few dead pigeons lying on what was left of the floors.

Rodney propped up an old chair next to the wall and had me hold the burlap bag and shine the light up towards the ceiling so that he could see as he began reaching into holes in between the floor joists of the ceiling. It was the luck of the draw, because sometimes you'd find a bird, sometimes not. Tonight we weren't having much luck.

"We will have to come back another night," he said.

"Let me give it a try."

Unfortunately, I couldn't feel anything. But on my second try, I felt a little fat squeaker and pulled him out. It was a little silver pigeon that looked to be about two weeks old. We decided to leave after our find since I still had a long walk home in the dark.

On our way home, Rodney told me that this bird was too young to eat on its own and I would have to feed it by hand. When we got to his house he showed me how to open the young bird's mouth to put feed in. After a few weeks of hand feeding, the young bird was eating and drinking on its own. He turned into an ash red bar self.

After learning the new method to catch pigeons, it didn't take long until I had an entire box of pigeons of my own, which meant that I needed more space to cage them. So I took an old kitchen cabinet, set it up on legs, and added some wire in the front. My plan was to start releasing them once they'd gotten used to their new home.

One night, I decided to take my brother Greg along with me to catch more pigeons. It was a condemned building I had been in before. After we dodged the rotten steps and climbed to the second floor, we caught a few squeakers that were big enough to hand raise and a couple of adults. I reached in between another joist and felt a big one. I could not see it, but I grabbed it by one of its wings and pulled it towards me. It was putting up a good fight, but Greg had the sack ready.

After I got it out of the hole, we could see it was solid white and one of the biggest pigeons we had ever seen in our lives. Its eyes were all black with orange circles around them. It weighed around three pounds and looked as big as a duck. After this catch, we decided to give up the hunt early so we could get home and mess with this big guy.

After we returned home, we noticed that the weight of the birds had caused the loss of two of the squabs. I hated losing the birds and knew to be more careful in the future.

After this magnificent find, I decided that I would clip his wings so there would be no chance of losing him. It didn't take long for word to get around, and soon other kids would come around to see the "giant pigeon." It was a very memorable time.

Fifty years later, Greg and I still talk about the night we caught the giant white pigeon. It was probably a Giant Runt. In later years I've seen pictures of Giant Runts that looked like the bird we caught.

Not long after, I started releasing my birds. Surprisingly, they were coming back. I was finally reaching my dreams of having birds you can release that will come home. On the days I let them out, I would just leave the door open and they would be in by dark. Grandpa was right; pigeons will come back after you let them go.

About a week after letting my pigeons out on their own, a solid black showed up on the top of the neighbor's house. He was beautiful. When the sunlight hit him, you could see green and purple colors in his neck. I thought he might be the same bird I used to watch from my grandmother's window. He would land and watch my birds and then fly away after they came in for the night.

One day I went out to feed the birds, and there was the beautiful black on my pigeon pen. As I got close to him he flew away. When I released my pigeons he would hang around on the house across the street and leave again as they came in for the night. He did the same thing every day. I really wanted that one, because I had no black pigeons at the time.

One day I decided to try to trick the black. Instead of letting my birds out, I put a piece of wire in my pen as a divider and had all the pigeons to one side. I opened the door but my birds could not get out because of the divider. In a little while the black came down to investigate. He looked in the open door and walked right in. I hurried and closed it before he figured out it was a trap. That was another great pigeon day for me.

This was a very robust bird and a very shiny black, not the dull black that you see in most pigeons. He liked to chase some of the other birds around. He would strut and coo and fan his tail with a little hop. After a couple of days I thought I would release him with my other birds. By dark, all of my birds were inside the loft but the shiny black. I never saw him again.

Not long after losing the shiny black, we moved again. This

place had a bigger house and a bigger backyard. I thought I would like it here. Once we got settled into our new house, I decided to build a bigger bird house. I needed materials, so I found a couple of old wood pallets that local businesses would toss out to be hauled off by the garbage trucks. I took them home and slowly pried them apart. It was a lot of work but would be worth it, because I was going to build a big pigeon pen this time.

I ended up with something I could be happy with, a 4-foot by 4-foot square and five-foot-tall loft with wire on the front top half and a nailed tarp above the wire I could roll up for sun on nice days and drop for bad weather. I also hung a couple of orange crates on the wall to make nests for the birds. My pigeons looked good in their new home. Though I didn't know it, I was about to move into new territory: roller pigeons.

— *My First Roller Pigeon* —

One day while taking a shortcut through a yard, I noticed a well-built loft with some pretty pigeons in it. I went up to get a better look at the pigeons and noticed they were well kept and had little silver bands on their legs. Little did I know my city was full of roller pigeon fanciers every few blocks.

I knocked on the door of this house and a young man named Bobby Nagle answered the door. He was very nice to show me around and answer any questions I had about his pigeons. This was the moment I first found out about roller pigeons, and again my life changed forever. I wanted my own roller pigeons. Mr. Nagle said he would sell me a pair for four dollars.

I rounded up enough money to buy a pair and was now a roller fancier. I bought a red grizzle barred cock and a red checkered white flighted hen. I later named the cock "Big Dude." This was mostly because he could whip any other pigeon that gave him a problem.

I would return to Mr. Nagle's house from time to time and buy more pigeons. I finally had several in the loft and thought how much prettier they were than the wild ones I had been keeping.

I was raising a few young birds and flying everything, even the breeders. One day I noticed a wild dove building a nest in the tree next door. The wild doves in our area are called mourning doves. They are light brown with narrow tails and some checking in the wings. I would look for the nest building dove every day to see how the progress was coming and noticed the bird had finally settled in. I figured it had laid eggs.

I climbed up to the nest and found what I was looking for. Only one egg; she hadn't laid the second one yet. I had a pair of rollers that had laid at the same time and thought I'd see if I could raise the dove under them. I tossed both eggs from the rollers to make sure the little dove would have a better chance in the nest not having to compete for food with the larger roller youngster.

I was very excited to see if the dove would hatch out. The little guy finally hatched. It had black skin and yellow down. Down is first born fuzz to help keep it warm. All my young pigeons had yellow skin, so it was a surprise to see the black skin on the young dove.

The roller pair I had put the dove egg under were great parents to the little guy. He grew fast and strong. After he feathered out to where he could almost fly, he would jump out of the nest when I would go to check on him. At first he would sit in the nest very still, like he was invisible. But, once he realized I could see him, he would make a wild dash out of the nest. I would pick him up and put him back in the nest before I went back in the house.

Unfortunately, that only lasted a couple of days; he jumped out of the nest once on his own, and one of the other cocks in the loft killed him on the floor. I was very sad but thought I might try it again sometime if I could find another dove nest.

— The Library Discovery —

A few days later I thought I might go to the library to see if they had any books on pigeons and doves. I spent some time sitting in the aisle looking through every book I could find. While I was wandering around the library, I noticed a glass dome with a bird inside it. There was a little sign made from paper in front of it that read, *Extinct Passenger Pigeon Shot on Offnere Street Hill in Portsmouth in 1882.*

I was fascinated with the bird. I thought it looked a lot like the mourning dove I had tried to raise, but larger than a dove and longer than my roller pigeons. It was a beautiful pigeon, with red on his breast like a robin and the rest marked like a mourning dove. I was so fascinated that I decided to look for a book about the now extinct passenger pigeon. There was plenty of information on these birds from the past. This now-extinct bird once numbered in the billions.

The birds migrated from Canada along the east coast, going south down and around as far as Texas. The sky would darken for hours when these numerous birds flew over during migration. There were thought to be more passenger pigeons on earth than all other birds combined. The cause for their extinction expressed by many varied from deforestation to being dumb, with the most obvious explanation to me being that they were hunted to extinction for their meat and feathers.

A great industry was created by selling their feathers, which was second to goose in the feather market. The meat also was a profitable endeavor; it was pickled, smoked, or salted and packed in barrels to be shipped. From the 1800s to the early 1900s, human participation in hard unregulated hunting pretty much brought them to their doom. They were trapping them by the thousands at a time, like commercial fisherman do today.

By September 1, 1914, the last known passenger pigeon, Martha, was gone. Her mate, George, had passed away four years earlier. I was looking at one of these great pigeons in front of me thinking I would never be able to see them in the wild for myself. In one hundred years, one of the earth's most common birds, whose fossils date back 100,000 years, were gone.

I was sad knowing they were wiped from the planet. My mind ran wild with thoughts of them in my own loft. Then I had a great thought. I would make more by crossing the mourning doves raised under my rollers in individual nesting, to bring back a pigeon that looked very close to the extinct bird. If I did it right, with a little planning, I could do it, I thought. So I went to a man named Bill Berry, a veteran pigeon fancier.

— Meeting Bill Berry —

I met Bill Berry through my cousin Rodney. Bill was a custodian and basketball coach at our local high school, but more importantly, he was also in the Portsmouth Pigeon Club.

Bill was a very nice gentleman, who gave us a tour of his loft and birds and then his garage, where he kept his breeders and young birds. He gave us this same tour multiple times and always got a big chuckle out of handing us a young bird out of the nest with its rear facing you as you held it, because a young bird pulled out of the nest will soon relieve itself. So always be aware of which way the rear is facing. Over the years, Bill would do this to people and get the biggest laugh when it went the way he had planned.

Bill was the only guy I'd ever met who watched his birds fly from a lawn chair. There always seemed to be somebody around in one of Bill's lawn chairs with Bill, all leaned back watching and talking about rollers.

Bill Berry was a great promoter of rollers in Portsmouth, and any time you would mention roller pigeons, people would ask if you knew him. He was always helping somebody get started with rollers or helping some rollers find a home. He would call up all the local boys when he had a bunch of birds he thought we would be interested in.

Once, Bill called me to come over to his house to see some birds that he had from a roller fancier going out of the pigeon hobby. When I arrived, my friend Steve Gambill was waiting too. While we waited for Bill to come outside we had some time to look at the birds. There were about 30 of them, average colors like blues and reds both in check and bar. I noticed a beautiful red mottle. He was a rich red recessive with the white feathers on his wings spread out very nicely, not many of them close to each other. He also had white flights.

Soon, three other neighborhood boys came into Bill's yard. One of the boys spotted the red mottle and said he wanted it. But I had dibs on the bird. Since we were not good friends, a heated argument ensued. It had just started when Bill came out and asked, "What in the world are you guys arguing about?"

After calming us down and sorting out the problem, he decided to settle the argument with a coin toss. I thought for sure I would lose the red mottle in the toss. To my surprise I won the toss! Bill divided the remaining birds with the other boys and I had a great ride home on my bike with my new roller.

I found many rollermen's lofts in the city, but I spent more time at Bill's house than any other. He was a true mentor. One day during one of my visits I asked Bill his opinion of my thoughts on bringing back the passenger pigeon or at least one that looked like it. I told him about the mounted bird at the library and my plans for breeding a mourning dove with a pigeon to get the body size similar to the original passenger pigeon, probably needing to breed back into one side or the other a couple of times to try to get the body type and color locked in.

"Do you think it will work, Bill?"

"Well, John," he replied as he rubbed his forehead. "If memory serves me right, guys I've talked to that have bred pigeons to doves tell me that you get the mule effect from the offspring."

Seeing that I was puzzled, he added, "The mule effect meaning you will not be able to breed from the offspring of the crossbreeding of the two birds. Just like when you cross a horse and a donkey you cannot breed from their offspring, the mule."

"Are you sure, Bill?"

"I'm pretty sure that's what they said, John."

What a big letdown. I thought I was going to help bring back the passenger pigeon, but my big plans were dashed. I was crushed. After that day, I never mentioned them again, But I was still a big fan of the 1882 mounted bird at the library, which I would stop in and check on from time to time over the years.

1882 Passenger pigeon: Portsmouth Library

*Bill Berry and his son Jim Bob Berry in front of the
pigeon loft, June 1964.*

Bill was always very helpful in my early years with rollers. He would
show me how to take care of the birds, how to check eggs for fertility,
what to feed them, and how to medicate them if they needed it. Bill
loved to tell stories about the old bird guys he was around when he

was a boy in the city. He also liked talking about bird guys of the times like Bill Pensom, Charles Albaugh, Paul Bradford, Carl Silvey, Paul Vaughn, Stan Plona, Frank Lavin, and many others that he admired.

Bill was a flyer, and when you stopped by he would always release the birds. He loved deep birds and always had one or two a year that would go several hundred feet without hitting the ground. Eventually fate would catch up with the extremely deep ones. Like most roller flyers, you would see one roll down now and then at his house. When a roller would hit the ground Bill would holler out, "You big dummy" and shake his head. He always hated to lose a deep one.

B ecause of Bill, I made many friends in the roller community. In my early teens, Bill told me about a man named David Staebler, who wanted to start a 4-H pigeon club for local youth. David was a local policeman and roller enthusiast. He took a half dozen of us down to the Portsmouth Pigeon club. It was the first time we had ever been to the clubhouse.

Before the clubhouse was built in 1953, club members would take turns having meetings at their homes. There was a lot of debating on what the name of the club would be prior to the members building the clubhouse. It was a pretty even split between the Scioto Valley Pigeon Club and the Portsmouth Pigeon club.

A member by the name of Grant Daniels had a stone block engraved without the others knowing. Grant raised Oriental frills and Domestic flights and when it came to his frills he was a top national judge. When the blocks were being laid for the club, he had his engraved block placed without the others knowing. From then on the club was called the Portsmouth Pigeon Club.

The clubhouse had a storage room for show cages with a restroom and concession-type kitchen attached to a large meeting room with mounted animals on the walls, including squirrels, a raccoon, and a few other critters. It was a pretty neat place for a kid, and we were all glad to be involved in the clubhouse with our newly directed pigeon endeavors.

Mr. Stabler said he would show us how to have a meeting and would let us name our group whatever we wanted, and we would learn a lot about showing rollers. Back then (around 1971-1972) all the rollermen in the club were very much into showing rollers. They spoke of dual-purpose birds, which meant they wanted them to perform well in the air plus do well at the shows.

Mr. Stabler's new group of kids voted me in as president. After a little head scratching on what we wanted to call our new kids club, we voted to call our club the "4-H Pro Flyers." Looking back, I don't remember ever talking about flying; mostly show and general care were the topics.

We always liked seeing our 4-H club mentioned in the

newspaper when we had our meetings. Dave was a great mentor, serious about the meetings and our discussions about rollers. He explained everything we needed to know about showing our rollers. We learned how to make them look more attractive by cleaning their bands and rubbing a little mineral oil or Vaseline on the bird's beak and feet before a show.

He also reminded us that name bands had to be taped over so the judge would not have any idea who the birds belonged to. We learned about points taken off for birds with odd eyes or bull eyes. We learned about how a bird's keel should tuck into the vent bones, and we talked about feather quality like hard and soft feathers. Dave also spoke of back skull feather and cover feather over the rump, compact tails, station, and just about everything we needed to know from the show standard.

After some time, Dave said we were ready for our first show. He set it up at the county fair, with a local rollerman to be the judge. We were very excited and had a great time. By the end of the show, I had won the grand champion prize. A tortoise shell cock and his nest mate (also a tortoise shell) won best opposite sex, which I had given to one of the other boys before the show, a great friend of mine named Mark Delabar.

We were two very happy campers that day. After the roller pigeon show, we got to be in the 4-H parade at the fair. All the guys had a great time and we made some great memories.

Dave also set us up with a national roller show to attend. Our local Portsmouth club would be sponsoring the show. The 4-H boys would be allowed to gather the birds up for the judges as they were needed. We were also in charge of watering and feeding them. We had never seen so many rollers in one place. There were over 1,000 roller pigeons at the show that year. One or two did get away from us during our task of taking them to and from the judging area, but the men were very understanding.

A year later Dave moved away and the boys 4-H club was let go. When Dave left, we continued to visit with each other at our houses and do our favorite thing, trading this bird for that bird. We felt like big traders. In fact, all of the boys had the Red Mottle pair at some point. They were a power pair, very beautifully marked. If you had the Red Mottle pair, you were always in a good trading position for just about anything you wanted with the other boys.

We were always wanting another pigeon, and Bill Berry would sell or trade with you for whatever you might be after. Over the years he gave us more birds than we ever had to haggle for. I visited Bill for many years until his passing away. I always enjoyed his company, and in his memory, if one my pigeons rolls to the ground, I always holler, "You big dummy!"

The years of my youth, guided by the likes of Bill and Dave, definitely had an impact on my roller knowledge. Some of us later returned to the clubhouse as adults and helped with the transition to a flying club. We all missed Dave Staebler and brought his name up for many years after he left.

— Jack Shaw —

One day on one of our bicycle journeys, Steve Gambill and I found a new roller pigeon guy. He had a nice cottage with a garage. Attached to the garage was the telltale sign of a pigeon man, with wire cages attached to the garage for pigeons to come outside to enjoy the weather. Some pigeons were outside in the cages.

We had no problem knocking on this guy's door right away. We did it all the time when we found a bird guy. Most of the time it worked, and if our luck prevailed we would end up with a new pigeon.

"What can I do for you boys," he asked as he answered the door. We introduced ourselves, and he told us his name was Jack Shaw.

"Well, Mr. Shaw," I replied, "would you care to show us your pigeons? We have pigeons too."

"Call me Jack," he said before showing us to his garage loft. Jack had most of his garage equipped with several wired sections for old birds, young birds, cocks, and hens. We had walked into a loft full of beautiful roller pigeons. The place was nice and neat with wood shavings on the floor. He was using tuna cans with red bricks like Bill Berry used for watering his rollers. They would place one red brick in front of the can for the pigeon to stand on, and another one on top of the can positioned with just enough room for the pigeons to get a drink. This kept them from getting in to take a bath.

By mentioning that Bill Berry had the same watering setup, we found out that Jack knew Bill too. It was almost impossible to find a roller enthusiast around our area who didn't know Bill. Just like my friendship with Bill, I developed a bond with Jack too. He was fun to visit because we always got to go inside the loft to get a close visit with the pigeons.

Getting a pigeon from Jack was impossible though. He had paid top dollar for most of his breeders, and he valued all of them more than we could afford. He had been swept up in the dual-purpose roller shows of the time. But he did fly his birds regularly.

We would often pull up on our bikes while they were flying. Jack would be lying on the ground watching them. Jack was the only bird flyer that we had seen around Portsmouth that would lie on the ground to watch his birds fly. We thought it odd at the time but have now found it to be a common thing.

Over the years Jack got away from the dual-purpose rollers and now flies strictly flying rollers from the Pensom line. I have had a lot of good visits with Jack over the years, almost 50 years now. He is not as tight with his pigeons as he used to be, ha-ha. In fact, Jack has given me several good birds over the years. To this day we still talk on the phone about once or twice a week about what's going on with our rollers.

— Berle Adams —

Another pigeon man in our area, Berle Adams, had some nice-looking rollers that a kid could get for a good loft cleaning. There is a picture of his loft on page eight in a book called *Roller Digest* by the Pensom Roller Club. (Illustrated in 1967).

Berle lived on the west side of town, 15 miles or so along the old towpath, which is alongside some of the last remnants of the Erie Canal that went through our area. The Erie Canal was started in Cleveland, Ohio, and went for 309 miles to the last lock here in Portsmouth, Ohio, lock number 55.

Once or twice a year I would ride the towpath to Berle's house where I would work in exchange for some pigeons. Mr. Adams used sand on the floor of his loft. He would rake the sand for a time then change it when he thought it was needed. He had nice dowel rod dividers for his loft sections and used box perches for the birds. He also used the old military-type breeding boxes, like the ones used in World War II.

After I scraped the perches, I would shovel out all the old sand and replace it with fresh sand. After I finished, Berle would take me to a section he had for his lesser birds and allow me to pick three. He always had many colors to choose from. I would pick my birds and put them in a brown grocery sack, after I tore some holes in the side of the bag for air. I was always eager to make the long bike rides on the towpath home to see my new birds in my pigeon loft.

Berle's last few years were spent as the president of our pigeon club. Berle Adams had become a part of my childhood pigeon experiences. So, too, had many pigeon kids from around the city. Names dear to my childhood memories include Rodney Cade, Mark Delabar, Steve Gambill, Andy Copley, Johnny Meadows, Henry Reynolds, and Walter Bowman.

We had a lot of rollermen throughout the city to learn from, which was great for all of the young pigeon enthusiasts. Guys like

Bill Berry, Bob Horton, Ray Schaffer, Jack Shaw, Bobby Nagle, Frank Moore, Grant Daniels, and John (Duck) Dadosky to name a few.

It was a pigeon kid's paradise back then. But when I was around 16 years old, I put pigeons aside for almost a decade. When I returned to the hobby, little did I know how much my life would change with Birmingham Rollers. That's also when I made a new friend, Joe Roe.

— *Joe Roe* —

After eight years, memories of my youth brought me back to the pigeon hobby around 1984. Then around 1986-87 I stopped by Bill Berry's house to see if he had any spinning birds to let go. I had already gathered up a few over time but was always looking for another good one. A lot of guys flew their pigeons, but not many had a performer in the group. Good performing rollers were rarely seen, mostly due to more interest in showing rollers. The men just weren't too keen on how to fly, feed, and select rollers for their aerial qualities.

I knew that my best chance for some spinners would be Bill Berry. Unfortunately, he didn't have anything to let go at the time, but he told me there was a guy named Joe Roe who might be able to help me. Joe lived in Wheelersburg, Ohio, a little town about ten miles from Bill's house.

I pulled up to a white house in the curve of an old country road called Hayport Road. It was a nice summer day when I got there. I knocked on the door, and a clean-cut, serious looking, red-headed guy came to the door. I mentioned that Bill Berry had sent me to see if he had any rollers to let go.

He said, "Yeah, Bill called, but as far as letting any birds go, I don't think so."

"Well, then could we go around back and look at your birds," I anxiously asked.

He didn't seem too thrilled about it but nodded.

Joe lived close to the Ohio River in a farming area. He had a cluster of trees out back, fairly close to the loft. While walking me around to the loft, he didn't have much to say. Finally he said, "That's my young birds. Here's my old birds. Over there is the old hen and cock sections."

The whole first experience felt very odd, like he didn't know me, so he didn't like me, and he would rather be doing whatever he was doing before I got there. I thought it would be tough to get a bird from this guy and figured I was wasting my time. Then he said, "I'll fly them for you if you like."

"Sure, that would be great."

After the birds were released and gathered together, I was impressed with how many he was flying. It was the largest group of rollers flying I had ever seen. While most guys were flying 15 to 30 birds at once, this guy was flying 100 or more. The best part was that all of them were rolling. Up to this point, when I stopped at a guy's house I was lucky to see three to five birds spinning in a flock. But here, the sky was falling with rollers.

While we watched the birds, I asked again about purchasing a bird or two. He didn't answer me, he just kept staring out into the sky watching his birds work. After the birds landed, with still no reply, he walked over and grabbed a light red grizzle off the top of one of the fly boxes and handed it to me.

"Here," he said. I was set back a little on how fast this guy could snatch up a loose bird. After realizing what had just happened, I offered to pay for the bird, but he said it was okay. I was thankful and we parted ways.

Eager to find out what I had, I took it home and released it with my birds during the next release. The bird settled at my loft easy, and I watched it fly for a couple weeks. Unfortunately, it was a dud. It flew great, but no roll. Knowing where the good ones still were, I could not resist going back. Each time I did, I noticed Joe was a little nicer and would talk a little more. But there always seemed to be a slight reluctance in his comments. Like he was guarding his knowledge.

I felt like he was evaluating my sincerity each time I stopped by. One of the things I wondered and wanted to know was how he got so many birds to spin like he did. I finally got the courage to ask him. For a short time I wondered if he heard me or just didn't want to answer.

He finally muttered, "It's all in the feed can."

That was a pivotal moment for me as a guy who wanted to watch them roll. He gave me a clue to what he was doing, but it was only a clue. I didn't know for sure what he meant, and he was reluctant to say more. I could see that this pigeon guy knew things that others didn't, and I knew it would take some work and time to get it out of him.

Pushing for more on the next visit, I asked if he would elaborate a little more on his statement from my last visit.

Finally, he began to open up—or so I thought.

"Sure," he replied. "Along with flying, the amount of feed makes a big difference on their frequency of performance."

I waited, thinking he would go into how much feed to give them, but he stopped short of that. I figured it was best to let it go until another day.

Showing rollers came up in conversation on another one of my visits. Joe told me that was how he got into rollers. Before that, he had started with wild common pigeons he caught in the old buildings in the city when he was around eight years old, like I had. Later on in life, after he had married, he bought some show rollers for him and his son to have something to do together. His son lost interest, so Joe took charge of them and decided to fly them out to see if they could perform.

After flying them and not being happy with the results, he started searching for strictly flying rollers. Joe explained to me that show rollers had the wrong body type for proper spinning. They were twice the size of a flying roller and could not roll like pigeons that had been bred just for their performing abilities.

Joe shared that he had started his particular group of birds from a Pensom pair of rollers, white cock and a black flight hen. He purchased the birds from Ray Schaffer, who had gotten them directly from Bill Pensom. The pair in turn produced a lavender hen and a red grizzle cock that he was very fond of. He said that both birds were great; the hen had a little extra speed in the rotation and would show a dime-sized hole from the side view.

Later on, Joe said he went out to search for new blood to incorporate into his stock. He had found a blue bar and a black self that suited him, and that's how he started the line of birds he was flying for me that day. I noticed over the years he called that line of birds his old blacks regardless of what color they were. I was pleased to see that the more I came around to visit, the less reluctant he seemed in sharing his knowledge.

The more he talked of roller pigeons, the more impressed I was with his knowledge. He discussed things concerning rollers that I had never heard before, like kitting, breaking together, tightness in the spin, velocity, control, and wing placement. I was excited to have found someone who knew so much about roller pigeons and how to get the most beautiful work out of them.

From then on, I made it over to Joe's house at least once a week to ask questions and try to talk him out of one of his birds. Most of the time I would leave with nothing but a headache from trying to understand and remember his replies to my questions. In all our conversations during our competition years, he still would never mention (and I decided not to ask) what and how much he was feeding his birds to get so much work from his performing pigeons. I figured with all the information he shared with me on performing rollers, it would remain a mystery, and I would never ask.

Still, I will always appreciate our time together. He was never much on bragging on his birds. Most of the time he would refer to them as nothing but junk. But I knew he knew he had some great roller pigeons.

Now and then one would roll to the ground, and he would dispose of it as soon as he could get his hands on it. I would try to get to the birds before he could do away with them and try to talk him out of it, normally failing. He finally got tired of me nagging him for his roll-downs and would let me have them. I would take them home and settle them to my loft and fly them. Sometimes they would roll down and sometimes they didn't.

One day Joe stopped by to visit me, so I released my birds. That day I flew almost every one of the birds I had gotten from Joe, and every one of them rolled down. We never got to watch them fly and perform because they were all too rattled to go back up.

Joe said, "Now do you see, John, why roll-downs are useless? You can't fly or breed from roll-downs."

Another lesson learned from Joe. From then on I never kept a roll-down or bred from a bumper.

On observing Joe on my visits I noticed he never looked down when his birds were flying. He was always very studious of them and rarely said anything unless I asked him a question. But this particular day, he asked me if I could pick the best bird in the group. They all looked good to me, performing as they were. It had never occurred to me that one of them was the best one.

"I can't tell, they all look great to me."

"When you go to a roller flyer's house, always look for his best bird in the air. You never know, you might be able to talk the guy out of it. What if his birds land, and he says, John pick you out a bird to take home? What then?"

That statement caused me to think about a roller pigeon's performance individually. Yes, I would want the best one, but how to pick it for sure, I didn't know. On a similar visit, I asked about one of the birds that came out of the mob of birds he was flying, really spinning nice.

He responded by asking if I could see the position of the wings when it was rolling.

"Wing position? How can you see the wing position?"

"With the velocity of the performance, the bird will show the optical illusion of a pattern," Joe replied. "But you have to catch them flying away or flying towards you to see it. If you can catch it performing at about a 45-degree angle, it works out best."

He then very patiently explained to me the pattern styles from axle to tight H. I tried to see the patterns that day, to no avail, and left again with another terrific headache.

After about a week of flying my birds, waiting for one of them to show me a pattern, I finally saw what he was talking about. I couldn't wait to call him and let him know I was seeing high and low X's from my bird's performances. From that moment on, I was always looking for the fast birds with control that had the highest wing placement.

One day while at Joe's, I saw a nice deep spinner that had some good velocity roll out of the mob of over 100 birds. It was frequent and had high wing placement, with the performing depth of around

30 feet. I locked my eyes on the bird for the entire flight, which was very difficult in a mob fly of so many. Once in a while I would lose the bird in the mix of the others but would pick it back up again when it rolled. It seemed to take forever for the pigeons to land, and all along I was trying not to lose it in the mob of birds.

Once they fluttered down onto the loft, I noticed it was a beautiful ash red bar with white flights and some white on the head, with a nice white streak down the front of the bird's neck. When it turned around I saw that it had a full white wing on one side. It was the prettiest red bar odd side I had ever seen.

"Joe, what do you want for that bird?"

"I don't know if I want to get rid of it. That's a really good one."

"If you ever do, I would like to buy that one."

When the birds trapped in, he walked over and reached in and grabbed the red bar odd side. He handled it for a little bit, then said, "Here, you can have him."

I offered to pay for him for the bird, but Joe would never take any money.

I felt like I finally had a good bird. As time went on and our friendship grew, I was able to get about whatever bird I was after from Joe. When we visited we always talked of body structure, big versus small birds, the keel, flight feathers, chest width, and other things as it pertained to the best performers we saw and could examine. I learned through handling and studying the best performing birds over time, the best body type will reveal itself to you if you are observant.

Joe was a great mentor. Looking back, I realized that all those headaches were worth it, because Joe was teaching me to see what he saw, but with my own eyes.

— *George Abner* —

One day on a visit to Joe's house, I mentioned I had seen a certain color of roller in a magazine that I had never seen before called a blue lace roller. Joe said he had a roller pigeon friend named George Abner who had some lace birds a few miles down the road.

After a quick call to George, we were on our way for a visit. George had the largest loft I had ever seen. It was a large building with many sections inside to house his many birds. Upon first glance, I would guess that he had 300 to 400 roller pigeons.

That day, George released close to 200 flyers for us to watch. He had some good working birds and a few H or better in style patterns in his mob. After flying, we viewed some blue lace birds he had set aside for me to choose a pair from. They were very attractive birds, a light powder blue with each feather trimmed in black.

I didn't know anything about blue lace birds, but George assured me that they were all good working birds started by a rollerman named Roger Baker. The story goes that Baker had some good rollers and had bred a couple of black selfs together and had a mutation in the color of one of the offspring. By breeding it to black pigeons he started the blue lace color in rollers.

I purchased a pair of birds, then took them home to settle them both. I had to see if they had any roll in them, and it didn't take long to see that I had made a good choice because the cock and hen both rolled to suit me. The cock was around 30 feet, and the hen was 15 to 20 feet.

After our initial visit, I knew that George was a knowledgeable rollerman. He would (and still does) drop by to talk rollers. I eventually found out that both Joe and George were in a national roller club called the I.R.A., the International Roller Association. The club was strictly flyers. I had never heard of the club. I was in the U.R.C. at the time, the United Roller Club. They talked mostly about showing rollers.

Not long after, I joined the N.B.R.C., the National Birmingham Roller Club. They were also a flying roller club. Joe also became a member, and later we joined the Piedmont Flying Roller Club too. I would even write some articles on rollers and send it to their magazine from time to time. I had the bug bad, and all I could think about was flying rollers. The roller magazines were great to read and learn about other roller flyers thoughts.

— *My First Flying Competition* —

One day I was visiting with another roller pigeon friend named Donny James. I had met him at a roller show a couple years earlier. I was stuck in the snow after the show, and he helped push me out.

I greatly appreciated the help and never forgot his kind act. I visited him to view his birds. Donny had dual-purpose birds. We became good friends and would visit other roller guys to talk shop. He was always upbeat and fun to hang out with. One day, he mentioned that his brother-in-law, Steve, had won the last roller flying competition in Portsmouth, around 1972.

My birds were working fairly well at the time, so I asked Donny if he thought we could talk all the local guys into a flying competition. In agreement, off we went to visit around 20 roller flyers. It had been 15 years since the last fly, and they all were reluctant to be flying in a roller competition.

A little discouraged, we stopped by Joe Roe's place last. We told him that there didn't seem to be much interest shown by the other roller guys.

Joe said, "I'll fly with you guys."

That made three of us to compete, so we set a date for the competition. Not long after we announced a flying competition we picked up eight of the guys who had previously turned us down. This was the first flying competition in 15 years, and it was my first competition too. We now had eleven competitors for an eleven-bird fly, with George Abner, a well-known roller flyer around our area, as our judge.

In an eleven-bird fly, George would judge by an individual point scoring system:

- 10 ft. = 1 point
- 20 ft. = 2 points
- 30 ft. or more = 3 points

The birds would have to roll from the team in a manner worth scoring. Now was time to put to use what I had learned from Joe on flying my rollers with the right amount of exercise, rest, and food manipulation.

I knew I was flying some good birds and had a chance to place in the top three. What most of my competitors didn't know was that I was flying their birds. All of my competition birds (except for Joe Roe's) were picked up at around the same time by a friend of mine who gets their culled birds every year. After a little haggling, I ended up with all the birds the others didn't want that year. I thought they might have missed some good ones in their haste to thin out their birds.

After flying them into shape, I found out that I was right. There were several keepers in the bunch.

With my new knowledge about rest, exercise, and feed manipulation, I had made a good group of workers from my opponents' presumably bad birds. In preparation, I made a point to visit all of my competitors to watch their birds leading up to the fly. I was feeling confident about how the competition would end, guessing that Joe Roe would take first place, with me taking second at the finish of the fly.

During the competition, we would travel from place to place to watch the guys fly their birds. Everyone was in a good mood and enjoyed the camaraderie. By the time we reached my house, the cat was out of the bag, and everyone knew I was flying my opponents' discarded birds. They were shocked when they were released and started working. So far, no flyer had come close to the work rate I was getting out of my birds.

Joe was last to fly. Once he released his birds, I thought to myself, "Joe's birds look brilliant! They are definitely going to beat mine." They were fast and frequent into the performance. That day, the speed of the roll was extremely faster than what I had seen them do before on my visit. Even though he had a couple out flyers, they were great to watch. Still, the birds had great style and velocity.

To my surprise, I took first place. Joe could have won that day, but the couple of out flyers that started giving him kitting problems allowed mine to prevail.

This was a big day for me. My first roller competition and win. There was no trophy, but for me it was (and still is) one of my best wins. I had a lot of pride knowing I was on my way to understanding how to get roller pigeons to show what they are capable of doing in the air.

I will never forget one of the older pigeon flyers kicking the dirt and leaving halfway through my fly. I always wondered if it was because he knew he lost so bad or because he got beat with one or two birds that he had discarded. Over the next few years they never mentioned it, but that was the last time I was ever able to collect all the others' unwanted birds. The jig was up. They were wise enough to never make that mistake again.

After the competition, the roller flyers had a renewed excitement about the roller hobby. We even picked up a few new members. Soon afterwards, we decided to get local club jackets and hats for our members. Donny and I were both officeholders in the club, and we were very excited that we had pulled it off. Now the members were looking forward to more flying competitions.

The club decided we would have trophies for first, second, and third place for future flying competitions. I handled club organization, booking judges, and coordinating flies.

Club dues and competition fees had to be paid in order to compete. We also had one winter show to raise money for the club treasury and give us something to do together in bad weather. We also promoted the flying competitions through the local newspaper. We were now an official roller flying club.

— *Carl Hardesty* —

After our official "club fly launch," Joe Roe stopped by my house with Carl Hardesty. Carl was the president of the National Birmingham Roller Club. They wanted to look at my birds. At the time, I had birds from just about anyone around the area that would let a good one go. I had some basic colors in the loft but mostly recessive red.

As I released my rollers that day for Joe and Carl, one hit the ground on the way out, a blue check white flight. She was always a little hot on the way out, and I was embarrassed by the crash.

"Don't worry about it. If you don't have a roll-down or two, you don't have any roll," Carl chuckled. "I think the bird's band was a little too heavy anyway."

Still, the birds worked well that day and we had a nice visit.

A few days later, Joe told me that he had met Carl Hardesty in Louisville, Kentucky, at a pigeon show. Carl was one of the flyers that was flying birds that day for visitors. Joe told me he liked the Hardesty birds he had watched fly that day. Before he left, he bought a certified hen and another bird he liked, known from then on as 4611. Both were blue check white flights. 4611 was a tight check in his check pattern. That was the beginning of the Hardesty line in our area.

A little later on Carl and Joe coordinated six pairs of their birds to lay at the same time. After all the birds were down on eggs, Joe and I went to pick Carl's eggs up, then brought them home to Joe's fosters. Eleven birds made it out at hatching. Some were ash red in check and bar and some blue checks, both in open and tight check pattern with white flights. Some of the blue tight checks had a brown type of bronzing, lightly in the wing shields. 4611 had the same in his wings.

Joe raised many from these thirteen birds. As time went by, Joe realized his roll-down percentages were too high with them and crossed his old black line into them to help with stability.

One day Joe called to tell me he'd bought another house and wondered if I would like to rent his old place. I really liked Joe's place and pigeon loft. So I moved in as soon as Joe was set up in his new place.

I was glad to have Joe's old loft. I could do some work with the birds with this setup. It had nice large old hen and old cock holding sections. This would allow me to house more stock for breeding. With the individual breeding sections, I would be able to do both open and individual breeding.

The front of the individual breeding sections had two flying sections attached that would comfortably hold 20 birds each. I could also feed them from inside for competition without fear of losing one during feeding. This would allow me to work a second group of backup birds for competition, which I called my "B team." Every year I would raise 100 to 120 young rollers, breeding from both open and individual nest breeding. Over the years, I got into a yearly pattern.

After a hard year of flying, I usually kept the best 20 for breeding along with my proven producers. Everything else was removed from the loft and I would start over the next breeding season. Moving into Joe's old place and having his old loft to work with was a big plus in helping me to produce a lot of good birds in a shorter amount of time.

I would also compete in our young bird flys when the birds were peaking in performance. That usually happened between seven to nine months old. They were always faster in the rotation their first year of performing and were very hard to beat in competition, even against old birds.

Carl Hardesty was the judge for our next local flying competition. Soon guys like Wally Fort, Jimmy Sherwood, Richard Miller, Ron Banks, Walter Harter, and Jim Miller became regulars. We had visits from Tony Dasaro, Joe Marlette, Ferrell Bussing, Sam Vulgamore, and way too many other flying roller people to remember.

Every year, right around October when the weather was cool,

we would schedule our local competition. The yard was always full of observers at our flys, including visitors from other countries, which always made for a great day. I usually ask one of our regular visitors to judge the birds in our local fly. Jimmy Sherwood from Northern Ohio was one of our judges. All the birds in our local competitions were that year's birds.

During these times, our club also put together another eleven-bird flying competition with the Sandusky Valley Performing Roller Club and the Canton Roller Club. We called it the All Ohio State Fly. Our club won the first year's competition. Most of the time, Joe Roe's score, as an individual flyer, would be the highest in the old bird competitions with the other two clubs. Joe was a hard man to beat in that one. I did pull a second-place win in 1992.

Our Portsmouth members also tried our luck at the National Birmingham Roller Club Certified Spinner Award. In this roller test, we would fly one marked bird with four others, and the marked bird had to roll with good style and depth. The bird had to gain a certain amount of points by the end of the fly in order to win the title of a certified roller, and it had to be judged by two qualified judges. This was not an easy task to pull off. First, you must pick the roller you wish to certify, and then you must try to find four birds that will kit with it. The bird was required to roll from the kit of four it was flying with. With that small number of flyers, it's a challenge to get them to kit for the contest.

Donny James was the first to get a roller certified with a rusty dun check self hen. There were a couple of others, but they were few and far between. It did cause a trainer to push his or her skills a little more, and we were all for that. Refer to picture on next page.

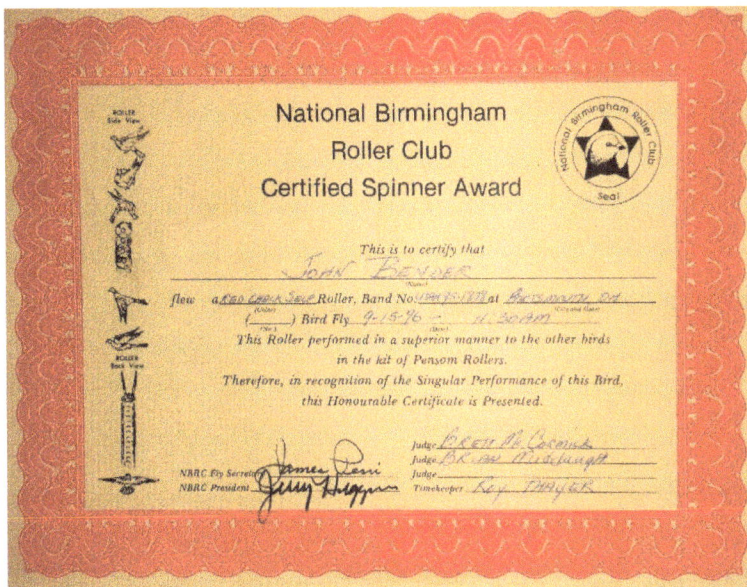

In 1991, the National Birmingham Roller Club put together a world flying competition. We now had a world champion in roller pigeon competition by the name of Monty Neibel from Canada. It made me wonder how I would do with my birds in a world competition.

The rules were different from those of the eleven-bird flys, and nine more birds were required in the team. My birds were ready to try to qualify for the 1992 regional competition, or so I thought. Joe Marlett was the judge for our region. After he arrived, I released my group of 20. They went up and performed beautifully. I was happy with what I was seeing, but with one minute to go they all landed early, which is known as a "big goose egg." They worked hard, with good velocity and style, but ran out of energy.

Joe Marlett could see the pain of this loss for me. I had spent days and hours getting my team ready for this qualifying fly and I failed. I would not have another chance for an entire year to get into the world cup fly.

Joe Marlett said, "Keep your head up, John, and don't quit trying. From what I have seen in your birds today, there is no reason you cannot win the world cup fly. You will have another chance."

Those words put me back on track with a renewed focus. All I could think about was getting my birds ready for the 1993 regional qualifiers. When the next qualifier was ready for me, I would be ready for it—and I was! In 1993 I was able to pull off a first in the regionals; I was going to be in the finals. What a great feeling it was to win such a prestigious fly. I was elated knowing I was going to fly against the best in the world.

By the day of the World Cup Finals, I felt pretty confident. The birds were looking great and everything went as planned. They did the time and put up a good score. After all the best had flown their birds in the finals, I ended up with tenth place. That was another great day for me as a roller pigeon flyer.

My mentor Joe Roe won the world cup that same year. He had to work the day of the fly and asked me to release his birds. Norm Reed from California was the judge and Richard Miller was our regional director. They both stayed overnight at my place. In the morning, we flew my birds. Being so close to Joe's house we waited for my team to land and trap before we left for Joe's.

All our locals and some from out of town were at his place waiting to see his birds perform. I wish Joe would have seen his birds work that day because they were phenomenal. The birds came out hot and working hard as they were trying to climb. I wanted to let them get some height before I called time. If I called time in too soon when they were low and a couple hit, it would be the end of it. I needed them to climb to a safe distance before I could call time in. I had five minutes to work with, so I waited. They were working so hard that Bill Berry urged me to call time so as not to miss all the points we could be getting. But I had to make sure; I felt I needed just a little more height.

Finally, at about 100 feet, I called it.

"Time in" I yelled.

They stayed fairly low at about 300 feet and were working harder than I had ever seen them before. I was afraid they might not make the time because of the work rate they were showing. The tightness and velocity of the spin, big breaks, and high wing in this group of birds was something to see. This was the best working team I had ever seen.

You could see it in Norm Reed's eyes too; Joe was kicking butt with this team. The birds did the time, and it was a great win for Joe, our club, and the United States. We were all very proud of the progress we had made since we started competing seven years earlier.

Joe was the first to win the World Cup in the United States. He was featured on the cover of the National Birmingham Roller Club magazine. It was a big deal for us to have accomplished so much in the roller pigeon world. Joe's 1993 World Cup team birds were a combination of Hardesty and Joe's old blacks, some hybrids of the two families, two Ken Payne birds, and one Indigo hybrid cross from his blacks. The team consisted of ten hens and ten cocks.

— *Roller World Cup Trophy* —

When I saw Joe next, I mentioned his win and the trophy he had won.

"You don't get to keep the trophy; it's a roving trophy," he said. "They put my name on it and send it to whoever wins the world fly next year. I think a World Cup winner should get to keep more than a twenty-five cent piece of paper for his efforts."

I agreed, and after some discussion, he convinced the powers that be to his way of thinking. From 1993 on, all winners of the world fly got to keep their world champion fly cup trophy.

After Joe's World Cup win, many people wanted to get Joe's birds. One day, as I pulled in for a visit, three rollers guys were leaving. Two of them had some of Joe's birds. I asked Joe why one guy left without any of his birds.

"John, there are so many people trying to get my birds," Joe replied. "I want to help them out, but I only have so many I can share. I have to be selective on who gets them. I would like to see them go to people who can appreciate them and manage them properly. The one guy who didn't acquire any of my birds today talked a good line. I made my decision whether I would let any go to him after we flew my birds."

"How's that?" I asked.

"I flew my best workers for them. He was the only one who would not look up to watch them perform. He just wanted to talk. A guy like that would never make a good rollerman."

Joe was like that; if you didn't fit his profile of what he thought was a good rollerman, you were out of luck getting a good pigeon from him.

— *The Roller Video Project* —

After the World Cup competition, I spent most of my weekends for the next year filming a roller video for the cub with two of our local roller flyers, Donny James and Jeff Snook. We thought a roller video would help raise money for some repairs to our clubhouse. We had already filmed one video the year before, titled *The Way of the Rollerman*. We had fun shooting it, and the roller guys who had seen it liked it so much they asked if we would film another one.

With the experience gained from the first video, we knew we could shoot a better follow-up. Jeff would be the cameraman and Donny would assist. We shot on the weekends, but since the weather was not always agreeable, it took us a year to finish. The idea behind the roller video was to interview our local members and film five minutes of their birds flying.

Everyone was eager to participate, but filming was tedious. This was back before digital recorders and iPhones. We were using videotape, and copies needed to be recorded one-by-one from a master tape that ran for a little over six hours, which meant that my video recorder ran constantly for weeks to keep up with the orders.

We finally finished shooting right after the 1994 world fly. We ran an ad in a few roller magazines, and *The Way of the Rollerman 2* became a hit. They were ordered by roller pigeon guys all over the U.S., Canada, and Germany, including Mike Tyson. We were amazed, because we didn't think it would be that well received, but our plan had worked out much better than we had thought. The sale provided enough funds to cover the repairs we needed for the club, including a new roof, aluminum siding, and new electric running in our clubhouse.

— *John "Duck" Dadosky* —

John Dadosky, or, as we call him, "Duck," was a national roller pigeon show judge and was strictly a Pensom guy. He was one of our locals who kept me very competitive with my rollers, a good rollerman who had won his fair share of local pigeon flys in his day. Duck loved to get me riled up at our local club meetings during our competitive days. We would argue the finer points of what we thought was the correct body type of a good spinner to the point that I would have to walk outside to cool down. Duck leaned towards bigger birds and I would argue for the smaller ones.

I always enjoyed beating him in our local competitions, only because he was arrogant and cocky, and nothing pleased me more than to smoke him when my birds flew against his.

On one of the days I was outside the pigeon club cooling down, Duck worked his way outside to say, "Bender, it isn't that I don't like you, I just like to debate."

I thought he didn't like me and just wanted to argue. I had been doing very well in competition and it seemed to me that he didn't like me because of it. Looking back, I hadn't considered that the amount of beer he normally drank before meetings might have played a part in his tone when he was "debating" with me.

After a little clarity that day, I started seeing Duck in a different light. I began to see him as a roller flyer who was set in his ways. Trying to be a little more open-minded about his comments, I went to his house to visit a few times. Duck was a WWII war veteran and was a true red, white, and blue kind of guy. Duck invited me in, which was very rare for a bird guy. Not because they didn't trust you, but the birds were outside. After Duck led me into another room, I understood why he invited me into his house.

To this day, I've never seen so many pigeon trophies together. There must have been a couple hundred of them. I wondered how many he actually had.

"I don't know," he replied. "I've lost count. My wife calls them dust collectors," he chuckled.

"Show trophies."

"Yes, most of them."

Considering that most of his trophies were for show, I asked why he was so adamant about what he thought a top flying roller body type was.

He replied, "The show standard was the original flying standard for body type, and it has never changed. My birds meet that standard."

I did agree they were not the big dual-purpose birds that I had seen winning in the shows in the past, but they were all at the maximum size limit that I would want for competition.

"I liked my cocks to look like a cock," he responded sharply.

Not wanting to stir him into another "debate," I let it go. We ended up agreeing to disagree. Duck was dead set on the show standard type being the type that should be required to compete.

In all fairness, he did have good rollers. But he never went around during any competitions to see what Joe Roe and I were flying. He always stayed home on fly days. He missed out on what the good ones really felt like in the hand. If he could have seen how they looked when trained and fed right, he might have changed his mind.

If I had his birds, I would try to get the size down on the breeders I selected. Then I would bring the feed down more during training. His birds were less frequent because of too much feed. One thing that also would have made Duck more competitive with his birds is learning to read the performing styles in the sky. He had some high-wing birds but never enough to help him place. I believe he just read the side view, which was what most of the guys did in the day. Mostly because Bill Pensom never spoke of the front and back view other than to draw it. So most thought it was of no consequence. Take it from me; a good flying judge notices wing placement.

I've found through personal experience that both small and large pigeons can perform correctly. As I mentioned before, the true size and type for the best velocity and style will reveal itself to you eventually if you fly the best, but in my experience, they were always smaller than what Duck thought they should be. Joe Roe and I called them cobby birds. This term is used for the small-cast, nice-chested birds that we liked.

I will always give Duck the credit for keeping my competitive fire lit with his close-minded comments during my competition years. Because of him, I felt that I always had something to prove with my rollers. In hindsight, it only made me a better flyer. He and many other devoted roller pigeon enthusiasts from Portsmouth in my roller pigeon journey have passed away. All are missed today by me and the few roller guys that remain in our area. You can find a photo of John "Duck" Dadosky and his loft on page 12 in the 1967 Roller Digest by the Pensom Roller Club.

— *Roy Thayer* —

If you have raised pigeons for any length of time you have probably at one time or another had your pigeons stolen. If so, you may get a smile from my friend in this story. Roy was one of our competitive flyers who took over as club secretary after Ray Schaffer left the club. Roy had an old modular schoolroom in Kentucky that he had bought and converted into a roller loft. He also had several other small lofts sitting around his property. Roy always flew great pigeons and had a wide selection of good roller strains to work with. He had birds from Carl Hardesty, Joe Roe, Monty Neibel, James Turner, and a few other well-known roller flyers.

On occasion he would lose some of his birds to a local thief who lived not too far from his place. He thought he knew who it was, but after two raids on his loft he still couldn't prove it. One night, Roy's wife spotted some headlights close to his main loft. Roy grabbed his twelve gauge and slid in a couple of high brass number 5s before heading out to see what was going on. He quietly slipped up on the car and found the car empty with the keys still in it. He recognized the car as belonging to the man he suspected of stealing his birds. Roy reached in, pulled the keys out, and put them in his pocket. He looked over towards his loft and could see some quick flashes of light coming through his roller loft's window. As he got closer, he could see the outline of a guy using a cigarette lighter to look over his birds.

Roy slipped into the loft and shouted, "Freeze! I have a gun and if you run I will shoot you. Get down on the floor now!"

The intruder decided to run. Roy shot him and he went down. In Kentucky you can shoot someone if they enter one of your property buildings unwelcomed. The thief quickly jumped up and started running again in the dark, running full blast into the chain link fence, bending one of Roy's fencing posts. After bouncing off the fence and onto the ground, the pigeon thief sprang up and jumped the fence. After he got to his car and found he had no keys, he disappeared into the dark. The thief left town for a couple of weeks, then returned only to be arrested.

Roy found out later that the guy took some buckshot to the chest and several more in one of his ears. As the time approached for the thief's court date, he called Roy to apologize and offered several hundred dollars for Roy not to show up. Roy took the money, and laughingly told me he should have charged the thief for the shotgun shells too.

— Building the World Cup Team —

As time moved forward, I began thinking of the upcoming flying competition to qualify for the 1994 World Cup finals. I had been flying a little over 100 birds. They flew almost every day, at different ages, and I was keeping them on the strong side. They would fly for a couple hours or longer, seldom with action. I cut back the feed and the flying and waited for them to become more frequent so I could pick out all the workers.

After a couple of weeks, they started being really frequent, and I found 40 that were good enough to make an A and B team out of. One was an outstanding spinner, an ash red checkered cock, faster than most, and nice high wing. Another that caught my eye was a nice, deep, black, white flight spinner, with a real nice fluid spin of 3.0 and 4.0 seconds.

I was hoping they would be in my final selection for the A team. But, after flying the 40 birds together for a while, I found that the ash red bird would fly just outside the kit. When he decided to go into a performance, he went over nice from start to finish and would regroup with the kit as directly as he could but stop just short of entering the group of birds. I hoped he would come out of that bad habit before competition. If he did not roll from the team, then he would not be able to score. There were a few other birds that did not kit consistently in the group or would take more time than necessary to get to the kit of 40. Some of them were pretty decent spinners and no doubt could score.

As the releases continued, I realized I should pull out the out flyers except for the ash red that flew with the group yet just on the outside of them. He really was a treat to watch, and I was wanting to use him in competition. One day while flying the hopefuls, a good friend and fellow roller flyer, Jeff Vernier, stopped by to visit. He noticed the birds flying and watched them with me while we talked. He was always good about looking up most of the time when the birds were flying. Jeff had gotten bitten by the roller bug and was always asking questions. I told him that I was trying to get a handle on selecting enough good performing birds to use in the upcoming qualifier. I pointed out the red check and said that it would be great if they all performed like the red check flying slightly outside the kit.

Jeff zeroed in on the red and watched him go into a roll. "Wow, he is really good."

"Too bad I'm going to have to pull him," I said.

Being fairly new to the roller hobby, he asked, "Why wouldn't you consider using the red in the final selection?"

"He couldn't score if he did not perform with and from the team. If five went over at the same time and the red was one of them, but is a kit width away, no points can be scored. So he is coming out."

"How much would you take for him," Jeff asked.

"Nothing, you can have him." I explained that the bird was a waste of time, but Jeff took him anyway and was happy to have him.

A year later, Jeff told me he had raised several out of the red check and all of the offspring flew as the red check did; a kit width of entering the team. He ended up culling them all. This is why I recommend that all rollers with performance faults that keep you from scoring in competition should not be bred, because performance faults are hereditary.

As I watched the remaining birds over the next few releases, I decided I would split them into two teams. They were all kitting and working satisfactorily. It was time to see how they would kit in smaller teams of two. As I had always done in past selections of my competition teams, I selected the highest-winged performers for the A team from the remaining group. Just as always when I had done this move, the smaller teams were not kitting as well as they had been. I ended up pulling a few I really wanted in the A team and replacing them with the better kitters from the B team. They were of lesser quality but good kitters. As I continued flying the two teams, I was able to swap a couple of them back into the A team before the competition. I wanted to keep as many of my original selected birds for the A team as I could.

I moved the black white flight cock I had been keeping an eye on to the A team. But the amount of depth along with his rolling a little sooner than I preferred when released made me concerned that he might not work out for the A team. So far, however, he had been doing a good job, except for finishing his first couple of performances right over the trees in my yard. I loved to watch him go deep with such velocity and thought the judge on fly day would also, but I worried that he might cost me the competition by hitting the trees. I decided to leave him in the team as long as he didn't get any deeper and hit a tree.

The family mixture of birds I was working with at this time was a mixture of several families. Among them were two birds I had been flying that I had bought from my old friend Bobby Nagle. Both birds were of the Richard Jaconette family. One was a very attractive black mottle cock with white flights. The other was a tortoiseshell self hen. The mottle cock was a three-second spinner while the hen was a two- or three-second spinner, depending on what she felt like doing on the turn. I was glad I had spotted the birds and brought them home. They would be very helpful, and it looked like they were going to stay in the A team.

Another good move I'd made a few years earlier was crossing the Carl Hardesty blue checks onto some of the black selfs I had. One of the key blacks in the breeding was band numbered 399 y from Donny James that went back to Terry Rhodes's line of rollers. I ended up with six tough black selfs that I could use in the A team. They had been helpful in past winning teams.

Another good pigeon I had selected for the team was a Larry Cohen bird. This bird was around 1.5 seconds and had been doing great. As time got closer to my fly, I thought of all the great spinners I had in the stock loft I was using for breeders. I thought of how much easier it would have been to fly them back into shape and pick the A team. But I had learned from past experience never to use birds that made it to the stock loft, so I picked from what I was flying at the time, which always worked best for me.

When I selected the 40 birds to pick 20 from in the beginning, I selected a five-foot, fast, high-wing opal bar that I was hoping would get deeper by the time I had to compete. I had used other opals from that line, but this bird stayed at a five-foot depth up until the end. Needing at least ten feet in the performance, the opal stayed in the B team almost to the end of training.

While watching the B team fly right after the A team trapped in, I noticed the opal bar always broke from the front. Anytime he performed, he would fly back to the team coming in from the rear and work his way through the team back to the front. Most of the time when he went over, a lot of them would turn with him.

The next day I flew him with the A team instead of the B team. Wow! My team frequency greatly improved. Over the next few training fly releases, I pulled the opal from the team and put him back just to see if I was getting a reliable reading of increased frequency. I most definitely was.

Not wanting to use the bird because it was too short in the performance, I decided to do it anyway for the potentially extra points it would induce. This is what you would call a good lead bird. Some flyers call them trigger birds, which are birds that will fly to the front of the team and roll, causing most, if not all, of the others to go over with it.

Though I had flown many winning teams, I'd never seen one bird stimulate so much action from the rest of the team as he did. He had to stay. That was the only time I had ever used a bird shorter in the performance than competition rules called for. I pulled a scorable bird from the A team and put in the opal bar. Yes, I knew he could not score on a turn, but the frequency of big turns he prompted the others to do more than made up for it.

When the big day arrived, he and the others I had selected for the A team did not let me down. We finished second in the North Central East Subregion and made it to the finals. I was content with that and hopeful I could finish better than Tenth Place in the world this time.

— *1994 World Fly* —

After making it to the finals, I rested the A team and upped their feed. I knew I would have to build some fat back on them and get them strong so that I could bring them down in condition to peak them out again. I was proud of the team and hoping not to lose any to weather or predators before the finals. If I could maintain the team properly until then, I thought I might have a shot at improving my world roller flying position in the finals. I didn't think I would win because I had flown better birds in the past. But, if I could attain a better final position than tenth in the world, I would be happy.

After a lot of rest and feed, the birds were back on schedule. I flew them on the strong side up until 30 days before competition but was getting more time in the air with less frequency of performance out of them. This is to be expected when adding more food. They continued to kit well and looked great. So far, they were looking good, until we had a 40 mile per hour storm move in on one of my releases. I lost the entire team. When I let them out, the weather seemed fine. But after 15 to 20 minutes, the storm moved in so quickly that my team was caught up in it. My birds had flown on windy days before, but never anything like this.

I had lost teams in the past when getting them ready for competition in hard winds. The closer you are to peaking your rollers out the less likely it is that you will keep them. The birds will get so caught up in performing and kitting that they do not give any thought to fighting the wind and getting closer to the loft. Being light in weight and in a weakened condition didn't help.

I had lost my A team again. I was devastated. But, miraculously, my entire team returned after about an hour of being blown out of sight. If it had been closer to fly day, I think I might have lost them forever.

As the days passed, I decided to replace the opal lead (or trigger bird) with a scorable bird. The switch didn't seem to make much difference with the team. They continued to be breaking together well, so I left the deeper scorable bird in.

At 30 days, I started cutting back the feed and staying on an every-other-day schedule. The birds were doing well, except I seemed to be underestimating their strength when I made cuts to their feed to bring the time down right up to the fly.

I thought it was interesting that with such a diversity of roller family genes in these birds, they worked so well together. I had always heard that it takes a close family of birds to pull off a good team. There is nothing wrong with that way of thinking, but it also can be done with unrelated good rollers given proper selection of aerial traits from the sky and the right amount of exercise and feed.

On my last couple of releases before competition, the birds were still stronger than I wanted, sometimes flying a little over an hour. So carefully I made cuts on their feed. But if I cut it back too much, it could cause them to land before 20 minutes. Then I would have to increase feeding proportions to catch the fly time of 40 minutes, which I wanted on the last fly before competition.

I had always brought the birds down to peak them out for a fly. I had never had to try to catch them on the way up. I was hoping this would not be the first time I had to try it. My fear of missing the peak and trying to build them up in endurance was with me right to the end.

Because of my memory of not getting the required time with my 1992 team in the qualifiers, I was always too reserved in cutting back the feed to reduce fly time to where I wanted it. I ended up flying them twice on their last two releases to tire them along with cutting the feed again to help ensure they would fly less and roll more on competition day.

A couple of days before the fly, our regional director, Richard Miller, called to inform me of some scheduling issues and to ask if I could release my birds for the fly a day later than scheduled. But everything I had been doing to train my birds was geared towards flying on my scheduled day and time. I could not change my release day and time so close to the big dance and still have my team perform as well as I hoped.

I was sympathetic to Richard's dilemma. If he wanted to skip me to get back on schedule, I understood. In the meantime, I would continue to fly my rollers as if the original time and date still applied. Richard worked out the problem, and I was able to fly at my loft as originally planned.

As part of the plan, Richard and the World Cup judge, George Kitson, along with Les Bezance, the timekeeper, came over the day before the fly and stayed at my house. When they arrived, Richard introduced George and Les. Both were great guys, and we all had a good time talking about pigeons. With some daylight left, I asked them if they would like to go to Joe Roe's house to view his birds and his setup. Joe wasn't going to be home, but he said if they wanted to see his birds I could show them around. As I showed them around, I pointed out Joe's best birds. When we left the stock loft, I took them out to see what Joe was flying, again pointing out the best ones I had watched many times in the sky.

Thinking that one of the gentlemen would want to handle them, I offered two of Joe Roe's best flying rollers to be inspected. After shaking their heads, George replied, "We don't handle birds."

I was at a loss for words. It never occurred to me that a rollerman would not want to handle two great rollers. I knew it was not meant in a mean way; it was just their way. I enjoyed the rest of the night listening to George and Les talk back and forth to each other with their English accents.

Sunrise the next morning came with my game cocks crowing out back to start off the day. With enough time before the birds were to be released, we all decided to go to a local restaurant called Pop's for breakfast. Other local and out-of-town flyers came into the restaurant to eat, including Joe Roe. Soon the place was thick with roller flyers, including the guy currently holding first place.

By the time we got back at my house, there were people everywhere. The sky was overcast, with a slight morning crispness in the air. The weather was in my favor, but I wasn't sure of the hawks, and a strike during the release could blow it for me and my team. The roller enthusiasts were excited as I made my way to the loft, asking how I thought the rollers might do today.

"Good," I hoped. "I think it might be a good fly."

After I released my birds I waited for them to climb to their working height of 300 to 500 feet before I called time. They were active on the way up, with some breaks. I hated to miss the possible points, but knew once they stopped climbing, they could make up for it. After time in was called, they were ready to do some big breaks together and they didn't let me down. The breaks were looking like half and three-quarter turns, and some breaks looked to be all of them.

The judge started off with calling six, then another six, then five, then another five. The judge called six after the next big break, and Joe said to me, "What the hell is he looking at?"

I leaned over to him and said, "He is a tough judge. But if he has been consistent in judging up to and with my team, I should get the points the birds deserve in the end."

Reluctantly, with a few comments under his breath, Joe held his emotions, though he wasn't too happy with some of the calls made by the judge. But he held his tongue and things turned out well by the end of my second world final competition fly. After the fly I was informed that I was now in the lead with only four or five flyers left to go.

After an exciting morning, I checked on my rollers before calling it a day. Later some of the flyers who had traveled with the fellow in first place told me he was in disbelief about what he had just seen. He verbally struggled with the defeat all the way home. I understand he had flown some really good pigeons before my team flew, but this day belonged to me and my birds.

The long wait to hear when the last flyers had flown their birds was tough. I had a couple of calls from colleagues expressing what they saw as political unfairness towards me and special treatment toward one of the other finalists. I appreciated their concerns but said we should be patient and wait and see what happens in the end.

The long-awaited phone call finally came.

"John, congratulations. You are the winner of the World Cup Roller Flying competition."

What a great thing to hear! I was ecstatic! I thought of how well everything had come together, the training, the feed, the weather. It all worked out for me and the team much better than expected. This was way better than tenth place. After being declared the world champion flyer had sunk in, I made my way to Joe's house to share my good news. When I got there, someone else had beaten me to it. Joe was in his stock loft looking at his hens. When I walked in, he said with a big grin, "Hey, champ. Two world champions in the same loft. Pretty cool, huh?"

"Yeah, Joe, pretty cool."

We thought back over the years prior to us both winning the world cup fly and all that had led to it. What satisfaction it was for us both as roller flyers, being a mentor and protege, to both have won such a prestigious competition fly one after the other.

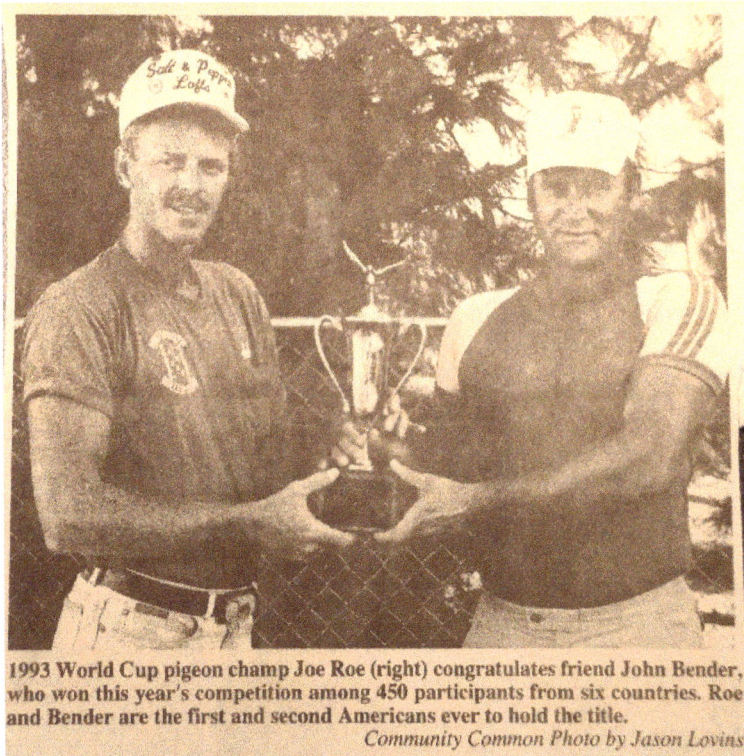

1993 World Cup pigeon champ Joe Roe (right) congratulates friend John Bender, who won this year's competition among 450 participants from six countries. Roe and Bender are the first and second Americans ever to hold the title.
Community Common Photo by Jason Lovins

Within a few days I got a surprise call from Dave Staebler, my past 4-H advisor. He had heard that I won the World Cup fly and wanted to congratulate me. It was nice to hear from Dave. It had been many years since I last saw him. I had always wondered what became of him. Since then, we've kept in touch, and I still talk with Dave from time to time.

— *1994 World Team Bird Information* —

In the 1994 finals, seven cocks and thirteen hens were flown in the team. The names associated with the 94 winning rollers is as follows:

One bird was a Larry Cohen bird I traded for. Two were Richard Jaconette birds I bought from Bobby Nagle. Six black selfs were my line, which I had been working on for a few years. They had a strong Carl Hardesty influence, with a key bird that had been from Terry Rhodes's line of rollers. The white pigeon went back to three families: Paul Platz, Wright Miller, and Carl Hardesty. The rest were a combination of these flying names either bred or not bred together: Joe Roe, Joe Marlett, and Charles Albaugh.

'94 Bird Colors	'94 Bird Depth
One white self	1 roller would perform for 1 second
Six black selfs	1 roller would perform for 1.0 to 1.5 seconds
One red check self	4 rollers would perform for 1.5 seconds
Two black white flight	3 rollers would perform for 1.5 to 2.0 seconds
Two red check baldhead	3 rollers would perform for 2.0 seconds
Four blue check bald	1 roller would perform for 1.5 to 3.0 seconds

One tortoiseshell self	2 rollers would perform for 2.0 to 3.0 seconds
One black mottle white flight	3 rollers would perform for 3.0 seconds
One blue check beard	1 roller would perform for 2.5 to 3.5 seconds
One blue check mark	1 roller would perform for 3.0 to 4.0 seconds

— *1995 World Cup Competition* —

Joe Roe trained a nice team for the '95 World Cup competition and placed third in the finals. I did not make it that day in time to watch the birds. Since Joe had to work this day, Richard Miller had released his birds for him. I did stop by later in the day just in time to meet Monty Neibel, who was visiting with Joe. Monty Neibel is one of the great flyers of the World Cup and was the judge for the World Cup finals that year. Photo by Richard Miller.

Joe Roe - John Bender - Monty Neibel
Photo by Richard Miller

Not long after the '95 roller fly, Joe left the sport. It's been over 20 years now, and I still visit him. In 2000 Monty died in a car crash, but not before making great progress in roller pigeon competition with three world flying titles. I went through a divorce in 1996 and moved from Joe's old place. Having lived at several different locations and moving my lofts around here in Portsmouth, I still have roller pigeons out back and hope to compete again after I retire. I also have a few racing pigeons. At present I'm just a backyard flyer and enjoying it.

For those of you who want to be successful in roller competition, remember you have to be serious, focused, and play to win because there are many tough competitors in this sport.

Regardless, always be a good sport, whether you win or lose. Be ready to handle a loss, think it through, and ask, "What went wrong?" Just like any game, there are aspects of the preparation or the team that may have been the problem. What kept you from doing what the winner did? Why did your plan not work? After some reflection at the end of the competition, adjust your plan and be more determined for the next competition. In my mind, the most important factor in winning is good birds, then a good feeding and training program. The lack of either will show on competition day.

I was very lucky not long ago to befriend a young scientist named Ben Novak. Ben is the lead scientist working toward bringing back the extinct passenger pigeon. I have been collaborating with Ben on the project. The project is called Project Revive and Restore (ReviveRestore.org).

With the progress scientists are making, it should not be too long before we will see them back in the sky. I may be breeding some here at my place in the near future.

Remember not to let your glass get too full. Read other roller writings too and learn what you can. It all will add up, and you will find yourself being very competitive in the sport of roller flying. I highly recommend *The Collected Writings of William Hyla Pensom* by Tom Monson, if you can find it. Joe Roe and I spent many days in our lofts chewing on Pensom's thoughts. You might find a couple of contradictions in his writings, but keep in mind that people do change their perspective on things as time moves forward. I would also recommend roller magazines for keeping up with what others in the roller world are doing. They cover the many aspects of rollers and will keep you up to date on rules, upcoming flys, political thoughts, bands etc. *The National Birmingham Roller Club Magazine* would be a good choice for this.

I would like to finish writing my history and thoughts with a quote from Carl Sandburg:

"Nothing happens unless first a dream."

In the meantime, keep looking up!

—John Bender WC/94

PART TWO

— *The Ins and Outs of Roller Care* —

Now it's time to dive into the ins and outs of raising and training roller pigeons. Before we get started, first understand why I believe rollers roll:

Why Rollers Roll

I think most would agree that rolling is the result of a genetic mutation. It appears to have no beneficial value to the pigeon. But we desire and cultivate it, because it is an oddity and very pleasing to watch. One theory was that if the pigeon rolled at the right instant during a hawk attack, it would thwart the attack. Which makes sense, but a roller will not roll during a strike because of its mindset of fear and focus at the time.

From my observations, the trigger to the roll is mental, a feeling of relaxed, slightly excited contentment. When a roller pigeon has that "glad to be alive" feeling and is happy and content, it is more prone to perform. Some will roll as soon as they are released because of the excitement of getting out and flying. Pigeons have a natural instinct to kit or group with other pigeons. When they do, they feel more content, which in turn will help them go over in a tumble or roll. The more there are in a group of flying rollers, the more frequency, or so it seems to me. If you toss a roller up and watch it return to the team or flock, they usually will roll after getting to the others because they feel safer after getting in with the group.

Our birds also very much enjoy the water, as you may have noticed by watching them take a bath in a pan of water or seeing them lying on their side with a wing up in the rain. They love light, misty rain, and are more frequent in rolling while flying during a light rain. It triggers them to roll at a more frequent pace.

I have also noticed that a team of frequent rollers will shut off the rolling when they observe a predator or another large flying bird. Once the large bird or predator has passed and our rollers feel secure again, the performing quickly returns.

I have seen a confirmed roll-down fly beautifully and outmaneuver a predator in the air, not rolling for the entire chase. But as soon as the chase is over and the threat is gone, the now content roll-down quickly goes back to his old ways, rolling so much he cannot fly.

I've also seen it at other times. For example, when watching a roller returning home from a distant loft of another fancier who had acquired the bird from me. The bird, realizing he is in familiar territory and is home, will knock off a good one or two before landing. The bird appears to be relieved and content that his journey is over and in turn is triggered to roll.

Another performing trigger seems to be fright. Occasionally you may see this in a roller pigeon, but not often. The highly excited or fright trigger response is very prevalent in Parlor roller pigeons and is similar in fainting goats. This type of triggered response is undesirable in rollers and should be avoided.

In summary, a good roller pigeon performs because of a past genetic mutation triggered by mental contentment. Of course, these are my personal thoughts based on my observations and what I believe is the trigger of rolling, and I may be proven wrong in the future.

Pensom Rollers

The majority of Birmingham Roller pigeons here today came to the United States in 1936 by way of Bill Hyla Pensom. He and the original imports were from Birmingham, England, in an area called the black country due to it being an industrial area. Bill Pensom grew up around pigeons. His father and many others in the area flew rollers. Bill grew to be very knowledgeable about roller pigeons and recorded his thoughts on the roller subject. He passed away in 1968. He was, and still is, highly revered by most roller flyers, especially in the United States.

The information he has passed on to the roller pigeon fancier has greatly helped roller flyers understand and promote the breed. You will hear and read many things about William Hyla Pensom from other roller flyers. Most roller pigeons in the United States are descendants of his birds brought into this country in 1936 and again in 1946. Many who have records tracing their birds back to these original Pensom imports take great pride in that lineage.

150 14 Cock. Blue Tight Check Beard. Pensom bloodline.
This one, an outstanding spinner, was a gift from Tom
Monson

However, if you have a good group of birds, don't be discouraged if you can't trace their lineage to the Pensom line. You can't fly paper. As long as you stick to the flying standards when selecting your breeders, you and your birds will move forward at a rapid pace. Other roller families have been developed over the years too. As long as your birds will perpetuate rollers that meet the Birmingham flying standards, you will be in fine shape.

The flying standard set for the bird is the main thing. The handler should pursue this standard with his performing pigeons with great vigor if he wants to be highly successful. Doing this will not only make you successful as a roller flyer sooner but also guarantee the future of the Birmingham Roller qualities for years to come.

Difference Between a Kit and Team

You may wonder in your observation as a roller fancier why some are using the term "kit" and others are using the word "team." Before you start building your team I will explain the difference.

A **kit** of rollers is a group of pigeons that stay together during flight. Some may be performing and some may not be performing in a kit. In addition, the group, flock, or kit can be any certain number of pigeons.

A **team** of rollers is like a team of basketball players with a certain number required in the group that all work together to achieve points in a game. In a roller team, all members are working together and are athletes too, with each member being in the best physical shape, working together as a team to score points. So, the term "team" would apply to however many good birds you selected for a competition or exhibition.

A team and B team would be an example of two teams working towards the same competition or exhibition. The term "team" is not common in old roller writings but is commonly used with today's roller flyers.

Building Your A Team

The smaller the group of birds you are flying, the less a roller pigeon wants to kit or stay together with the others. If you picked fifty birds out of a group of one hundred, you need to see if they will all stay together while flying in the smaller group. You may find a couple that are not kitting. Go ahead and remove them from consideration for the competition team.

After the grading and pulling out flyers is complete, hopefully you will have twice the required team numbers you needed for the fly. If you do not, and your competitor does, he will have an edge over you. Odds are now in his favor, since he has more birds to work with. Remember, it is a percentage game. (How to grade rollers is mentioned later in the book.)

Now that you're ready to pick your teams, go down the list and put the highest-graded birds in the A team. Put the other half in the B team. Time everything you do as a roller pigeon competitor to make sure you have finished selecting the A and B teams at 30 days before your fly date. I repeat: you should have twice the number of working birds you need at this time. If not, try to get as close as you can. Once you have your A and B teams, it is time to prepare your birds for competition.

— *Preparing Your Birds for Competition* —
(Week by Week)

We now have four weeks before our competition, which means we can work through the preparation process week by week. If you follow my four-week layout, you should be successful in your competition:

Preparations for A and B Teams: First Two Weeks
1. Worm both teams.
2. After worming, put one tablespoon per gallon of apple cider vinegar in their water for two days.
3. Add cod liver oil on their feed by shaking it in a can just until the feed is shiny; do this for three days.
4. Dust all birds.

Note: When adding cod liver oil, the grain should not stick together. It should just be shiny. If you have put in too much and it sticks together, add a little more feed and shake some more. You can give any extra feed to your other birds.

You will want your A and B team birds at the right level of health to respond to your adjustments in their feed. At this point, we want to strengthen the birds. The worming medicine you are giving them to kill any internal parasites will weaken them. The vinegar you gave them will help replace some of the good gut bacteria they lost during worming. This will help them get the most nutritional benefits during digestion from the grains you're working with. The cod liver oil will help you get your birds back on the strong side.

The goal now is for the A team roller members to have a lot of strength and endurance to work with. Sprinkle a little grit on the feed every day. Give them all the feed they want and pull the tray for the first two weeks. You will want them on the strong side because you are going to gradually bring them down in condition later. If they are flying a couple of hours or more and are infrequent, it will not hurt them at this point of preparation. That's what you're after.

After you have your A and B teams picked, dust the birds for feather parasites. A parasite can cause unnecessary energy waste by irritating the bird and keeping it restless. When not flying, and after feeding, you will want to keep the teams calm and still in a semi-dark fly box, with just enough light to see to eat and drink.

Selecting your A and B teams is not as easy as going through your notes and picking your best from your notes. But that is what I always do first in the hope that I can nail the team down on the first try with my highest-graded birds. Some of the first birds I pick are never in the final selection for the A team. The team members are always a combination of birds from the A and B teams. You should fly both teams every day by releasing the A team first. As soon as your A team has trapped in, release the B team. Now that both teams are in a smaller group, you might have another out flyer in the A team. Put it in the B team and replace it with a B team member that's kitting. Sometimes, by competition day, they will adjust to the smaller team and can be put back into the A team.

From thirty days up until your fly day, I strongly recommend that you use a calendar and fly your birds every other day. I've ALWAYS used a calendar in every competition. I recommend you do the same until the release for competition day.

Your observation of your birds and their protection is crucial from here up to the release on competition day. While flying them, notice if any of your A team members are landing early. If so, replace them with ones from the B team that you think will land with the A team you are building. If you notice a bird in the B team outperforming one in the A team, switch them. The A team will reveal itself to you as the days pass. Oddly, certain birds in your team will make a big difference in the frequency of turns to be scored by the team. Even though their performance may not be as good as some of the better ones, in some cases the team as a whole will be better by them being there. Keep this in mind as you pull a bird from the A team and replace it with another.

If the overall action declines from the replacement you made, you may want to put it back and see if that causes them to work together like they had before you pulled the lower-quality performing bird. This type of bird is known as a trigger bird. They will spur the others to go into the performance when it does. They most generally are short in the performance and will fly to the front before going over. The rest will follow its lead. Some also call them "lead" birds. Watch for these while you are adjusting your team members. A good trigger bird can make a big difference in your final score. Even if its style isn't the best, if it's scorable, leave it in the team. If this bird helps your best be more frequent in breaks, it will be worth it. Sometimes your A team member adjustments will go right up until the last fly before the competition day release. So study both A and B teams until competition day.

Of course you would generally want your fastest and highest-wing performers in the team, but do not be too concerned if they do not all make it. Your goal is to build a team that has frequent big breaks. By "breaks" we mean five or more turning over together, also known as "turns." If one of your high-wing rollers is not breaking with the team as you think it should, replace it with a lesser bird that will break when the rest do and still be able to score (if that's all you have to pick from). A high-wing bird you catch rolling by itself will not score for you in a team competition in which you get a score only if five or more birds roll together. But the same bird will score in an individual competition team where rolling together is not required.

Normally, in individual team competition you will fly eleven pigeons. In team competition geared for breaks you will fly twenty. The process for building both types of teams is the same except you can get by with a little more depth in the performance with your individual team members. Too much depth in a turn competition can cause you to lose some regrouping time in the birds returning to the team.

Generally, a good 20-bird team will be a mix of both short and deep performers. You will be chasing the best show you can get out of a mix of your A and B team until your scheduled fly date. Ideally you would want them all to have high wing from the front or back view in the performance, rolling tight as a ball from the side view inconceivably fast, and rolling together frequently in big breaks as a team and regrouping as fast as possible.

Watering Flyers

If you are just maintaining your birds and using the feeding method of "all they want to eat, then pull the tray," place the water in after they have all started eating. Pull the extra feed out when the first two or three birds go to drink but leave the water.

When giving measured amounts of feed, I suggest that you put the water in after you pull the feed tray as opposed to putting in the water container at the same time as the feed. Especially if you're prepping your birds for competition. This assures that all the birds will start eating at the same time and get their fair share. Many times, working birds will get a drink as soon as they come in, before going to eat, and then cough up water back into the feed tray. Some birds will miss out on their measured amount of feed while getting their drink first.

In addition, always give a fresh change of water every day. If you know your water will freeze that night, you can dump the water after all the birds drink. This will save you from having to deal with busting the ice at the next feeding. The birds will do just fine on one drink of water until the next day. If you're competing or showing off your workers the next day, it is a good idea to dump the water after they have all had a drink. They will put on a better show if their crops are not full of water.

Feeding the Flyers for Competition

The feed is key for competition. Some trainers of rollers say they are trying to raise rollers that can compete without cutting back the feed. They tend to think a roller is of lesser quality if the feed is cut back to get it to perform more. Others just can't cut back the feed because they believe their birds are starving.

All athletic champions eat and exercise a certain way to achieve the best results or peak performance. I have never had a roller pigeon die as a result of cutting back the feed to get it ready for competition, so don't worry about that happening. Keep in mind that if your birds can fly for 30 to 40 minutes, they are not close to death. If they can do the time, they will be fine. The guy competing against you who does not cut back the feed on his team during training will be giving you an easy victory.

On the other hand, a flyer that is trying to catch the peak performance from his birds on the way up in physical strength can give you a run for your money if he hits it right. Either method will work if you have the know-how. This method of getting them strong first and catching the peak in the birds' physical condition on the way down has served me well many times. What most flyers that catch the peak on the way up in physical condition don't mention is that they had to bring them down in condition before they took them up.

Bottom line, different flyers have different methods of peaking out their team. I personally believe that if you try this method and take good notes, you will have a good start. Also, don't be afraid to try things you might think would make this method better. One way would be to experiment with different grains. Some trainers just use wheat in training, some will just use milo. Others may add peas at a certain time. We will be using mixed grain on this training method.

Using a Calendar

As mentioned earlier, you need to use a calendar! So before you start, get a calendar to work with for this training period, one with space to write notes each day as needed. Keep the calendar (or notebook if you didn't use a calendar) after the competition for future reference. You will be glad you did by the next flying competition.

Mark down your scheduled release and count backwards 30 days on the calendar until the present day. The best way to get you on the right track is to fly every other day until the big day arrives. Start with your competition fly day by writing down an F to represent flying that day. The day before mark 0 to represent an off day of no flying. From there go back the entire 30 days, mark F 0 F 0 F 0 F 0 F 0 F and so on.

This is the main reason you will want to find out as soon as possible when your birds are scheduled to compete; it allows you to plan out your flight days. Next, nail down the fly time for your competition. The sooner you get this information the better. Your fly date and scheduled release time can be provided by your regional director.

Once you know your flight time and date, fly your team at the time you will be releasing them on competition day. If you can do this on every release, it will help you be closer in judging their feed to get the correct flying time for the big day.

Starting at the 30-day mark, feed them all they want and pull the tray. Be sure to sprinkle a little grit on the feed when feeding.

Preparations for A and B Teams: Last Two Weeks

Through my years with rollers, I have heard that you can make a good bird better, but you cannot make a bad bird good. I found this to be true. In other words, if the bird is a cull there is no certain way of feeding that will fix the bird. But a good bird, one that has made the team, will improve its wing height, frequency, velocity, and depth by gradually decreasing the feed during training. This bird can be brought to his maximum physical capabilities.

As you will recall, this is referred to as "peaking out" by most flyers, and that's what you're trying to do by the time your scheduled fly time arrives for the release. The last two weeks before the competition is when we want to do this, by cutting the grain back gradually. With this approach, you can take average birds and make them great or great birds and make them excellent. Remember that gradually reducing the feed after you have them strong in condition is the key to peaking out a team of pigeons. Trying to do it in a week or so will not allow your rollers to show you their true capabilities.

As you've previously read, you will be feeding them up for the first 15 days. This is to get them through the last two weeks of preparation. They should now be flying strong for a couple of hours or more and probably out of sight. That's okay; that's the plan.

However, watch out for the jet stream by keeping a close check on your weather patterns. If your team gets caught up in the jet stream, they're gone. You've lost your birds and there goes the competition. By feeding a full feeding and pulling the tray when they go to drink for the first two weeks, you are preparing a champion team.

At 15 days to go before the competition, start bringing your birds down in condition. This is accomplished by putting both teams on two spoons apiece of mix feed per bird. I suggest a mix of wheat milo and yellow peas.

You must follow this feeding protocol for the best results, which means no grit, or no vitamins; nothing but the feed and water you intend to train them on. This will cause them to be more frequent and cut some of their time in the air. From now until the competition release, make sure to keep track of your team's time in the air. Don't forget to use a longer than needed tray when feeding them and spread the feed evenly across the tray. As long as they have room to pick up the grain they will get their fair share if pushed to the side. If your feed tray is too small, use two feed trays when you feed.

Some roller trainers are concerned with fast peckers, birds they think may be picking up grain faster than the others. This allows a roller to get a little more than its share, which can unbalance the team. Such trainers will build individual slots for the birds to eat from to make sure that each bird gets only the amount it was intended to receive. Some trainers even count the grains, only giving a little extra to a bird if he thinks it will help the bird stay in balance with the team. I have never had to resort to this way of feeding before a competition, but I do see the logic in this method, which is time consuming. If you do feel one or two of the team members need a little extra feed to help them get through the training, pull them aside and provide a few extra peas.

At times you will have to cut back a little more on the feed by shaking the spoon a little to lessen some of the feed amount in each spoon. Yes, keep using the spoon. I have always used only the spoon method for measuring the feed for competitions. You will get a better feel for what you're feeding the team instead of marking a container lower than what you were feeding prior. If you feel you must use a container rather than a spoon, that's fine. If your judgement is right, you can still be successful. In the end, all you are trying to do is slowly get the birds' flying time down to as close to twenty minutes as you can by your competition release day, trying all the while not to cut back the feed too much and not make the time.

Your feeding amounts in the two spoons per bird will depend on your team's time in the air. By the last week, you will still want to be above one hour, and you probably are. Don't forget, if you cut too much feed too soon, you may not make the 20-minute time you're after. If they are flying over one hour on competition day, you will not have the frequency you will need to win. So wherever your birds are currently at on flying time, with only one week to go, you had better guess correctly on the amount of feed per day.

When you started at 30 days, your spoon amount is closer to three. Your spoon at the two-week mark is two heaping, and by the last week, as you still are cutting back feed, the feed in the spoons should be level. Continuing to cut feed to bring them down in condition, keep in mind that the last few days before a fly, you will normally have barely enough grain in the spoon to cover the bottom. The total amount will fit in one spoon, but don't deviate from using two spoons shaken when you're cutting the rations back. On the last couple of releases of the A team, you will do very well if they are at 40 minutes in the air. But, if one of your competitors gets his birds to 30 minutes on fly day, his birds could be more frequent than yours.

So it's a big decision. Do you get as close to 20 minutes as you can and risk an early landing (before the required 15 minutes) and disqualification? Or do you train them to fly 30 to 40 minutes on their last couple fly releases to ensure achieving the full 20 minutes during which your birds can score?

If you go with the 30 to 40 minutes it may cause the judge to score yours with a little less frequency if your competitor nails his at 20 minutes. But if your birds' overall style is better than that of your competitors, you may still have a chance to overcome, but will it be enough to win? That's always the gamble you must consider.

Those are the considerations that you will have to deal with as a roller pigeon competitor. I have dealt with them too. In fact, after a disqualification in the 1992 World Cup Regionals for landing one minute early, I started training my future teams for a 40-minute fly instead of a 20-minute fly and did well.

Note: Keep in mind that, if needed, you can fly your birds twice a day on the last two days of scheduled flying if you think they might be too strong by fly day. If you do, remember to feed just one day's rations. Do this by feeding half a day's ration after each release. One spoon on the first release, and then one spoon after the second release. On the last day of feeding your team before the competition, pull the water out after they eat and all get a good drink. Place the water in after they eat, not before, but watch to make sure all of them went to drink. The reason for pulling the water out is to help guard against it becoming a possible problem during the next release. A few may get a drink right before you release them. No athlete wants to be full of water during their best performance. The water sloshing around may cause the performances to be cut short.

Hopefully, by the last couple of fly releases, you'll have the A team members selected. Good luck in your fly. If everything went right during training, the only thing you will have to worry about is the weather or a raptor to mess things up for the team on fly day. This 30-day way of training towards a peak performance with my teams has always worked for me.

Through good note keeping and experimenting with the feed, you may come up with a different method of peaking your rollers. This method—getting them strong in condition and then slowly bringing them down in condition until they peak—is something I picked up from Master Flyer George Mason years ago as he was being interviewed by John Huntington, and it was the method I used to win the big one in 1994.

There are also opportunities to tweak this method and make it better. There is always room for improvement on any feeding and training method. These tweaks will be for you to find through observation and good notes. When rollers peak, they will fall apart in the style of roll a few days after. In order to peak them out again, you will have to get them strong again and repeat the process. Getting them right on the exact day you want will always be the challenge.

One thing to consider before you compete is using a quick-release door for competition. The sooner your rollers are out, the sooner they can group together and start their ascent. If you have been releasing them from the trap door it will take a little longer than what you might desire. They can't all get out at the same time, and the first ones out may have already started climbing before the last few are able to get through the opening. This takes more time for them to group, and some time and energy can be lost.

You may want to consider building your competition box to allow the whole side of the box where your trap door is mounted to be opened at once, providing a quick release of all the birds in the team. The larger the release opening, the better for competition.

— *Preparation for Fly Day* —

1. If you are worried about certain birds in your team hitting the ground on release on fly day, get some of the guys at the fly to help you toss them up together with the others when they are high enough. You will want them all to get together as soon as possible, so toss them up at the same time. Everyone toss on three—one, two, three, toss.
2. If you think you have a better spot to release them other than from your fly box, then box them up and take them to the better spot to be released. The judge will have no problem with that. Also, you'll want to have the best vantage point for the judge to view your birds while flying, so figure that out before the judge gets there. Missing a break from the team because the judge was not in the best viewing spot can make a big difference where your team places in the end.
3. Don't call time in right away. You have five minutes to call. The team will have to climb. They will start rolling their best after they stop climbing and level off. Make sure to watch them during training so you know about where that will be.
4. Everybody wants to be friends with the judge. Guys who stop by to watch the fly sometimes will keep talking to the judge while he is trying to watch the team. Don't let one of your competitors or friends do this while your birds are being judged. Points can be lost. Some judges will look to answer a friend or competitor's question and miss a break. It could mean the difference between first and second place in the fly. You will have to say something, because no one else will speak up for you.
5. To be a champion trainer, you need to do everything you can to win. A lot of little things can add up to a big difference. But, win or lose, one should be a good sport in the end.
6. If you want to be successful in roller competition, you have

to be serious, focused, and play to win. There are many tough competitors in the sport you are getting into. Always be a good sport, win or lose. Be ready to handle a loss, then think it through, asking yourself, "What went wrong?" Just like any game, there are aspects of the preparation or the team that may have been the problem. What kept you from doing what the winner did? Why did your plan not work? After some reflection on what just happened, adjust your plan and be more determined for the next competition. To my mind, the most important factor to winning is good birds first, then a good feeding and training program. The lack of either will show on competition day.

Flying Stock

Some breeders like to fly their stock; I beg to differ. A good rule of thumb is to never fly your stock. They should be well maintained, but never flown. They are too difficult to acquire and should have already proven themselves in the air to have been placed in the stock loft. If you do fly your stock, be sure to cut back their feed for a few days to get some of the fat off. Even then, you may have to flag them for a couple of days or so to help them rebuild some flying endurance. Try not to be disappointed if the breeder you put back up in the sky did not have the same quality spin that it used to have. Most never look as good as when you first stocked them. Generally, some of the velocity will be lost when a bird is flown after being bred from or on a long lockdown.

Maintaining Hold Over a Kit

You can maintain your old bird team by feeding them two spoons of grain every day and grit sprinkled on their feed every couple weeks. You will find that they're rolling with more frequency as they get close to grit time again. Your birds will roll less frequently in the performance after you give them grit. Grit is a necessary staple for pigeons. They need it to digest the grain properly. Tests have shown the grit to last approximately two weeks in the crop. As long as you give them grit every two weeks, they will stay healthy. Grit is fortified with vitamins and minerals for pigeons, which will make them stronger. After eating the grit, you will notice that your rollers will have more resistance to the roll. This boost from the grit will slowly wear off over the next two weeks and the birds will become more frequent in the performance. You will have more frequency in your rollers if you do not give them access to grit every day. If you let your rollers eat all the grit and feed they wanted, they would fly for hours, higher than you can see, and would roll seldomly. This is where you come in as the trainer. Feed them what they need to handle the aerial performance properly, not what they want to eat. Many roller flyers have assumed they had bad rollers, when all it amounted to was bad feeding practices, generally too much.

Taking Rollers Up in Condition
If you want to keep your old birds strong for an upcoming competition, feed them all they want and then pull the tray. This is done by pulling the tray after the first few birds drink. Giving a working team an extra day off will also help make them stronger. Sprinkle a little grit over their feed every day. The longer that grit is introduced to your roller pigeons, the more that performance will decrease and they will fly higher and longer.

Taking Rollers Down in Condition
When you are ready to increase the frequency of performance and bring the birds lower in flying height, again go to two spoons of feed. This will slowly weaken them, which will induce frequency and less flying time. Rollers that are strong first and then gradually weakened by gradually cutting back the feed will peak out better than rollers that are cut sharply in their feed rations. You can fly your rollers every day and fly them twice a day from time to time to burn off extra energy. When flying twice a day, feed only one spoon per bird on each release. No grit, vitamins, or supplements (like pigeon builder) should be used when bringing them down in condition.

Rest Requirements for Working Pigeons
Working (performing) birds should have a day off to rest. Working

birds are rollers that roll, not ones that just fly and flip. Depending on what your working birds need in terms of rest, you might want to give them two or three days off from flying now and then. When fed right, your birds can put on a good show after a couple of days of rest. Generally, for working birds, flying them every other day works out well. But keep in mind that too much flying time off will affect your pigeons' kitting.

Flying the Roll Out of Your Rollers

Rollers perform with more frequency in a weaker physical state than they do in the reverse. Feeding rollers all they want and flying them every day can cause them to stop rolling because they are too strong. This is called "flying the roll out."

If you have flown the roll out of them by overfeeding and over flying, take the following three steps for two weeks:

1. Feed ONLY two spoons (shaken) of feed per bird per day.
2. Do not give your birds any grit or vitamins during the two-week period.
3. Fly your birds only every other day.

These three steps will bring back the spin within two weeks. Simply cutting back the feed and going to every other day of flying will assure the roll will return. Cutting back the feed will take off some of the fat. The day of rest will help revitalize them and stimulate more mental excitement on the next release. This will normally increase their frequency.

Correcting Sloppy Performance

If good rollers are kept in a weakened physical state for too long, their rolling performance deteriorates because their fat is gone, which starts to affect the muscles. At this time, you will notice sloppy spins from rollers that normally display quality spins. At this point, more feed and rest is required to get working roller pigeons' quality performances back.

Peaking Out in the Performance
Seeing a roller at its best (or peak performance) is normally noticed when you are either at a point of taking the bird back up in strength or when you are bringing one down in strength. Again, this is best done by gradually adjusting the feed. Usually you can maintain a roller's best performance for only a few days. These few days are called "peaking out." When rollers are peaked out, they are in top form and giving the best performances they're capable of. Some also call this physical point "roll fit."

Weather Concerns (When Flying Rollers)
The weather and feed can be your friend or your enemy when flying rollers. Try to get into the habit of checking the weather every day when you're flying your rollers.

When checking the weather, you will find Doppler radar a helpful tool for many reasons. For one, many times hawks will stay in front of an approaching storm. We don't want to lose a bird to a hawk. Another reason would be to let you know when to readjust your flying time to ensure that you can fly your birds. There may be an approaching storm for instance. In addition, check humidity. A combination of high temperature and high humidity will drastically affect your flying time.

Personally, I like to fly my birds at 65 degrees and below because the birds always work their best at cooler temperatures. Bottom line, a few degrees up or down in temperature and humidity can play a big part in your flying time.

The amount of feed, mixture of grains, weather, prior exercise, and the right amount of rest always factors into what your flying results will be for the day. This is the constant challenge of a roller flyer who wants to show his rollers performing at their best and keep from losing them.

The easiest way to fly and make adjustments in flying time with both feed and rest is to stay on schedule. Keeping in mind that weather conditions in general play a huge role in this schedule, you should fly and feed at the same time every day. By staying on schedule you will be able to make more precise adjustments. Early in the morning is the best time to fly your birds to take advantage of the cooler weather. If you are hot and sweating by the time you walk to your loft, don't expect too much work or flying time from your rollers. They always perform better when the weather is cool.

If you have been flying your rollers in the heat and they are doing the time, be aware that a ten degree drop in temperature can trigger either an overfly or a flyaway. For instance, if you have been flying your birds all week in 75-degree weather, and then you release them when the temperature is 65 degrees, many times it will cause your birds to fly way higher and longer than they had been during the 75-degree flying.

Dealing with Snow and Wind

Another weather-related factor to consider is the wind. Never start flying young birds in the wind, which, if overdone, can influence them to fly low as adults. Once the young birds have been on the wing for some time, it is not much of a problem to fly them in the wind. Anything past 10 to 12 miles an hour your taking a chance losing your young birds.

Another potential wind-related problem is flying good rollers in the wind when they are peaked out or getting close to peaking out. The spinners may regroup just fine after performing, but the team will be pushed out of sight in the direction the wind is blowing, most of the time never to be seen again. Be sure to consider these things when getting a team ready for competition.

Never fly your birds when it is snowing! They can be blinded by the snowfall, resulting in a high chance of losing them all. You can fly them after the snowstorm but only after you have cleared the snow from the top of your fly boxes. The birds should be able to see the rooftops for landmarks, which helps ensure you get them back home.

Flying Out of Breath

Rollers flying a short time and landing out of breath (like the birds in previous picture) is normally a sign of one of two things:

1. They are not being flown frequently enough and have become overweight and out of shape physically;
2. It is just too hot. When the heat and humidity are high, your rollers will land with their wing butts wide and their beaks open, panting hard.

To help prevent your birds from landing out of breath, fly your rollers early in the day when the weather is best. If your birds still do this when the heat and humidity are low and the weather is great, then it is a sign that they are out of shape. Let them sit until they get their composure and are looking normal again, and then chase them back up. Do this every day until they fly for some time and land breathing normal. When your rollers can fly the time and are doing the work, and they land without open beaks and wing butts wide, they are back in shape.

Flying an Exhibition Team
If you are thinking of competition in the future, an exhibition fly for your friends is a good place to start. There are no rules. Build an exhibition team for your friends to watch. This will help you focus your training skills for competition without the pressure of deadlines or wins and losses. When you get them where you want them, as far as working well together in the air, call some of your friends to stop by and watch.

Once you can see progress with your rollers and gain confidence with your managing skills, you will be in a good position to compete, which is where you can make them shine.

Don't forget to take day-to-day notes whenever you're getting your birds ready for exhibition or competition to keep track of important things like how you fed them, when you rested them, the temperature, wind, air traffic, humidity, etc. All are key factors to help you understand why your rollers did well or poorly on a certain day. Notes will allow you to make better decisions on your training techniques in the future.

Wing Flight Feather Concerns

Wing flight count knowledge is extremely important for flight/spin excellence in your kit. A roller pigeon wing will have 20 flight feathers, ten primaries and ten secondaries. The condition and count of your bird's wing feathers must be considered if you're going to compete. When a pigeon drops a feather in the molting process, the new feather will be tender while it's growing back. It will be the most tender in the blood stage. Your main concern will be when the eighth, ninth, and tenth primaries are growing back. If one of these is in the blood stage, it can cause some good birds to outfly. They will try to avoid the team, trying not to roll because of the pain caused in the blood stage. The blood stage in any of the last three primaries to molt can also cause a good roller to roll to the ground. Other rollers, however, will stay with the team and work right through this stage. It will affect some birds, while others it may not.

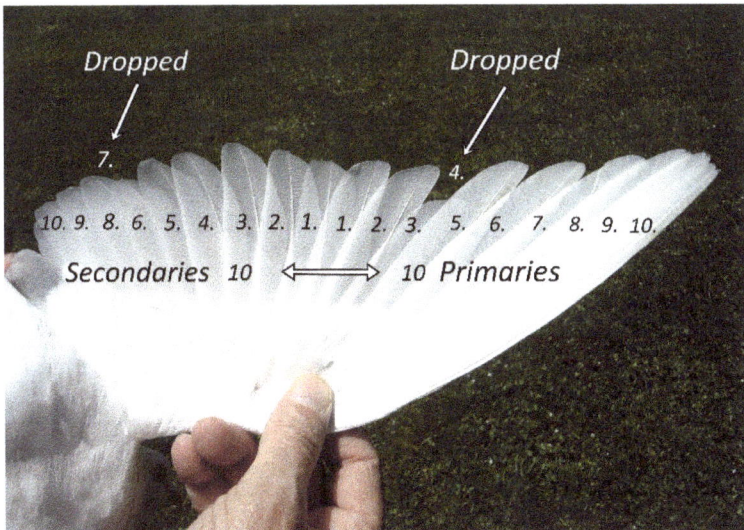

Some rollers that are hard spinners will at times burst the feather quill in the blood stage during performing and trap in with blood on their wings. You may think the bird is injured and wonder where the blood came from. But it was just a busted primary in the blood stage.

One option with the primaries (if you need the bird in a competition team) is to puncture the feather with a needle while in the blood stage. With just a little squeeze on the quill, you can remove the blood. (See next photo.) This will cause the feather to start drying out and in turn stop the sensitivity to the pigeon. The feather will still grow in naturally and be of no more concern to you or the pigeon after it dries out. When the growing feather is around three-quarters grown back, the next higher numbered feather will drop. They will molt from number "1" towards number "10" on both the primaries and secondaries (as labeled in the last picture).

Some trainers will pull the tenth primary when the number 1 primary drops, then pull the number 9 when number 2 drops, number 8 when number 3 drops. This helps the pigeon get through the molt of the last three primaries sooner so you won't have to worry about it during competition time.

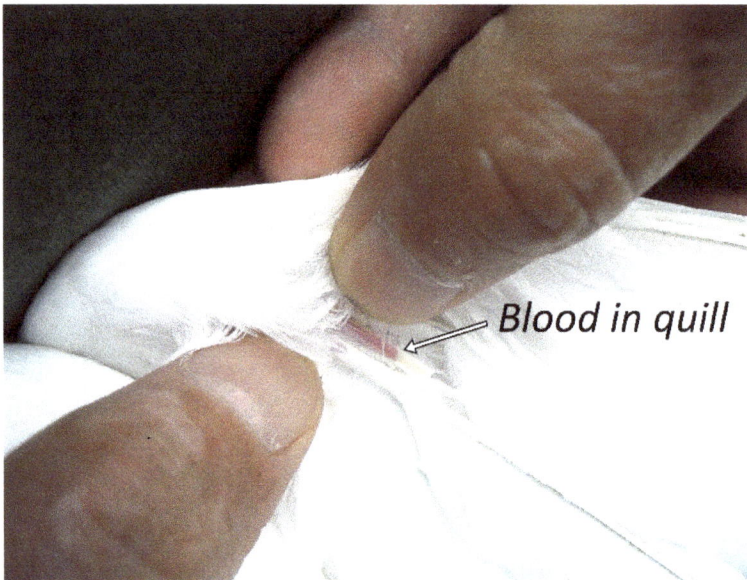

Blood in quill

When getting ready for a competition, you will need to grade your flyers. Most competitors will use old birds for a competition fly, mostly because they are a little easier to manage. Others will use young birds, which are birds in their first year of flying. They tend to show more velocity in their first year of performing.

Whether using old or young birds, they need to be checked or rechecked in the air to see if they are up to par for competition. Sometimes rollers will change their frequency or style of spin, or for some reason may not be rolling at all. You will need to go through them and evaluate each one for prospective team members. This is where you'll wish you raised a hundred or more birds this year.

It will also cross your mind that maybe you should not have taken up breeding space on that color project. At this time you will not care what color they are or how big or small they are. You want all the workers you can find. If you have enough birds to pick from in the air, you will want to double the number of birds needed for the team. For best results, you will want an A and B team. For example, if you're competing in an eleven-bird fly, look for twenty-two workers. In a twenty-bird fly you will want forty workers.

Let's say you're competing with another flyer and he is just as knowledgeable as you. He raised more birds than you did. You will have less chance to beat him in competition. Play it wise and raise plenty to be competition worthy by having a wider selection of workers to pick from. If you're flying one hundred birds, send them all up together. If they all land at the same time after a good flight, then grade these on your next flight. If they split into two groups and one group lands earlier than the other, grade the stronger of the two groups for competition selection.

When competing with young birds, keep in mind that the average young birds are seven months and up in age before they may be worthy to compete. However, there may be the occasional exception that is younger. If you were wise, you bred your birds to be in the roll by this competition. For some reason, this is overlooked by many competitors. Most competition flys are at the same time every year. If you know what age your rollers come into the roll, then breed them to be that age or older by the time of the competition fly. This gives you a big advantage over the flyer who does not breed his birds in the same manner. If you raised the same number of young as your competitors did but put your birds together to breed at the right time, then you beat your competitors as soon as the eggs were laid. These young rollers into the roll can also compete with other flyers' old-bird teams. Peaked-out young birds will have great velocity in their first year, and you can be very competitive with them.

Grading for Competition
Before we get into grading, you must consider where your birds may be in condition. If you have been feeding your birds to allow them to fly for more than one hour or longer, you will want to cut them back on the feed for grading. A few days of enough feed to cause them to be around one hour or a little less in flight will work out fine for grading purposes. You will want them down in condition to help promote the rolling we need to grade. After the grading, you can raise the feed amount back up to get them back over one hour or more in flight.

Gather all the birds to be graded. Asking another flyer to help you grade your birds will make for an easier process. If you can't read wing styles yet, hopefully the other flyer can. Be sure to have a watch or timer and be prepared to take notes on each bird. You want to see for sure what each bird is doing. If you are the only one grading your birds, it can still be done even if you can't read style or wing placement yet. For a better understanding of style and wing placement, go to the section on wing placement further ahead in this book.

You will be watching for your workers and you will want to mark down three things:

1. How far it rolled, or for how long in seconds
2. Wing placement
3. Overall score from one to ten (your personal opinion of how well they performed from one to ten)

One of your graded birds may have rolled two seconds with a high X pattern, and you gave it a six. Another may have rolled three seconds with an H pattern, and you gave it an eight.

It doesn't matter what numbers you give them as long as you are consistent with each bird in your judgement of the overall visual effect that you observed. If you can't read style of the roll yet, just remember that a roller pigeon competition is a visual game. Pick the ones that look the best to you in the performance. Chances are, they will also be the ones that look the best to the judge.

After your competition, pick the judges' brain to learn what you can do to improve your team. Always ask questions when you have a sharp judge or experienced flyer around. There is always something to be gained.

Hand Toss Grading

You will be hand tossing each bird as you grade them. This comes in handy for a quick check of your birds, especially if you have raised 100 or more birds. If you did, and your youngest birds are a year old, you will also need to find the workers and get rid of all the non workers. This is also a quick way to find potential team birds for an upcoming competition. The key to this is not to lose sight of the pigeon after the hand toss until it gets graded. If this happens, you can try that bird again on the next release. The released bird will need a group of pigeons to fly to on the release (10 or more). The 10 birds used to produce a group for grading purposes can be graded tomorrow or the next day. After you have sent up the group and they level off, take one of the birds to be graded, write down the band number and color, and then toss it up in the air. It should make a direct effort to get to the group or kit. If the kit is high, allow enough time for the pigeon to get to the kit. Make sure to keep the bird in sight until the grading of this one particular bird is finished.

Keep in mind that the bird may roll before it gets to the kit. When the bird rolls and you catch it from the side view, write down the depth by seconds and consider whether or not the bird had a nice, tight spin. If the view of the performance was from the front or back, consider wing placement and depth of roll. If any bird has a deviation in the spin, like a twizzle or change of direction of the downward fluidity of the performance, disregard the grade altogether and mark the bird as unworthy to use in your team.

Once the bird reaches the team, your timing for grading is essential. You will need to use your watch or timer and have someone else watch time for you. If the released bird does not perform within one minute of reaching the team, disregard the grade and mark it off your list as "not worthy" at this time, and then move to the next bird to be released for grading. Repeat this process for the remaining birds.

When you are done, go down your list and pick out all the workers that were graded and put them in the same fly box or boxes. Don't forget to grade the 10 you sent up in the beginning of the grading day. The birds you have finished grading can be the group for them to join on the next performance grading day. You can usually wrap up the grading in two days. If you have to skip the next day because of bad weather or feel as if your birds need a day of rest, it won't hurt anything. However, keep in mind that when you're getting ready for a competition you should try to have your birds picked one month prior to your fly date.

Grading with Tape

With tape on the tail of your pigeon you can keep track of it for the entire flight without losing it in the mix with others that are the same color. If you have seven blue check pigeons with white flights in your flock and one of them is rolling, so many of the same color makes it hard to know which one it is. Placing tape in one of these three different positions on their tails allows you to check three of them each time you release the birds. If all seven of your blue check white flights are rolling and one of them is outstanding, you will want to know which one it is to make note of the pair it came from. Also, if you're checking the consistency of quality performances from a pigeon during its flying time, tape on the tail will make it easy to follow for the entire flight.

Refer to the prior photo for reference when taping your birds. I suggest that you use around twelve inches of masking tape (painter's tape), preferably one inch wide. The tape comes in several different colors if you prefer. Place three strips of tape in a ready position before getting the birds to be marked. Place approximately one inch of the tape on the bird's tail in one of the three positions pictured. Be sure to place the tape slightly over the edge of the tail feather for a fold under. This will help keep the tape secure during any spins the bird does. Take the tape that is hanging from the tail and lay it on some powder or press the tape to any surface in your loft that may have pigeon dust on it and peel it off. This will keep it from getting tangled to itself or sticking to the bird. Do the same with the next two birds in the remaining two positions. The tape rarely will come off until the birds land and you take it off.

When the birds land and trap, take the tape off right away. The other birds in the fly box may step on the tape a few times and cause the feather to be pulled from the tail. Placing the tape in the three different positions (far right, center, and far left) will allow you easy recognition of each of the three birds to be evaluated in flight. Be sure to write down the band number of the bird and where you placed the tape on the tail, i.e., Left-1691, Center-1687, Right-1672.

Grading with Hair Color and Paint

Some roller flyers use spray paint to mark their birds for grading. The problem is that spray paint will stay on the bird until it loses the painted feathers in the next molt. If you're okay with that, use spray paint. After you run out of different places to mark the birds (i.e., right wing, left wing, tail, and whatever other combinations you can find), you can do the same with a different color.

Some roller flyers use hair spray colors to do the same. This will eventually wash off of the birds you marked. Others will cut certain feathers to mark a bird. Again, this will last until the next molt.

Grading a Bird by Its Color or Markings

One of the easiest ways to check a bird's performance for the entire flight of the kit is to fly it with birds of a different color, for example, a light bird with a few black or blues. Another would be to fly a flighted bird with self-colored birds.

PART THREE

— *Breeding Pigeons* —

If you're new to breeding, you will want to breed your birds after the worst of winter has passed, starting in the spring when the leaves begin to bloom on the trees. This will make things easier because you won't have to worry about the young and water freezing in the loft. However, you can breed any time of the year if you have the right setup. I have raised rollers in the harshest of winters. The main thing you will need is electricity to your loft. Having lights in the loft will allow you to raise young fairly easily. You can set timers to control how long you want the lights on.

Using Timers

Some timers have faders to allow the birds to return to the nest by the time the light goes out. Setting your timer to 16 hours on works well for raising young.

I stopped using timers (and leave lights on 24/7) because a bird will occasionally get off the nest in the dark. If a mouse gets into the loft and spooks the hen, she will get off the nest and not find her way back. In the winter, you want them to return to the nest as soon as possible. This is why I suggest leaving the lights on twenty-four hours, seven days a week during the breeding period.

Raising young is stressful on the breeders. Therefore, try to avoid breeding more than four rounds out of a pair without a good rest. Over-breeding your stock can weaken them, and they may get sick and die.

Color Concerns

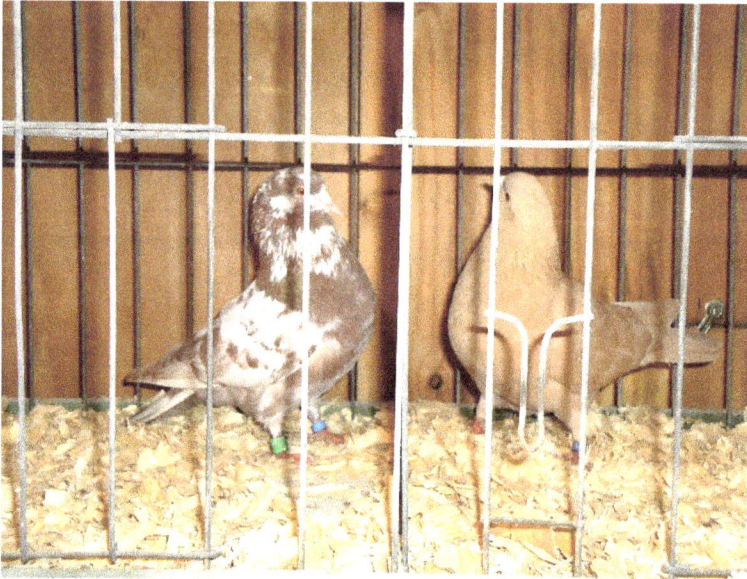

When choosing your breeders, pick your best from the sky first. When breeding rollers to competition standard or for your own backyard entertainment, some things need to be remembered. First and foremost, when breeding for performance, one will progress faster if he or she is colorblind. In other words, for a performance pigeon breeder, color should be the last consideration when pairing your birds. If all else is satisfactory regarding the flying and performing traits you need in the two birds you are pairing, only then may you consider your possible colors, patterns, and modifiers they may produce. Breeding from attractive pigeons will not set a flyer back as long as they are good birds in the air to start with.

If you are blind to the colors in your pigeons while breeding and only pick breeders for their aerial qualities, great gains can be made in a shorter amount of time in your stock loft. Chances are, if you only consider the colors when breeding, you will end up with colorful birds that are weak in aerial abilities. Very strong knowledge of both the quality traits in the air and color genetics on the ground is necessary to succeed in breeding colorful rollers with good performance at high percentages.

Some roller flyers only have one color in their performing rollers to preclude it from being a consideration while breeding. They want no other influence in their decision making other than the rollers' aerial traits. This is not a must, but it is helpful. While a big part of the roller sport or hobby is being able to see and appreciate the wide range of these colorful birds, to each his own.

If I were to go with only one color in my rollers, it would be black. I have noticed that solid black rollers set a better visual appearance while performing on an overcast day. On a sunny day, black white flighted rollers are the easiest for reading wing position when watching.

Necessary Flying Standard Consideration Before Pairing Birds

Another important consideration is that the ability for a roller to roll is due to the action of multiple genes. This was first brought to my attention by the Pensom writings. We have no control over this action of rolling or which genes will be passed on or in what order other than being a decent selective quality trait breeder. Many aerial traits make up a roller pigeon, some good and some bad. Understanding which are the most desired is best done by understanding the accepted roller flying standard and picking birds as close to the set standard as possible.

One should always keep in mind that a good roller is discerned from the sky, not on the ground. All the birds you are breeding from should be observed and graded in the sky for approximately eighteen months while you're training them. This will allow you time to ensure your birds are stable in the roll and consistent in the performance. From these I would suggest you pick your future stock birds. I will also add that with good knowledge and hard flying of the roller pigeon, a handler can stock his birds after 12 months of hard flying and do very well.

The flying standard which is accepted for flying competitions is a good guideline for picking your breeders from the sky. It goes as follows:

"The true Birmingham Roller is a performer which turns over backwards with inconceivable rapidity through a

considerable distance like a spinning ball."

— Lewis Wright

Lewis Wright, who was a pigeon historian, once wrote our present-day standard as a description of a roller pigeon from his observations. Bill Pensom, who was a great roller pigeon enthusiast and teacher, used Wright's description as a guide for explaining what our flying standards should be for a true Birmingham Roller.

The flying standard is what determines whether or not the roller pigeon should deserve to be called a Birmingham Roller. A Birmingham Roller pigeon is called a roller by the name of its breed. Only when it can meet the flying standard should it be called a true Birmingham Roller. In a group of Birmingham Rollers that meet the flying standard and have attained such status, some will be better than others in the performance. The best are called Birmingham Roller champions. They will show exceptional style and velocity above all the others with their high wing placement, great speed while tight as a ball with control while performing. These are the ones we are all striving for.

Some contend the title of champion should include great depth. I see no problem with either a good short one or a good deep one carrying the title of a Champion Birmingham Roller as long as it exhibits the performance that the standard describes. One of each depth would make a great pair for breeding.

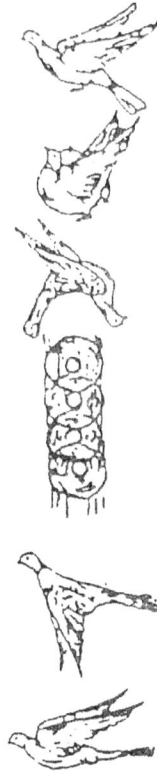

Rolling side view
—from Pensom, William H., The Birmingham Roller
Pigeon, 1958

The previous illustration is the most common visual illustration used to represent the flying standard from the side view. This is one of two illustrations that Bill Pensom drew to help in our understanding of what the best roller pigeons are capable of. According to this visual standard, when viewing a roller's performance from the side, we want our birds to be tight as a ball when rolling, along with having very good velocity, as in Pensom's side view performing illustration.

While some rollers will be tight as a ball, which is good, other rollers in the spin will show the optical illusion of a hole in the center of the ball. This is highly prized by most roller flyers. Some will have loose, sloppy rolls from the side and you may sometimes see two holes. These loose, sloppy performances will not be scored in competition and should not be considered for breeding purposes.

Good spinners that do not show the hole tend to be of short cast in body type. The hole-showing performers normally are cast a little longer in body type. Sometimes a bird may be showing the hole in the performance of the roll, but the distance and angle of your view may be incorrect to see it. The showing of the hole is a good trait but is rarely seen. If two rollers present holes in their side view performances, one being larger than the other, the smaller-hole performer would be of higher value. This impresses on the observer to value a tighter ball in the performance. Keep in mind that a no-hole roller is still a good bird as long as it rolls tight as a ball and has good velocity.

Concerning velocity, an average bird would rotate over at around one revolution per foot. For instance, a ten-foot performance would be the result of approximately ten revolutions, with a very good bird averaging around 13 revolutions in a ten-foot performance. I personally have never counted the rotations. I only mention this because of information presented by good bird men who have filmed and counted the rolls in slow motion. Eight revolutions would be slow, with 13 being the maximum rotation in a 10-foot drop. I have even heard of up to 14 revolutions in the same distance.

The ability to attain 13 to 14 revolutions is the result of a higher-quality bird in the velocity trait area. Some may even see a very rare and exceptional bird in the rotation that may not drop at the same rate as an average spinner. They drop slightly behind the others on the break but have an outstanding amount of velocity, or an "exceptional rotation," in the performance. These are the ones you should always keep an eye out for. They spin so fast that they appear to hesitate briefly while spinning right before the descent of the performance. In all my years, I have only seen one bird with that kind of speed. The faster in the rotation the better. They can never be too fast. Always breed from the fastest you have in the rotation of the spin. You may have two rollers of the same body type and wing style in the performance with one being faster in the rotation. I would surmise these faster types are getting a quicker mental signal from the brain governing the wing stroke. If there is a gene to be captured that causes this, I want it, hopefully, to be perpetuated.

During a roller's performance, the drop distance in seconds (which is debatable) is said to be around ten feet per second, i.e., 20 feet per two seconds, 30 feet per three seconds. Keep in mind that this is an average; you can have one faster or slower in the drop, depending on the overall genetic makeup of the pigeon. To grade birds, for many (and I'm one of them) it makes more sense to time the performance duration in seconds rather than guess the depth. The argument against this is that one person may count one thousand one, two thousand, etc., faster or slower than you do. Regardless, I have always gone with measuring depth in seconds.

However, if you decide to guess depth instead, by all means do what you think will work best for you.

Note: For a more in depth analysis of feet per second, rate of descent, and RPS. You can look for the latest scientific work done by Tou Yang of Hickory, North Carolina.

"How far is too deep?" you might ask.

If the bird can maintain a good style from beginning to end of the performance and make a direct effort to regroup with the team, they are never too deep to watch.

Faults to Avoid When Breeding
The following traits should be avoided when breeding:

1. **Hitting the ground on release** - This type can be part of a good team if you hand toss them when the other team members gain some height, but they should not be bred from.
2. **Hitting the ground or rooftop while landing** - This bird should be culled. If this stops after a couple times, then fly the bird if you want, but it should not be bred from. These crashes most generally are deemed accidents. Roller flyers call birds that have an occasional accident in the

performance "bumpers." Some roller breeders will breed from bumpers because they do not recognize this as a trait to worry about. They will overlook this and not see it as a fault. If you have good birds that do not bump, you would be wiser, in my opinion, to breed only from them. Normally, what you put into a breeding project will reveal itself to you again in the future.

3. **Rolling down to the ground from the team** - These need to be culled.

4. **Birds that do not roll properly** - Examples of not rolling properly include mature birds that may tail ride at the end of a performance; axis changing or any deviation in the spin; and anything other than a nice, smooth, fluid performance with a quick stop at the end. Such birds should be avoided. Some birds will do everything right but have a little wobble at the end of the roll, which is a fault. All the ones I have seen do this were short in the length of tail. Your better rollers have about a thumb width between the flights and the end of the tail for a good stop or finish. Birds short in tail length should not be bred from.

5. **Out flyers (birds that don't stay with the team when flying)** - Out flyers are a problem if you're trying to move forward with your stock. They are useless to you no matter how well they do in the performance or how many other quality traits they possess as a roller pigeon. Remember, non-kitting is a negative genetic trait you are trying to breed away from.

Breeding from pigeons that are more than three seconds in the performance is your choice. But I caution that many competition flyers will not breed from rollers that perform more than three seconds. This seems to be the average limit on a good performance (percentage wise) while staying in a competition range. Very few roller pigeons can maintain a good performance after three seconds. They are out there, but the deeper a roller's performance, the less likely it can maintain the performance standard. Most do prize a good deep one when they get it. They are very impressive to watch. Just keep in mind that the more you play with depth of roll, the more roll-downs and bumpers you will have.

Balancing Depth of Performance When Pairing for Breeding
When pairing your birds for breeding, you'll want to breed deep-performing birds to short performers. Generally, when you breed deep to deep you end up with a high percentage of roll-downs. One should try to balance depth by breeding short to deep, which ensures that both types of performers will be available.

Breeding too much from either type of performer will result in more of the same. Most flyers use both short and deep rollers in competition. A combination of both types of rollers will make for a better working team in the air. What works well for me is 3-second performers bred to 1.5- to 2-second performers.

A roller breeder should select birds with a conscious effort to improve one's stock. It's all about the stock loft. When your stock birds are set and producing a high percentage of good performing young, you will be in a great position as a competitor.

"What about short birds? Can they be too short?"

Yes.

Remember, the flying standard states considerable depth. "Short performing" normally refers to a pigeon that is 10 feet to 20 feet in the roll. Anything less than ten feet is not acceptable. Five feet of action is not much to consider as a performer. The scoring depth starts at ten feet in competition. When choosing between the five-foot and ten-foot performer, one should always lean toward the deeper bird unless the shorter one has some trait that may be needed to improve the overall quality of your stock, e.g., has a higher wing placement in the performance or improved velocity, frequency, or body type that you may be lacking in your stock, etc. When breeding, one should consider all the traits that make up a good roller that may be needed or may help improve a trait that is lacking in your birds.

As a roller breeder, always consider your knowledge of rollers and the written flying standard as you mate and propagate your birds. Learn to discern which rolling style or wing placement your rolling pigeons are showing from a front or back view in the performance. This will help you further develop your stock.

Wing Placement

Many roller flyers have flown roller pigeons for years and still cannot read wing placement. Since the written flying standard does not cover wing placement, many believe it is unnecessary to master. Bill Pensom, one of the greatest authorities on roller pigeons, coined the written standard and is known for drawing two rolling illustrations of the standard (rear and side view) for a better visual understanding of the performance.

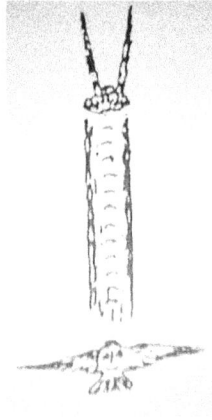

Rolling rear view
—from Pensom, William H., The Birmingham Roller
Pigeon, 1958. This drawing represents the H pattern style
wing placement.

Bill kept both illustrations on his letterhead for correspondence with other roller fanciers. With this in mind, I have always considered both illustrations (side and rear view) in selecting my best birds. I suggest that you master reading your rollers' performing patterns not only from the side view, but front and back view as well. Reading a roller's performances from the front or rear at a 45-degree angle will give you the wing placement.

You will be in a better position in flying your rollers in competition if you can read the side view and the front or rear view in the roll to get a reading on wing placement. The best flying judges do consider overall wing placement in your competition team.

Knowing how to read a bird's wing placement will be advantageous in both selecting breeders to further the development of your stock and selecting rollers for competition. There is much to be gained in a competition with higher wing placement. If your competitor's birds' work rate is as good as yours, but you have a higher average wing placement, you will win.

In the performance, rollers will put their wings in various positions. This is determined by the distance a roller strokes its wings while in the rotation of the spin. Certain positions of the wings in the performance are more desirable than others. They run from a low axle placement in the performance to a very high tight H position. H or better is your goal, with less space on the top and bottom of the H if you can get it. You want them to almost touch, like so: ( ). Bowing in from the H pattern, known as a tight H, is most desirable.

The illusion of patterns portrayed in the performance runs as follows:

(All these patterns are scorable in competition. Numbers 5 through 7 are the most desirable. The more you have in your competition team, the higher your quality points will be.)

1. **Axel** is what some call a corn cob roll—where the wings will point straight out to the side like a stick through a donut hole. Some have great velocity.
2. **Low X** is the next wing position up in quality.
3. The **High X** pattern is better on the scale of quality compared to the Low X pattern.
4. This **A** pattern, which is called the steeple, can score but is less desirable than the H or ( ) = tight H.
5. This **H** pattern up through pattern 7 produces a very "pleasing to the eye" straight line performance. This is a

starting point for most flyers that compete and consider wing placement when selecting their best performers.

6. This **( )** pattern is what most call a tight H. The closer the wing tips appear to be on the finish of the up and down stroke, the better visual in the performance. This tight ( ) pattern illusion represents a better than H stroke in the wing beats of the roll. This is one of the best of the pattern wing placements in the roll and is very desirable in a roller pigeon.

7. Sometimes rollers will slightly exceed this sought-after pattern of number 6. I refer to this pattern as the **Slim A. ()** The wings tips will be bowed in. The slim A is about as tight as the front or back view of the pattern can get. It appears to touch at the top and almost at the bottom of the illusion of the pattern. I believe that the reason for not seeing a comparable closeness at the bottom is because the bird is in the process of bringing the wings back up from the stroke at this point. Visually, the pattern looks similar to this (), with a little more space at the bottom and with the top touching. Keep in mind, we are not talking about the steeple, but the appearance of a very small gap at the bottom of the pattern that is not as wide as the steeple would show. It is more like two dinner plates set vertically on their edge touching at the top with a very small gap at the bottom. With this style of performance, you will sometimes notice rollers with the wing tips (primaries) of their flight feathers frayed or broken from hitting together.

Any of the above seven patterns that would involve any deviation of the start and finish of the scorable style are not desirable and would not be scored. One such deviation is called axis changing, which is missed by the untrained eye. A good example would be when a young roller does a flip, it will be facing the same direction when the rotation is completed. If the same bird does 30 rotations, it should still be facing the same direction at the finish of the roll. If not, the bird has changed its axis at some point in the performance.

If a roller has this fault of axis changing and is facing the wrong way in the performance, it should not be considered for competition or bred from. Some axis changes are very obvious to the observer while the bird is descending; some will take a keener eye to see. Occasionally, you will spot one doing an axis change and still end up facing out in the right direction when finished. This is still an obvious deviation in the performance and is an aerial performance fault.

You will see all these wing placement positions in different rollers in their performance. The ones that are consistent in high wing placement will always be of higher value to you. Remember, the wing placement positions are the result of an optical illusion portraying these visual symbols or patterns and depend on the velocity of the performance and the distance of the wing stroke. They are normally hard to read without a certain amount of experience.

When you start to learn to read style, good roller performances will all look like a blur. The struggle is to read the blur. It will help tremendously if you have plenty of time to observe rollers with another roller flyer who can stand with you under a team of rollers and talk you through reading the patterns. Even after guidance from another roller flyer, it may still take you many observation days to distinguish one pattern from another. But without putting forth the effort they may never be seen.

If you are on your own trying to see the pattern in a roller's performance, remember to view the roller performing while it's flying towards you or flying away from you when it goes into the spin. True wing position cannot be seen from the side view. The wing positions can be seen best by standing at a 45-degree angle from your birds while they perform. The first time you finally get to see a certain rolling pattern, seeing the others will not be far behind.

Speed and tightness in the rotation, along with high wing placement, plus control of their depth in the performance should be your constant objective as a breeder. At times you will see a roller exhibit more than one style or pattern in the performance of the spin. This is normal, for most rollers are not consistent in style. This mostly depends on how tired the bird is, and sometimes your viewing vantage point may be slightly compromised.

Always grade a roller on its consistency of style of performance. If roller A produced three high wing pattern spins out of ten performances and roller B produced four or more, then roller B would be of higher value.

Note: If you are struggling with reading style of performance and are getting ready to compete, just pick the fastest, straightest performers you have that kit. If you keep trying, one day you will see the wing placement. I have worked with roller flyers in the past on reading wing placement. I always enjoy the phone call the day the patterns reveal themselves to the flyer. They usually never see them until days or even weeks after our encounter. I experienced the same thing when I was trying to learn to read wing placement. So, do not get discouraged if you cannot see the patterns right away. For a little visual help in understanding rolling styles from the front or back view you can go to: Roller Legends New Era Episode 3 Art Martinez on YouTube. Towards the end of the video Art shows a tool he made to help people see the different wing positions. I believe it will be of great help to you.

I will remind you as a breeder that a bird with all the best qualities is useless for breeding and competition if it does not kit, or stay, with your team. In my experience, they tend to pass this trait on to the young and should not be bred from. Rolling pigeons should stay together in a tight group, and after a break (performance) go right back to grouping tight again. You will occasionally have a good roller that does everything right but flies out to the side of the team by the distance of the team's width. Even if it is one of your best performers, refrain from using the roller in your breeding program. This is a trait you do not want in your birds. Even though it is close to the team when flying, the pigeon is still considered out if it is out by the width of your team. These "slightly out" birds (almost kitters) can't score in competition. Before all else, a roller must kit first. The tighter your team, the better.

When breeding your pigeons, always breed from rollers with the best desired traits. Over time, this should help purge the bad traits and increase your percentages of good ones in the years that follow.

When breeding rollers, remember that we are using the best educated guess we can, keeping in mind that we can't be sure of the coming results. Some roller pairs will produce the good birds we were hoping for and some matings will not. Consider all you know about two birds when you breed them together. This will save you both time and money.

Rolling Pattern/Style Considerations for Breeding

Rolling pattern and style is very important when you are considering breeding champion birds. For example, if you have just one H-pattern roller, breed it to your next highest wing placement bird. Hopefully it is with another H or maybe a high X (if this is the highest you have to breed from). If you have no H-placement birds at all, then breed high X to high X. Sometimes high X birds will produce one or more H performers. Let's say you have a high H in the roll that you think could use more velocity in the performance, and the very fastest bird you have is a low X. Hoping to get a high H or better with the velocity of the low X, I would breed them together. Out of ten of their offspring, you should get at least one (sometimes more) with a mixture of the traits you want, which will help you move your breeding program forward.

If you have good birds but can't seem to produce the high H or better pattern in your young, then I would look around for a couple to bring into your breeding program. If you can read wing patterns, you can pick out and buy a guy's best performer when you spot it. If the flyer does not compete or does not read wing placement, you may get the bird at a very reasonable price.

If he is one of your competitors and he knows what he is looking at, it could cost you dearly. I have known of a champion in the sky that reproduces the same sell for one thousand dollars. Most will not sell them for any price, because they are too hard to come by, while others will give you a bird of great value at no cost because they know you and think you might need it more than they do. It's a good rule of thumb to never be satisfied with your birds, never let your glass get full. Always keep an eye out for a good one that may help you make your birds better. Thinking this way as you breed from year to year will move you forward very quickly for both backyard entertainment and competition.

When breeding pigeons, nothing is set in stone. You may breed two high wing birds together with the best of all the other desired traits and produce low-quality performers from that pair. On occasion, lesser birds may produce birds that are better than the parents in wing and velocity traits. Not all the birds you raise in a season will be keepers. Feel lucky if you get 10 out of 100 you would consider breeding from in a season. Keep track of how many quality pigeons you get in a season and from which pairs. Then adjust pairs accordingly. This way you should move forward very fast. The goal is to get a higher percentage of keepers than the previous year, never being content, always pushing forward. Keeping track of all the necessary factors to be a good flyer will depend greatly on your note keeping. Keeping good notes will more than pay you back for your time.

The most important notes refer to breeding and flying. Key breeding notations include percentages of good birds from the pair, what the parents' wing positions and depth are, if any eggs were infertile, if the parents are good feeders, youngsters' band numbers, etc. You may also want to take notes on what pattern or color modifiers the parents may be hiding. This would be handy for keeping the colors you like best or staying away from colors or patterns you do not like, not that any color would necessarily hurt or help you where performance is concerned. Color choice would be strictly up to the flyer.

Flying notes are important. The following are examples of notes that I personally keep:

- What age the bird started rolling, not flipping, but rolling. (This will be helpful when mating early to late developers.)
- Does it break (roll) with the others? (This is good to know when picking out the best to breed from or for competition.)
- Does it fly straight back to the kit? (Rollers that take longer than necessary to get back to the kit will cost you points in competition.)
- Where does it fly in the kit? (It's always helpful to know

which rollers fly in the front of the kit and are frequent. They help stimulate your kit to turn over.)

- What is the frequency of its performances? (The more frequent the bird, the better, as long as it does the time with the others. Some are too frequent. You will know them by their constant chasing of the kit.)

- What is the most consistent wing pattern the roller shows in the performance out of 10 spins? (The higher the wing helps make velocity more appealing to the eye.)

- Does it roll deep, short, or is it a multiple-depth performer, performing both deep and short performances? (The multi-depth would be best for breeding. These birds tend to show control when flying low.)

- Is the velocity of rotation fast enough to compete with? (Velocity is almost everything in good rollers and can never be fast enough.)

- Did the bird ever hit the ground? Was it an accident (bumper) or straight down (roll-down)?

- Is the bird a good kitter? (Without kitting, you have no pigeon no matter how good a performer. This note may cause you to reconsider breeding the bird's parents together again.)

- Does it land with the others or is it an early or a late lander? (Rollers should take off and land at the same time unless there is a good reason like being a little more frequent than the others and landing before the rest).

- Does it fly higher or lower than the kit? (You can forgive a bird that flies above the kit when it first starts rolling, but only for a while. You will know when it's long enough. I would stress patience to get a good bird for competition, but not for breeding. However, a pigeon that flies lower than the kit I have no patience for, especially if it is of the same age as the others that are flying.)

Keeping the notes I suggested and anything you want to add will help make it easier to know which birds to keep and how you are going to breed them. Without notes, chaos will ensue and all potential progress will stop. Always work with your best birds if you want to be competitive.

Type and Body Structure Considerations When Selecting Breeders

When considering what physical attributes may help to improve your birds, look at your best performers in the stock loft. The ones with the highest wing placement in the roll and best velocity are the ones to study. Also, when visiting other flyers, ask if you can handle their best three or four birds. Look for similarities in their body structures. It is important to note, however, that his best bird in fly shape versus stock shape would feel like a different bird in the hand. Birds are lean (or they should be) when in flying shape but will be a little on the fat side in the stock loft, because of the lack of flying and the extra feed they receive. The flying bird in its first year will be shorter in length and very light in condition compared with the same bird kept in the stock loft. The length of a pigeon's feathers will be longer after the first molt.

After some time of study and examination of the very best, you will get a decent idea of how you would like all your birds to be built. You will encounter good birds in both very large and very small types. If all the right physical traits are in place, a large roller pigeon will look as good as a small one in the performance of the roll. You will notice that they both will have a nice, wide chest for power to aid in the velocity of the spin.

Other things, like the feel of the keel of the best spinners, should be studied. The keel is the breastbone. You may not be able to notice the difference between a shallow or deep keel in the beginning of your interest in body type, but in time you will. If you're lucky enough to be around an experienced roller flyer to help you, it will save some time. Your interest in the keel is to discern between deep, shallow, and medium keel, medium being the right design of the best spinners.

A keel bone holds the muscles that power the performance. If a roller is deep keeled, it will have more muscle. These can be very good in showing velocity but tend to come in early and roll down. A deep-keeled bird rarely lives very long when flown regular. I have seen some deep-keeled birds make it, but I would suggest that you stay away from breeding deep-keeled birds if you have others that are not. Shallow-keeled birds tend to fly high by design of the keel. This keel is best designed for soaring or gliding, and they tend to fly high. A good example of a shallow-keeled bird is a hawk. A good example of a deep-keeled bird is a turkey or a modena pigeon. Short or long keels depend on the roller breeder. Some like them to tuck up into the vent bones, which is considered long, while others like a finger width gap between the keel and the vent bones, which is considered short. I like the keel to tuck up into the vent, but I don't think either will hamper or help the spin. Your main concern is to understand the keel fully and come to your own conclusion.

When handling a roller pigeon, notice the body; it should be wide in the front and taper back to the tail like a wedge.

Homing pigeons are a good example of a wedge type body.

You will see the wedge type in your best performers' body structure. You can also see it nicely by looking down on your birds when they are in the floor during feeding time. You will notice some may be narrow in the front. These pigeons are called waspy bodies, and the trait is not a desirable one in the body structure or type in a roller pigeon. If the bird does it right in the air and you need it, breed it to a wider-chested bird. If you have others just as good with the right bodies, shy away from the waspy-chested ones. They can display high wing in the performance of the roll but tend to lack the velocity of the wider-chested birds.

You will have roller pigeons that may be weak in certain physical attributes but still have good aerial abilities. Breed from them to improve them, but only if you do not have better birds to work with. While breeding to enhance any physical trait, understand that you may overdo your original intentions. Breeding rollers too wide in the front will affect wing placement in a negative way. Too wide in the chest will result in a lower wing placement in the performance.

Just because a roller is of the right type does not mean it will roll properly. Our goal should be to get the type on the ground and the necessary traits in the air together. After proper selection of these things, all your birds in time will look or should look the same if no other birds are introduced to your stock. Joe Roe used to say, like "peas in a pod."

Over the years, I have noticed in my very best performers that their primary flight feathers touch each other when laying over the tail, like the red checker pigeon in the prior photo. Sometimes they will slightly cross over each other. I have had rollers whose flight feathers cross too much, which results in a lesser style in the performance. Be aware that you cannot simply expect a bird whose flight feathers touch to be a champion in the air. But it is one of the things I like to see in the body type of a roller, because my best have always shown this wing placement on the ground.

Feathers on a bird can run from too soft to too hard. Stay in the middle with strong but flexible feathers. The feather should be flexible yet strong enough to handle a champion's spin without breaking in the flights. However, some damage will occur with some birds with high wing action regardless of good feathers. If by chance you have a good performer that is soft feathered, be sure to breed it to a harder-feathered bird.

If you acquired good rollers to start with, the body type and the performance that goes with it will most likely be there. But it is always a plus to know the best type and performance when you see it. Never ignore a pigeon that's superior to your own. Borrow it, buy it, or trade for it. If you think it may help improve your birds, use it.

Never be so caught up in your birds to think they can't be improved. Even flyers who have been flying the same family of birds for years eventually bring in some new blood. Picking the right one for this is always the challenge. I do, however, know a roller flyer who has bred his own family of rollers for 22 years without introducing a new bird, Ken Easley from New Mexico, a friend of mine for years. He has done very well with his rollers in competition, and I have been flying his family of birds for some years now. Ken is also a Master Flyer and now works with racing pigeons. He got his first rollers in 1967. I asked Ken to explain how he created his family of rollers. The following is his process.

— *Breeding a Family of Rollers by Ken Easley* —

October 25, 1999
Updated May 2018

Sometimes in the course of flying out young rollers, one will find he has in his possession a bird that exceeds all others. It doesn't matter at what level you are, this will almost always be the case. What is an excellent roller in your eyes today may be well below the mark in the future due to improvement within the family. All young birds will not show the success of your efforts, but improvement should be noticed in some individuals. This is the indicator of progress. The realization that your efforts have paid off is an exciting time. You have been careful, using only the best, when a youngster turns up that is beyond all before him. How many times do you get a roller that enjoys rolling and can vary the depth, with speed and stability? Not very often, I can assure you.

Another grand moment is when you see a huge break with definition. This would be a break wherein ¾ or more of the kit is coming down deep, in tight speeding little balls. A break without the typical filler slop. These are the tidbits of success we all patiently await. I have seen improvement in individuals over the capabilities of the parents. The cause for the newfound ability is due to the combination of the parents' genetic background. It could be that something new or old has been brought to the surface that wasn't visible before. Traits that were possessed by a bird in the past may be reintroduced, or a new unseen version could surface. Your family of rollers in this way can be considered improved. Such revelations are more possible with the constant switching of mates, increasing the odds of unlocking hidden genetic secrets. The evidence that will support this is the fact that a roller was once a cross between a tumbler and an Oriental Roller.

In speaking with a group of roller enthusiasts recently, an older and wiser counterpart mentioned the fact that knowing your family of birds for several generations is an essential tool for the development of a superior stud. Traits that were visible or the character of a past champion may be noticed in a young bird of that descent, giving an indication of what the future may hold.

My experience indicates that you can do almost anything you wish with rollers. I have at my command all the proof one could want. Do you suppose fantails just happened? How about Pigmy Pouters? These birds can be modified in many directions without question. Birds such as the above mentioned can be improved more easily because you can see the results quickly. Rollers, on the other hand, must be flown out to see what has happened. Working on a family of rollers is like chiseling the Titanic out of stone. Just a little here and a little there. Usually the proof of our efforts is very slow coming. I would imagine that, individually, as good as a roller can get has been achieved by someone, but that doesn't mean that you cannot improve upon your own family. There are many things one could improve on, such as frequency, depth, tighter kitting, simultaneous performance, etc.

The most efficient way to begin is by building on the solid

foundation of others from the past, being careful to start as high up the ladder of good stable rollers as possible. Then being very careful not to destroy, but to add to the end product. One should at the very least try to maintain what was started with. In the scheme of things, I would say I know almost nothing. I once asked my grandfather what valuable information he had to pass on to me at the age of 86. He replied by saying, "I am old enough to know, I don't know a thing." I was confused for some time, but that was the best advice of all. What we thought we knew at one time can change with age and experience. What we know about any given subject is equivalent to the success of our efforts in general, but we must be careful not to overlook new valid information that could affect improvement. Should you ask a fellow that builds race cars for a living about any piece of the car, do you think he will be able to answer?

Without question, what makes winners is passion, dedication, and the use of acquired knowledge coupled with hard work. Do you think he would be interested in new information that would increase the horsepower of his engine? Of course, but nothing is for sure until after the test drive. After many test drives one begins to understand what works and what doesn't. The only responsible and sure way to build and understand what is inside a roller is to fly them out and observe. I was recently requested to share my views on establishing a family of rollers. There are several ways to accomplish this. You could begin with several different families and selectively build a family. This can take years due to different body types, feeding, flying type, and many other considerations. If you are young and have plenty of time, this may be the path for you.

Another method is taking a couple of pairs from an established family and inbreeding them. If you are older and want quick results, this may be the route for you. I do not recommend this for long term due to the limitations in the gene pool. Chasing rollers from well-known families is not always the best path. Some of the very best breeders I know are quiet and relatively unknown. Be sure you can recognize a good roller, then spend time where you have seen the higher number of fast, stable birds. (Lots of good rolling and very few roll-downs) Try to get the best from the air or old proven stock birds from the same source. Most successful breeders have three to five different parts to a family. This helps to keep the gene pool strong, and it is not often that one bird possesses all the desirable traits that make up the perfect roller. The birds should all be related, but not too close, and may be mated many different directions for higher odds of success. Try to get all the pieces. Then begin pairing the birds. Raise three rounds of youngsters from each pair then switch mates. Do this until every possible combination has been tried.

Fly out the resulting youngsters for two years, only keeping the ones that fly in the kit and roll straight, clean, tight, fast, smooth, and instantaneously in the breaks. Depth can be regulated through proper matings. After two years, pick out the best rollers from your kit to use with the breeders you already have. You may only have one or two worth breeding. Switch mates every three rounds as before. Keep records of which parents produced the best so that eventually you will have a good idea of which ones are the good producers. Get rid of the originals that don't produce after all possible combinations have been tried. In about five to six years you should see the beginnings of a true family of your own. You will begin to recognize qualities and characteristics of ancestors from the past, as in your own human family. Be very selective about what you start with or you may find it necessary to start over in the future. Watch out for roll-downs and birds that won't fly in the kit.

These things don't just go away, it takes years and much effort to breed out bad qualities. If you want excellent rolling, don't be too anxious to use pretty birds. You will get a few beautiful birds that can do it right, and that is great, but remember, just because they look like a champion, doesn't make it so. One of the essential traits to watch for is stability. A stable bird may roll with extreme velocity, but not when close to the ground. They can vary the depth in which they roll. They will rarely if ever hit the ground when rolling. If a smart bird makes a mistake and hits the ground, it will be noticed that he will learn and not repeat the same mistake. Stable birds roll when and where they wish.

Stability must be watched for and maintained. Raising rollers is much like following a path with very few markers. If you don't see good, frequent, and stable rolling, don't go that way. When building a family of rollers, the pretzel method has been my choice for the best results. It's nothing special or hard to understand, in fact the opposite. It is very easy to do. My father and grandfather flew rollers, too. When I was growing up they would say, don't let those two mate up, they are brothers and sisters or father and daughter. When you're a kid and you only have one pigeon that can roll 40 feet like a spinning yoyo and go back to the kit, your options are limited. So I had to figure out ways not to break the rules they gave me and still somehow get many birds to roll like that one good one. So I would breed my prized blue baldhead cock with the best hen I could get my hands on. I would fly the youngsters and find the ones that rolled like the father. I would switch the father to many different mates so I could have lots of outside blood. I would get birds from Mr. Comstock, Mike Trainer, Terry Toliver, and others to cross onto the old cock. I would mate the best performers to "outside the family" birds, too. Then fly these and find a new generation of top performers. Then I could mate these back to others bred similarly that also showed the performance of the old blue cock.

In several generations, I had the old blue cock dominantly throughout the family without having bred mothers to sons or brothers and sisters together. I had fulfilled my mission when I bred 1981 NPA 50. He was everything I wanted and produced the same. Fast tight spinners that were deep. The only problem is that many would roll down by one year old. They were great for competition as young birds, but by the next year most were gone. I decided to start over in the late '80s. I picked up rollers from Frank Lavin, Jay Starley, Art Hopkins, and John Destout. I flew out several hundred, and after three years I had a cock that was a 30' smooth H-pattern dependable cock. He was 92-CTRC-374 from a pair of Chip Carter birds bred by John Destout given to me as a youngster by Art Hopkins. He flew lower than many of the old Pensom families I had encountered, so I really liked him. I also had a hen 93 Utah 370 dark check who was multi-depth up to 50 feet and smart as a whip and tight in the roll. Both birds had come home from overflies. They were strong and dependable. They had the rare trait of initiating the breaks on the turn. I begin looking at the pedigrees and realized they were highly related. The cock had 514 in the pedigree 13 times and the hen had 514 in the pedigree nine times. The youngsters from them were incredible spinners with the old 514 in the pedigree 22 times. I won the region the first year with 13 of them in the kit. Looking through the pedigrees I realized they had all the best Pensom birds in the lines. I was happy because I had flown them hard before knowing the background. They had proven themselves without any prejudices. They truly were amazing pigeons.

I sought out to find others from the same source and added in a couple of birds from Jay Starley who had also gotten his birds from John Destout and helped in acquiring the 370 hen from Chip Carter when she was a youngster in the nest. I carried her in my coat pocket on the airplane. I put her and her nest mate in the kit and forgot about her until I saw her spinning one day. She was everything my old blue cock was, and she flew several years without ever rolling down.

Jay and I became good friends over the years and traded pigeons many times. At one point he borrowed my 370 hen and put her on his best two cocks. I later acquired a youngster from each one. I picked them from the kit he was flying, and they were as good as they get. I also picked up two full sisters from Adam Hill's World Cup–winning kit to pretzel into my family. This was the finishing touches of my family of birds. I won the region many times, placed well in the national and world finals with them. A few ties receiving the highest quality multipliers of 1.8.

Breeding a family of rollers is like a long dance. We dance a little flying the birds, adjust, and dance some more. Breeding rollers takes a lot of patience and hard work. There are no shortcuts other than getting the best birds you can to start out with. Then it is up to you to breed them properly, fly them hard, and only select the right birds to move forward with in the breeding loft. Keeping a baseline of pigeons you understand because you built them is mandatory for continued success. Everyone wants to win immediately. Where is the fun in that? Enjoy the dance. Adjustments while dancing will include all aspects of raising pigeons. Maintaining feather quality, stamina, strength, spin, breeding ability, egg laying, longevity, smarts, homing ability, flying height, instantaneous breaking, depth, quality, and many other minor details.

I used to amaze my friends by being able to pick out the best rollers in the kit. I had a secret that I used to pick them out when it wasn't obvious in the air. The secondary feathers near the body will twist during the roll when the air is exiting through during the spin. The very best, the super-fast rollers, will break these feathers. This tells me the feather is too dry. The pigeons must be oilier with flexible feather. The ones with the best feather can spin like a bullet without tearing up these feathers. I figured that out when I had several high-quality spinners coming from the old 25 x 370 cross pigeons. I noticed that when they spin the feather would still twist and this would pull the barbules apart. They would quickly reattach but in misaligned way, due to the curling effect on the feather. It would leave small pin holes at the base of the quill. I could go through a kit and find the birds with these pinholes and I knew I had the spinners. I would put these in one kit to make a super kit. It is true what Bill Pensom said about putting too many super rollers in one kit, and you would have sore legs and tails in no time due to accidents. In the best kits it is advisable to have several 10–15 footers that break frequently that spark up the kit and will wait for the deeper birds during the breaks.

These birds are always more frequent and will help your kit put on a better display for the judge or home viewing enjoyment. These pigeons are the glue that holds the kit together. I had a cock one year that every time he rolled, his wings stuck out and his speed was medium. A friend gave him to me and I promised to fly him out. He didn't match the rest of the kit. I didn't like him at all because I like high H-pattern or balled up tight. I pulled him out of a kit that was breaking two times a minute and more. The kit completely changed and stopped breaking, or the breaks were completely out of time with two here and three there. Chemistry means a lot on a great kit and changing out a kit member can ruin the performance. I added the cock back to the kit, and they began to perform again but not at the same level. I hoped I could get them back, and we managed to win the regionals by a small margin.

When the judge came for the finals the first thing he said after the judging was, Why do you have that one with the wings sticking out in your kit? I had to lower your quality due to him. I told him the story, and he agreed these birds are a continual surprise and challenge. I gave away the kit and started over after he left. These are the kinds of things we as managers must do to train and maintain a proper kit. It doesn't just happen at the kit box door. We must also make subtle changes as the master of the breeding loft. Breeding rollers is not easy, and it takes a master breeder to maintain a top-notch roller operation. You are trying to keep a ball balanced on top of a needle. Yes, it can be done, but it takes great understanding of these birds and, in particular, your own birds.

Pedigree Example

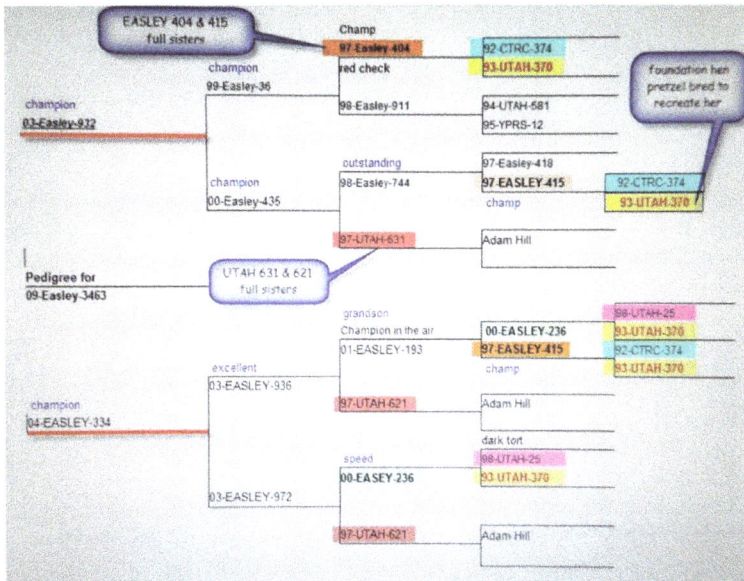

EASLEY 404 & 415 full sisters

Champ
97-Easley-404
red check
92-CTRC-374
93-UTAH-370

foundation hen pretzel bred to recreate her

champion
99-Easley-36

98-Easley-911
94-UTAH-581
95-YPRS-12

champion
03-Easley-972

outstanding
98-Easley-744
97-Easley-418
97-EASLEY-415
champ
92-CTRC-374
93-UTAH-370

champion
00-Easley-435

97-UTAH-631
Adam Hill

Pedigree for
09-Easley-3463

UTAH 631 & 621 full sisters

grandson
Champion in the air
01-EASLEY-193
00-EASLEY-236
97-EASLEY-415
champ
98-UTAH-25
93-UTAH-370
92-CTRC-374
93-UTAH-370

excellent
03-EASLEY-936

97-UTAH-621
Adam Hill

champion
04-EASLEY-334

speed
00-EASEY-236
dark tort
98-UTAH-25
93-UTAH-370

03-EASLEY-972

97-UTAH-621
Adam Hill

Pedigrees are a good way to check on a pigeon's background breeding. This pedigree is one of Ken Easley's. You can see how he went about pretzel breeding to get his best-producing breeding pair.

Size Considerations

For the best optical illusion in the performance, in my experience, medium- to small-sized birds on average are your best bet. Some roller breeders do not care if they are large or small as long as they roll right, while others prefer a medium-sized roller. I will say that none of the above matters on competition day as long as they are doing it right in the sky. But I do consider size when I'm breeding from them.

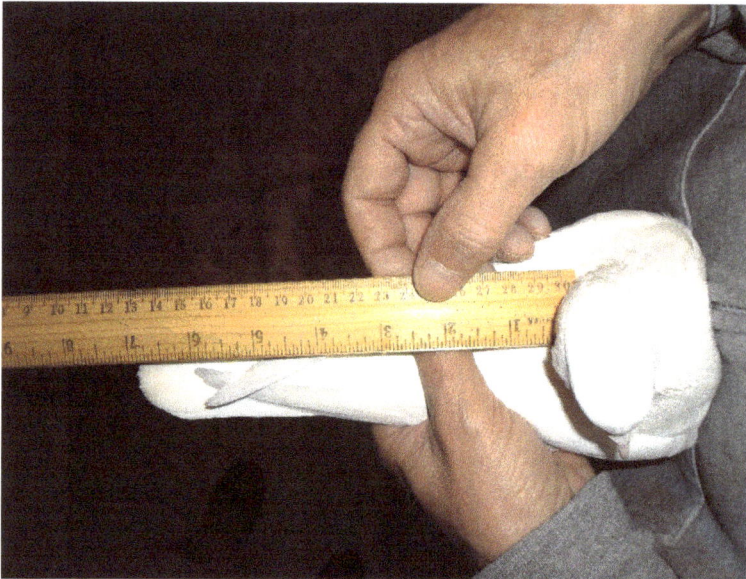

The length of the birds I prefer for breeders would be 6.5 inches to 7 inches on a hen and 7 inches to 7.5 inches on the cocks. This would be measured from the base of the neck to the tip of the tail, as pictured above.

Pairing Pigeons

With the knowledge you have now, it's time to put your pairs together. Begin by picking the best hen and cock you currently have in your loft. Then the second-best pair, third-best, etc. I suggest that you balance your pairings, with one being short and one being deep in the performance. You should be selecting the fastest and highest-wing birds for pairing. If all your birds are high wing, that would be great, but rare. Most are lucky to have one H or better in wing placement in their loft. However, having many birds with H wing placement or better would not be out of reach for any breeder through proper selective breeding.

Since we know that the correct way to breed is best-to-best matings, it should be noted that "best to best" is not your deepest to your deepest performers. You will be selecting them for velocity, wing placement, and frequency first, then breed deep to short. We as roller breeders are taking an educated guess or gamble that our selections will move our breeding program forward. So the more you know, the better. Educating yourself will gain you a higher percentage of quality roller pigeons in a shorter amount of time. Most of the more successful roller fanciers will raise 100 or more birds in a season, hoping to get some good birds for competition. The competition birds are where you will be selecting your future stock from. Raising 100 or more a year will increase your chances of quality keepers for breeding and competition in no time. If you're in a hurry to climb the roller ladder to success in competition, I suggest that you raise many until you get your stock birds and flyers where you want to be.

Working with Color
Now that we've covered competition, I'd like to discuss the breeding of different colors. One of the big attractions to me as a boy (and other pigeon enthusiasts) was the vast number of colors in roller pigeons. We have all desired another good bird in a certain color.

Without knowing basic color genetics, it could be a long time before you may get another pigeon the color that you desire. Color attraction, however, can be a detriment to becoming a successful competition flyer, especially if a roller flyer gets too caught up in the colors of the performing birds and makes wrong decisions in their breeding because of color interest. The superior rolling abilities of their pigeons can be lost if they're not careful. The ladder to success must be climbed with only the best capable air qualities if you want to win in roller flying competition. In flying competition, one would save time and progress faster if he were to be color-blind.

With that said, I am still a lover of colors. So I offer these next few pages to save you some breeding time if you have only one bird of a certain color and desire more. I have assembled 43 different color expressions of pigeons here, but there are many others. The desired color expressions will be pictured on the left side of the page, with the right side being the suggested bird to breed with it in order to get another of the desired color. This is a quick tip chart on how to get more of the color you may like in your loft. Before we start, it would be helpful for you to know that a pigeon carries two patterns, one showing and one not. This is referred to as hiding a pattern. For instance two check birds producing a barred bird. Both parents are hiding the bar pattern.

Again I would suggest that when breeding, breed short-performing to deep-performing birds for the best results. If you do not have this balance in depth, I would advise you to wait until you get another bird with the right performance depth, velocity, and style to work with on your color project. A pretty bird that does not perform properly is just that.

Speed Chart for Breeding Colors and Patterns
  Desired color and pattern on left   Suggested mate on right

Breeding a blue barless cock to a blue barred hen or vice versa will produce all blue barred offspring that will carry the barless pattern. Breeding a blue barred cock or hen hiding barless to a blue barless will produce some of both sexes in blue barless. Barless to barless matings will only produce barless offspring.

Breeding a blue barred cock to a blue check hen or vice versa will produce all checked offspring, unless the check bird hides bar, then you will get both bar and checked young. If not, all the checked offspring will carry the bar pattern. Breeding a checked hen or cock hiding bar to a barred bird will produce some of both sexes in the barred pattern. Breeding barred to barred pigeons will produce only barred young.

Breeding a blue open check cock to a blue barred hen or vice versa will produce some blue open check offspring.

Breeding a blue tight check cock to a blue barred hen or vice versa will produce some blue tight check offspring. You can also use a blue open check instead of bar.

Breeding an ash red bar to a blue bar will produce ash red barred offspring. You will also get blue bar young if the cock hides blue.

Breeding black white flight to blue check white flight will produce some black white flight young. You can use blue bar white flight, but the black will look the best on blue tight check.

Breeding an ash red tight check to ash red bar will produce ash red tight check offspring. They may also produce bar if the check is hiding the bar pattern. If some blue pops up it is because the cock also hides blue.

Breeding a black pigeon to any blue pattern pigeon will produce some black offspring. Breeding a black to a blue tight check (as pictured) will produce the best-looking blacks.

Breeding lavender to an ash red barred pigeon will produce some lavender young. This pair would also produce black or blue. Since the lavender cock has ticking showing, he is hiding blue.

Breeding a lavender mealy to an ash red check pigeon will produce some mealy offspring.

Breeding an ash red grizzle bar to an ash red bar will produce some ash red grizzle bar offspring.

Breeding a blue barred grizzle to a blue bar will produce some blue bar grizzle offspring. If you prefer them in white flights, use a blue bar white flight for higher percentages of white flights.

Breeding an ash red checked ticked grizzle cock to a blue check hen will produce some ash red checked grizzle offspring hens. Breeding the sexes in reverse will produce red checked grizzle cocks.

Breeding a dark tortoise blue check grizzle cock or hen to a blue check will produce some dark tortoise blue check grizzle offspring.

Breeding an ash red check grizzle to an ash red check will produce some ash red check grizzle offspring.

Breeding a blue bar grizzle with spread to a blue bar will produce some blue bar grizzle with spread.

Breeding a black grizzle to a black pigeon will produce some black grizzle offspring. Blacks look the best working with blue tight check base pattern pigeons. Blue check can also be used, but that would cut back on the percentages of black grizzle offspring. Some will be blue. Grizzle can vary on how much is seen on the bird's offspring.

Breeding a black mottle to a blue tight check pigeon will produce some black mottle offspring. A black pigeon can also be used on the mottle.

Breeding white to red grizzle will produce some white offspring.

Breeding a black grizzle to a blue tight check will produce some black grizzle offspring. Black can also be used on the black grizzle.

Breeding a classical almond to a blue tight check with bronzing will produce some classical almond offspring.

Breeding a blue almond to a blue check will produce some blue almond offspring. Don't breed two almonds together. This can produce young with bad eyesight.

Breeding a blue dominant opal check cock or hen to a blue check will produce some blue opal check offspring. Some may look like the blue opal check pictured above but will also produce other variations lighter and darker in color. Don't breed two dominant opals together. You will lose a quarter of their young. The opal color gene is a semi-lethal gene when bred together.

Breeding a blue dominant opal bar cock or hen to a blue bar will produce some blue opal bar offspring. They may look like the blue opal bar pictured above and may also produce other variations lighter in bar to all white in bar to some with reddish bronze bars.

Breeding blue indigo check hen or cock to blue check will produce some blue indigo check. The blue indigo color gene is a mimic of red. Some offspring may have more or less degrees of red showing.

Breeding an Andalusian to a black pigeon will produce some Andalusian offspring. Andalusian will also show variations with some being lighter than others. This one pictured is on the dark side. Always breed Andalusian to black for the best results.

Breeding a red indigo check cock or hen to a red check will produce some red indigo check. You will know them by their dark heads.

Breeding a homozygous indigo spread cock or hen to an Andalusian will produce homozygous pigeons.

Breeding a yellow open check cock to an ash red open check hen will produce some yellow open check hens. All male offspring will carry the color gene. Breeding any of the male offspring to a yellow open check hen will produce some yellow open check in both sexes. With checked pigeons, when any barred young pop up it simply means that both check birds hide the bar pattern.

Breeding a yellow grizzle to a yellow check will produce some yellow grizzle.

Breeding a yellow bar cock to an ash red bar hen will produce yellow bar hens. All cocks from the mating will carry the color gene but not show it. Breeding any of the cocks to a yellow barred hen will produce some of both sexes in yellow bar.

Breeding a yellow tight checked cock to an ash red checked hen will produce some yellow tight check hens. All of the offspring cocks will carry the color gene. Breeding any of the tight ash red cocks from the mating to a tight check yellow hen will produce both sexes in yellow tight check.

Breeding a recessive yellow cock to a recessive red hen will produce some recessive yellow hens. None of the young cocks from the mating will show yellow but will carry the color gene. Breeding the cock offspring from the mating to a recessive yellow hen will produce both sexes in recessive yellow. If two recessive yellow pigeons are bred together, all the offspring will be recessive yellow.

Breeding a recessive red cock to any color pigeon will not produce recessive red in the offspring unless the hen hides the color gene. All offspring will carry the recessive red gene. Breeding any of the offspring to recessive red or any pigeon carrying the gene will produce some recessive red young. Breeding two recessive red pigeons together will produce only recessive red offspring unless the cock hides yellow, the dilute gene. If so, you will get an occasional recessive yellow hen in the nest.

Breeding a recessive red mottle to a recessive red pigeon will produce some recessive red mottles. Don't breed mottles together. It tends to lighten the color more than desired because of the double factor grizzle. This would apply to all pigeons that carry grizzle. Mottles look their best in the single factor. This modifier combination will still produce different variations of mottle. Some may just have a small amount of mottling.

Breeding a blue reduced check cock to a blue check hen will produce blue reduced check hens. All the young cocks will carry the reduced gene but will not show it. Breeding any of the cocks from this mating to a blue check reduced hen will produce both sexes in reduced blue check.

Breeding a blue reduced bar cock on a blue bar hen will produce blue reduced hens. None of the cocks from the mating will show the gene; but will carry it. Cocks carrying this gene will produce blue bar reduced young in both sexes when mated to a blue reduced barred hen.

Breeding a blue reduced check with spread cock to a black hen will produce blue reduced check with spread hens, which is also known as "blue lace." Any of the male offspring will carry the color gene and when bred to a blue lace hen will produce blue lace in both sexes. Working with blue tight check base patterns gives the best results.

Breeding a brown bar cock to a blue bar hen will produce brown offspring hens. All the cocks from the mating will carry the brown gene; but not show it. Breeding any of the cocks from this mating to a brown bar hen will produce both cocks and hens in brown bar. Brown paired to brown will only produce brown offspring.

Breeding a brown check cock to a blue check hen will produce brown check hen offspring. All of the cocks from the mating will carry the brown gene but not show it. Breeding the male offspring to a brown hen will produce both sexes in brown check. Brown to brown will produce brown offspring only.

That covers 40 color combinations. The following three rollers are color patterns that come in many colors and are liked by many. The first is the bellneck, known for having color just in the back of the neck area. The second roller is called a saddleback, and the third is the odd side.

In case you only have one bellneck, the best choice would be to breed it to a saddleback.

To help promote more saddlebacks, you can breed to white wing odd side pigeons

The term "odd side" means a pigeon has a white wing on one side. This bird has a red wing on the other side. Bred to another bird with a lot of white feathering should produce more odd sides.

If you breed a blue cock, checked, barred, or barless to an ash red hen of any pattern, all the offspring that are cocks will be ash red and all the hens will be blue. She passes her color to the cocks and he passes his to the hens. This is known as a color sex-linked mating. A brown cock and a blue hen would also be a color sex-linked mating. The cock in the next photo carries the blue color gene on both sides. Showing and hiding nothing but blue. The hen is ash red and hides no modifiers. They are an example of a color sex-linked mating.

Pigeons with Black Ticks or Ink Spots

This cock is an ash red bar hiding blue. The black flecking or ticks on the feathers is a sign of two things. One, this is a cock, and two, it's hiding blue. Hens will never show tick markings (with the exception of indigo hens, that I know of) or hide another color. She will be as you see her. She can, however, hide another pattern or modifier like recessive red. Occasionally, you will see some ticking in the tail of a hen, but it is lighter than black in color and not very prominent.

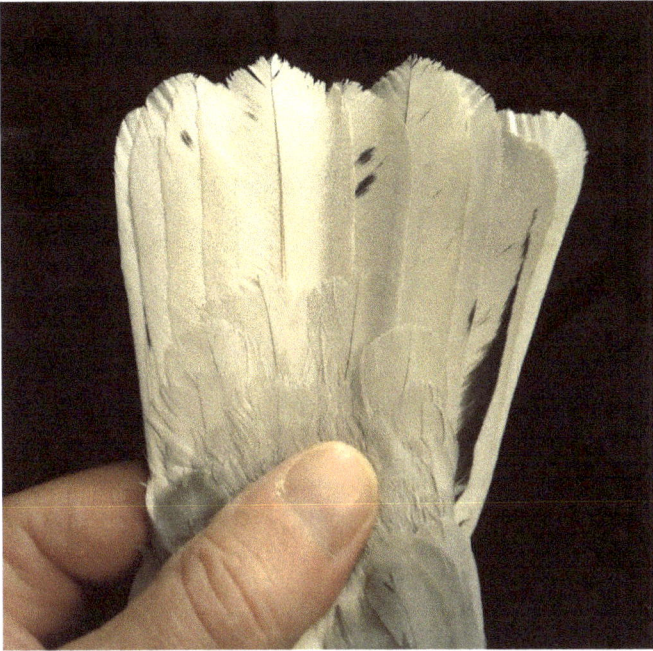

Some cocks will have ink spots or ticking just on the tail or wing flights, while others may have it all over their body.

This cock has ticking over his entire body.

This lavender cock is very slightly ticked. This pigeon is an ash red hiding blue with spread as the modifier, which made it lavender.

If this ash red bird was a cock with no ticks or ink spots, it would mean the bird is the same color on both sides (double factor ash red). Cocks can carry two colors. If he was hiding blue, you would normally see some ticking. Ash red hens cannot hide blue, only another pattern or modifier, such as bar or recessive red. Therefore, you will never see ticking or ink spots on an ash red hen or a lavender hen.

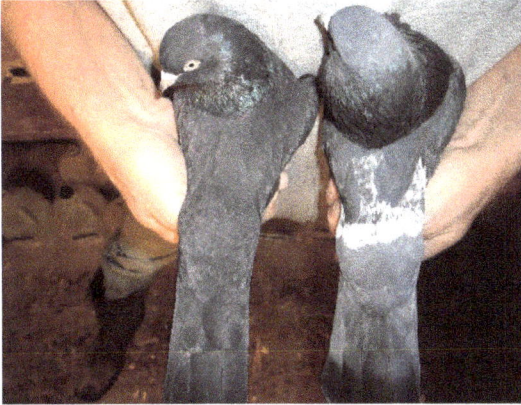

Sometimes a fancier will confuse a tight pattern blue check with a black pigeon. If you compare the rump to a true black to a tight pattern blue check, you will see the difference. Two blue pigeons will never produce a black.

This color and pattern is known as the "wild type." All of the colors and patterns we have today in our pigeons are

derived from this color and pattern, which is commonly
called a blue bar self.

If you would like to learn more about pigeon color genetics, you can search the Internet, using the key phrase "James Turner and Tony Roberts on color Birmingham Rollers." You will find a very informative and easy to understand video on the subject. It will last for about one hour. Before you do, memorize these three colors and four patterns and their order of dominance used in pigeon color genetics. Once you do, it will all fall into place and be very understandable:

Color in Order of Dominance	Patterns in Order of Dominance
1. Brown	1. Barless
2. Blue	2. Bar
3. Ash red	3. Open check
	4. Tight check

(The least dominant being #1 in both categories.)

Anything that is not one of the three colors or four patterns would be a modifier. By using combinations of the three colors and four patterns along with certain modifiers, you will be able to create pigeons in the colors you prefer. Learning these things from Mr. Turner's video and speaking with him has made my pigeon breeding a lot more interesting. Keep in mind, color will not help you with winning a competition. Only your flying knowledge, worthy birds, and a strong desire to win will help you win the competition. Done the right way though, beautiful roller pigeons can win competitions.

Egg Laying
Once your pairs are selected and introduced, they should lay one egg approximately seven to eleven days after putting them together. After the first egg is laid, the hen will skip a day, and then lay a second egg. The pair usually waits until the second egg is laid before they will set on them. The hen normally will set on them at night and the cock will set on the eggs during the day. They should hatch 18 days after the second egg is laid.

The previous photo shows the body posture of a hen close to laying. Notice the rump protruding up and the tail drooping down. This hen laid 24 hours after this picture was taken.

Checking Eggs for Fertility

A big time saver is to check your eggs for fertility at five to six days after they are laid by candling. Candling the eggs can be done by holding them up to a light to help you search for signs of growth. Place the egg at the base of your thumb and index finger gently but firmly so as not to break the egg or drop it to the floor. Cup your other hand up close to the egg with your finger together to help shield the light so you can better see inside the egg. You will be looking for some blood veins. Sometimes you might not see them right away and have to turn the egg to find them. Normally it will be on one side in these first few days. If veins cannot be seen by seven days, they are not fertile and should be thrown away. I generally see the veins at five to six days.

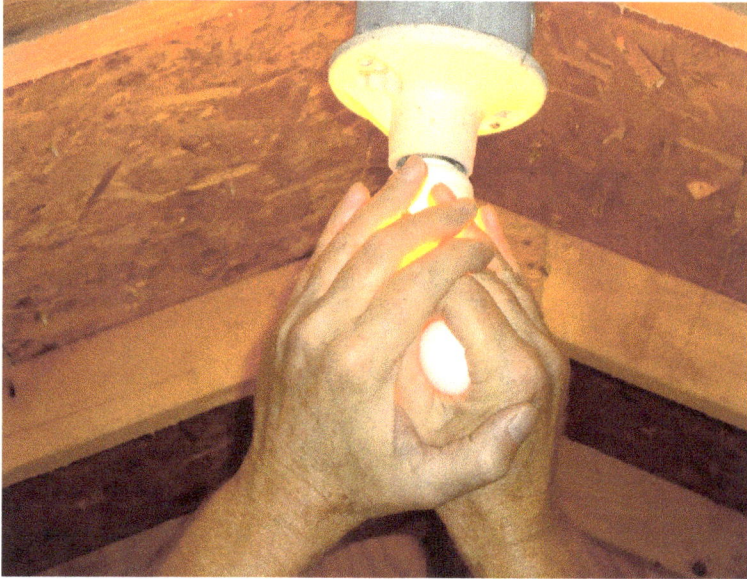

By throwing the infertile eggs away, you have only lost the days waiting to see if they were fertile instead of the full 18 days waiting for them to hatch. Hens should lay again in seven to eleven days. Hopefully, the next round of eggs will be fertile. Sometimes you will just have one that is fertile. I usually leave the infertile egg in the nest until the fertile one hatches and the youngster is a few days old. It will give the single youngster something to lean on and may help a little in not getting a spread leg. The most common reason for a young bird to develop a spread leg is a lack of sufficient nesting material, and when it does pop up it is most commonly a single young in the nest. If you notice one of the legs on the young bird is starting to spread out, you can correct it before it gets too bad to fix. You can do this by using some string to tie both feet closer together more in their normal position. Using a band on each leg to tie to works well. Catching it early is the key. If you do not notice the problem before you band the young bird, it usually will be too late to correct.

Spread leg due to lack of nesting material

A lot of times, the first round of your breeders will lay one egg or one infertile egg of the two. To ensure more fertile eggs, many breeders will bust all the first-round eggs and go with the second round. If you decide to do this, wait until the last pair lays during the first round before you pull all the eggs. By doing this, all of your pairs will lay at approximately the same time during your second round. This will come in handy on banding day. You will be able to band them all in a day, plus your young birds will be easier to train as a team, being the same age as opposed to a week or so apart.

Protecting Young and Eggs During Inspection

When pulling your eggs (or youngsters) out for inspection, you must be careful of the parents. They will be in a protective parental mode and will either peck at you, wing strike you, or both. Either of these reactions from the setting parent can cause you to drop or damage the egg. The best way to keep this from happening is to use the back of one hand to block with while getting your eggs out with the other hand.

Use the back of the first hand to hold up against the setting parent and push her back slightly. This way the setting bird cannot peck the egg or knock it from your hand with a wing strike. Repeat the same thing when putting the eggs back into the nest.

Hopefully, before trying to breed from your birds, you had them separated, rested, and fed in preparation for breeding. Don't expect to do well with breeding rollers straight out of the fly box. If you have been feeding and flying them correctly, they will not be in the right mental and physical state to breed from anyway. They will generally not mate right away like your well-kept and separated breeders. If your birds are mating and laying eggs in the fly boxes, then they are under flown and/or overfed.

When not breeding pigeons, you should always keep your stock cocks and hens separated from each other. If you decide to breed a pair or two at any time of the year, they will always be ready to get started this way.

The yellow hen in the previous photo is very anxious to get started into the breeding program with any cock put with her because of being separated from the cocks in the off season. Most of the time, the courtship of a pair will involve some head bobbing, with the cock fanning his tail and driving towards her, sometimes with a little hop incorporated into his drive. She in turn may or may not do the same. After being separated and first put together, the pair may or may not bill with each other before mating.

The hen will sometimes go straight to the squatted position, as in the previous picture, for the cock to mount or top her. Occasionally the hen in return will mount the cock. They usually start courting right away since they have been separated during the off season. Now and then a hen will resist the cock's advances and run from him. The cock will chase the hen and try to dominate her by grabbing and shaking her by her neck feathers with his beak.

Occasionally, when a hen resists the male's advances, by the next day the cock can have caused injury to the hen, normally to the head. She may have feathers missing and a bloody head. So it is important that she has a safe way to evade his advances if she is not responding to him. Having a perch for her to get up on until she is ready to mate is a must, especially in a small individual breeding situation. Normally, if she is not ready to mate at the time of introduction, she will give in to mating by the third day.

There are two ways to breed your pigeons, open-loft breeding (shown in the previous photo) and individual loft breeding. In the previous photo, there are twelve nests that would be used for open-loft breeding. The doors are closed because they are not being used at this time. When in use, the doors would be open with two nest bowls in each compartment.

The difference between open loft and individual loft breeding: If you put multiple hens and cocks together in an open loft where they all can fly down from the nest to the floor to eat and drink and return to the nest, that is "open-loft breeding." While a cock and hen in one loft or breeding pen is called "individual loft" or pen breeding.

Ideally, individual pen breeding is the way to go. Even though a pair of pigeons will mate for life, accidents in open-loft breeding are common. If you do not have individual pens for breeding, try to leave your pairings together by themselves for a few days before you release them into an open loft situation. Place them in some type of cage so they can fully mate. This will help ensure proper pairing. The hen will lay sometimes before seven days, so pull the pair out of the mating pen and put them in the open breeding loft after three to four days of being together. This will give them enough time to get set up in their new breeding surroundings before she lays.

Make sure to have nesting material ready. Put a handful of wood shavings in the nesting bowl and throw some straw or pine needles on the floor. Use two nesting bowls spaced together or some distance apart depending on their nesting area size. The cock will pick up the pine needles or straw and take it to the hen, and she in turn will place the material in the nest. Pine needles will also help with keeping pigeon mites out of the nest.

When using wood shavings, stay away from cedar. Cedar chips may cause respiratory problems in your pigeons. The nesting material will be necessary for an egg cushion and to help the young develop their leg muscles properly. Keep in mind that open-loft breeding will never allow you to be 100 percent sure of your pair's offspring. But it is easier to manage than many individual breeding pens. From time to time in open-loft breeding, your young birds will fall prematurely from the nest onto the floor, normally around two weeks old.

Cocks other than the young bird's sire will injure the young by trying to breed the young bird. By doing this act, the young bird will have damage to its back and head, and usually this damage will be fatal. If not, the young bird may have permanent damage that will cause feathers to not grow back or grow back abnormally. To save this from happening to your young birds, be sure to place a protection board on a couple of bricks for them to hide under until you notice they are not where they are supposed to be.

The young bird protection board should be high enough for the young bird to get under, but low enough so the cocks cannot. Sometimes you may have several on the floor or under the protection board when you go into your loft. They will need to be returned to the nest to be fed properly by their parents.

If for some reason you need to foster a young bird under another pair of birds for feeding, the rule of thumb is the younger the better. You can get a pair of pigeons to take a young bird that does not show color if it's at about the same age as theirs. But once the pin feathers bloom to show color, they normally will not accept the young bird and will kill it as an invader to the nest.

It would be wise to band your open loft young as soon as possible and take note of what nest that particular numbered bird came from. The best time is when a youngster is at the pin feather stage. Most breeders like to wait until they can tell for sure what color to write down in their record book when banding. This way they do not have to go back a second time to make note of the young's color. But if you have many birds, odds are if you wait for the color and pattern to be seen, a few unbanded birds may end up on the floor and you can't remember where they go. So put bands on them as soon as you know the size band you are working with will stay on. This will save you from making some regrettable mistakes. When practicing individual pen breeding, you can wait longer to band young so as to see their color.

Occasionally, you will find a young bird that appears to be dead from falling out of the nest or dying from exposure from the cold. Many times you can save one by warming the bird in your hand. Cup your hands around the young bird and exhale into your hands. The warmth of your breath will bring it back if it has not been exposed to the cold for too long. Gently massaging the bird a little will help with stimulation. If the bird shows signs of life, take it into the house to warm it up. After you're sure the bird is okay, place it back in the nest.

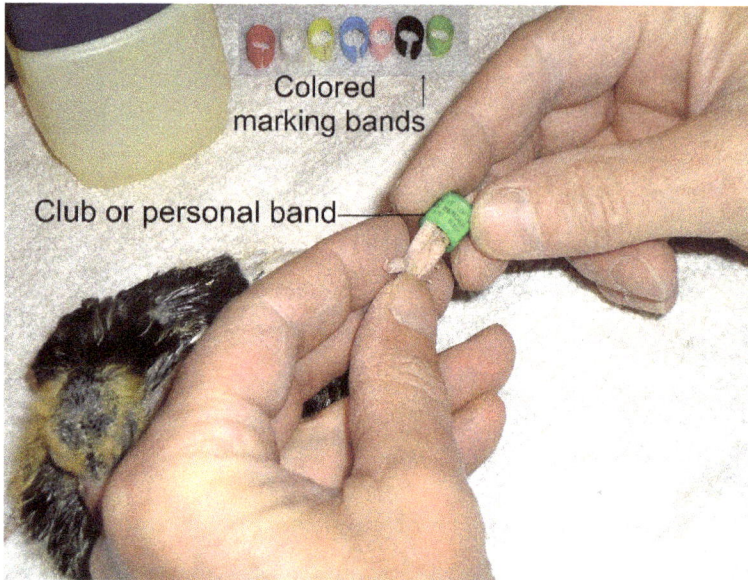

Colored marking bands

Club or personal band

Banding Your Birds

In the previous photo, the young bird is being banded with a fully closed permanent band. This one has the number of the bird and year of birth and will stay on its entire life. You can purchase these in a different color every year. This helps to associate years to colors at a glance. The color snap on bands helps with identifying cocks and hens in the stock loft. They can be taken off or on if need be. Once in a while the wrong sex bird may end up in the wrong holding section. Marking with a color band for sex identification will help you spot the bird quicker. You can also use them to mark early landers, A and B team birds, last round of young, etc. The most helpful thing for a pigeon flyer was the invention of the band for keeping track of the great ones and their parents.

If you ask how to tell a cock from a hen you will hear many different ways to tell them apart. Some will say a certain toe is longer on the cock than on the hen. Or that the hen will have wider vent bones. Or the cock is the larger one. I personally do not use these methods. The best way for me is observation. Cock birds are fully mature and can be bred from at three months of age. That, of course, is something you would not want to do because it is too short a time to be properly evaluated. But is good to know when looking for the males. By three months old they should be acting like males do, cooing and strutting around, trying to get some attention. When they do, you will see them strut around in a full circle. This is a sure sign it's a cock. Hens will act similarly from time to time but will never do a full circle. They will start to but will stop short of a full turn and go back in the opposite direction during cooing.

If by some chance you have two pigeons mate and lay fertile eggs when you thought they were both hens, again, you can find the cock through observation. The cock will be the one to set on the eggs during the day, and the hen will set on them during the night. You can also throw some straw on the floor and the cock will be the one to pick it up and take it to the hen on the nest.

Another sure method would apply to certain colors. Any ash red, lavender, or yellow pigeon with ticking or ink spots, whether it is on check or bar, will be a cock. I discussed and showed photos of ticking or ink spots earlier in the book.

I normally don't check for hens, I just watch for the cocks. By the end of the year, any bird that does not have a blue band on will most certainly be a hen. The hens will end up with red snap-on bands. When it's time to stock some of them, I will know what section to put them in; cocks on one side, hens on the others.

Banding

The banding process must be done correctly to prevent damaging your bird. It's simple: slide the band over the first three toes right on past the rear toe. The back toenail may catch a little, so be prepared to guide it through the band. However, the bigger the foot the harder it will be to pull the back toe through. Refer to previous picture.

You can order bands from many different pigeon clubs or have them custom made to your liking. Either way, a serious roller breeder will always band his young birds. Individual identification is very important for managing your pigeons. Without bands, your management is lost. If your birds have no bands you will never be a credible roller fancier in the hobby. You also cannot fly or show an unbanded roller pigeon in competition. Especially in young bird flying competition.

Banding is normally done in the first couple of weeks after hatching. Occasionally you will miss banding a bird or the band falls off in the nest. By the time you notice, it may seem impossible to get the band on. If this happens, put some petroleum jelly, cod liver oil, or butter on the foot before attempting to slide the band on. With a dry rag, hold on to the three forward toes and keep constant pressure on the band. Take your time and go slow. Nine out of ten times you can get the band on this way. You might skin the foot a little, which may cause some limping for a couple of days, but no permanent damage will occur. If this fails, you will have to resort to splitting a band or using a plastic snap-on band with a number. Please note that if you were to show a roller, it would be ejected from the competition for not having a permanent band. Split bands and plastic snap-on bands would not be accepted.

Individual Pen Breeding

With individual breeding I suggest a 2x2x2-foot square pen. Larger would be fine, but no smaller than 2x2x2 square. You will do better if you place two nesting bowls on a shelf in the pen so they will be off the floor. You should have at least one perch (inverted V) in the pen up off the floor. This will allow the hen a chance to get away from the male for a while if she needs to. It is also a great help to acclimate their young birds to a perch before weaning. If the young birds have never been presented with a perch, they will sit on the wire in the fly box for a couple of days.

With individual breeding pens you will have to decide what to put your water and feed in. You can use different containers for this, depending on what you like. I use quart milk jugs for the feed and water. I cut a hole on the side in the middle. If you cut your hole too big, the breeders can waste a lot of the feed by flicking it out looking for certain seeds in the mix. Not cutting the hole too low allows the birds to eat and drink with ease and allows you to keep ample amounts in the containers until the next day.

When building your breeding pens, you may want to consider whether or not to place the feed containers on the outside or inside of the pens. I believe it is very convenient and time-saving to place them on the outside of your individual pens. Your birds will not be disturbed as much this way, and it cuts down on one of your stock birds getting loose while changing the feed and water.

Note: Always make sure to keep your main loft door closed while changing your feeding and watering containers from the inside. If one of your stock birds makes it outside and a hawk gets it, you won't be breeding from that one again.

Once you place your pairs inside the individual breeding pens, they should lay in seven to eleven days. The same goes for open-loft breeding. The reason I use two nest bowls in the pen is for the next round of laying. After the first round of youngsters are around two weeks old, the hen will lay again. If she has another bowl to go to, she normally will. This will allow the hen to set on the eggs properly without the two young birds in the nest with the eggs. If the hen has not laid in the first two weeks of pairing her with a cock, replace her with another.

If you have two sets of infertile eggs with a pair of rollers, trim the vent feathers on them both. Rarely will you have to do this, but it does help in many instances. A lot of the time, the pair will start producing fertile eggs after the vent areas are trimmed. You can use scissors or a mustache trimmer to do this and it will not cause any pain to the bird. Be sure to clear away the vent feathers as close to the vent area as possible without touching the bird's skin. The feathers will grow back when the bird goes through the next molt.

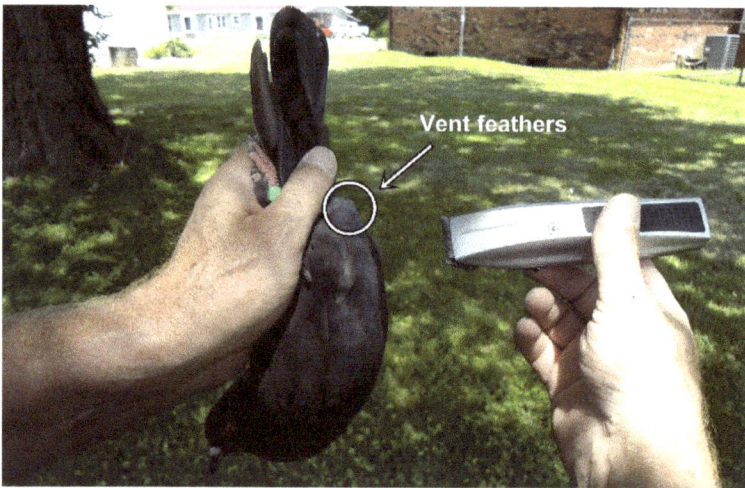

If another round is infertile, re-mate both birds to birds you know to be fertile. This will allow you to discover which one is the infertile bird. Birds that are laying for the first time tend to lay a couple bad eggs in the beginning. They usually will produce fertile eggs on the second round of laying. Old hens and cocks (from my experience)

tend to go infertile around nine years. However, I have heard of them staying fertile into their teens. Once your young birds are feathered or almost feathered under the wings, pull them out and place them into the weaning pen with a couple of old hens. This is the same action you would take in open-loft breeding when you pull the young. Do not mix them with a round of young birds you have previously pulled out, especially if the prior group of young birds are a few weeks older. Some will be bullies. They can be rough on the newcomers. You can mix all the young once they are up and flying well.

Advancing Your Stock
When wondering about your breeders and replacing some with younger birds, always replace the pairs that produce the lowest percentages of keepers. For example, if your best pair produced seven out of ten young that were keepers, put the rest of your pairs in order of how many good ones they produced. You are trying to replace the lower-number-producing pairs with better ones.

Another way to advance your stock is to try breeding some of your offspring as a test for possible replacements in the stock loft. You may also try another mate for both birds in a low-percentage-producing pair. Sometimes that is all that is needed to get what you're after. Some birds may produce better percentages on other birds with the same traits that you had in the previous pairing. By keeping good notes while breeding your birds, you can keep track of the high percentage producers. These are commonly referred to as "click pairs." Always watch for them.

Foster Parents
Foster birds are necessary if you decide to foster eggs from your best pair to save some time propagating their young. Sooner or later you will have a good pair that you will want to get as many out of as soon as you can. You can use your lesser stock for that purpose, or birds that did not work out in the air during their attempt to meet your flying requirements. Birds we would deem as culls that we would never attempt to fly any more, breed from, or even sell can still serve a purpose to you as foster breeders. Be sure to take notes

on which pairs do better than others. Occasionally you will find some great fosters. I had a pair that was laid out but would set on eggs any time I put them in the nest. They were wonderful foster parents. Some foster parents are also better feeders than others, so keep an eye open for these types of birds. I normally keep a certain number of culls around just to propagate my better birds.

Fostering Eggs

If you know before they hatch that two pairs only have one fertile egg and they are going to hatch on the same day, move one of the eggs to the other pair. Mark the egg before moving it. This way one of your pairs can be bred from sooner without having to spend all that time with one young bird. As soon as you know they are starting to break out of the shell, check it often to be sure which one hatches out first. You can mark one of the toes with a black marker to help you keep track of them until banding time.

When fostering eggs from your best pair or two, put together as many foster pairs as you can. Normally, one would think that if you put two pairs together at the same time they would lay at the same time. But Murphy's Law applies to everything. Some will not lay at all, while others will not lay on the same day.

Normally, switching eggs under a foster pair laying within two days early or later than when the selected pair laid is fine. Still, some pairs will get off the eggs if they go past their due date of hatching, the two-day difference being the problem. Most parents use an internal clock that tells them it's past time to hatch, so when they don't hatch they leave the nest. Others will wait a couple of days longer for them to hatch. You're always better off to have them hatch a day or two early under a foster pair than a day or two late for this reason.

If I want to be successful, I make sure the switch is with a foster pair that laid on the same day as the selected pair. To help ensure this, I would put three or more pairs of fosters along with the selected pair together at the same time. Then, I start checking all pairs to see if they have laid, starting at the five-day mark to play it safe. Sometimes your selected pair will lay eggs as early as the fifth day. Mark down when each of the foster pairs laid. If one of the pairs, or in a perfect world all of the foster pairs, have laid with your selected pair, switch the eggs.

Once you have removed a foster pair's eggs and replaced them with your selected pair, bust all the eggs from your remaining foster pairs. They and your selected pair should all lay back about the same time again. Then, repeat the process. This way, you can raise a lot more from your best stock pair in a shorter amount of time. One year during breeding season I raised 21 birds from one pair by fostering the eggs. I had a loft of twelve fosters pairs together, so I had something to put the eggs under as soon as they were laid. As soon as I switched the eggs, I busted all the remaining foster pairs' eggs and looked forward to seeing how many would lay at the same time as the selected pair did. It worked out beautifully.

When checking eggs for fertility or moving them to a foster pair, occasionally you will notice a chipped-out place in the egg. Sometimes the birds will be responsible, while other times you may be. In open-loft breeding, another bird can get into the wrong nest and a fight ensues, and damage to the eggs can occur. It may also be your fault by not guarding the egg well enough when you are getting it out to check it or putting it back. If you do notice a chip in the egg, as long as it does not go through the inner lining to the egg, it can be saved. A patch will help keep the weak area strong and protect it from getting any worse.

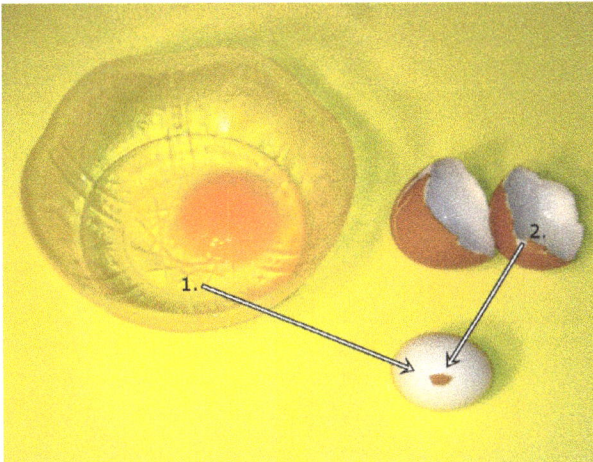

You will need another egg for patching material. You can use another pigeon egg for this. If you don't have a spare egg, you can use a chicken egg. It doesn't matter if it is brown or white. As you can see in the previous photo, I patched a pigeon egg by using a brown chicken egg. When patching, you will need to use the egg white as glue. 1. Place your finger in the egg white and rub it over the area you are going to patch. 2. Next, pick a piece off the eggshell that has the approximate curvature as the area you want to cover. Place it over the chipped area. It will dry quickly, and you can place it back under the parent. The young will hatch with no problems.

Fostering Young Birds

Once in a while you will have a couple of pairs of breeders with only one youngster in each nest. To save breeding time, you can move the young bird from one pair to the other. This will allow you to get another round of eggs from the best pair in less time. When moving a young bird to another pair, they should both be as close to the same age as possible. Move the young bird before the pin feathers bloom. If the new young bird is showing color on it, the foster parents may not accept it to the nest.

Special Care of Smaller Youngsters

The young in the nest will require special attention to assure their health and survival. Check your young in the nest every day or two to make sure they are doing okay. Occasionally, one will be a little larger than the other, which will require some attention to prevent the smaller one from getting starved out. One of the two may have hatched a day early and have too much of a head start over the smaller one. When the parents go to feed the young, the larger one normally gets fed first. The smaller bird sometimes will die because of the larger bird getting more than its share. You can take the larger of the two youngsters and pull it from the nest until the parents have fed the smaller one. The best time to do this is when you are feeding the parents. After they eat, they will go straight to the young and feed them after a good drink of water. Leaving the larger youngster out of the nest for about half an hour or so should be sufficient. In just a few days, the smaller one will catch up with its larger nestmate.

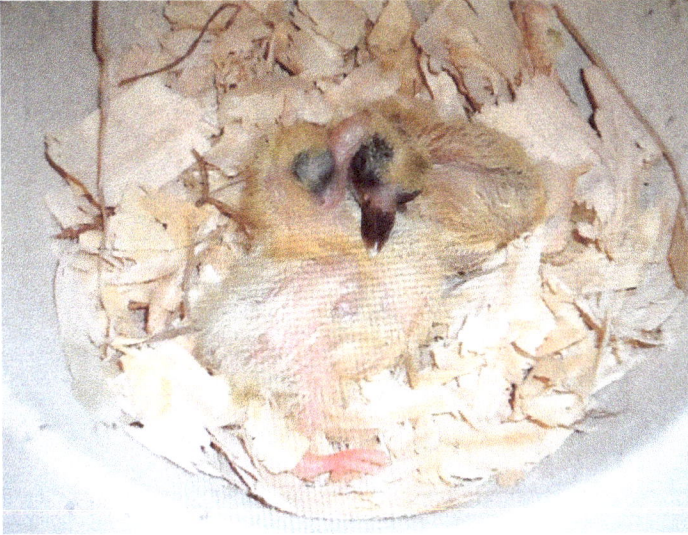

Sometimes the problem may not be that one hatched before the other. They might have hatched close enough together to be fine, but one may be sick with a pigeon sickness called canker. You will get this mostly in young birds, but old birds can be carriers as well. When you notice one is smaller than it should be, check it for canker. You can do this by opening up the mouth and looking inside. If you see a yellow, cheesy substance in the throat, you will need to treat the bird by giving it a canker treatment. You will also want to check the navel. Sometimes you will notice it there, too. Most of the time they will live after treatment.

If you find canker in one of the young, also treat the nestmate and the parents. You can also give a canker treatment once a month to the breeders as a preventative measure before breeding. If your birds are well taken care of, canker is not too much to worry about. It is said to be stress related and is easily remedied.

Another way to help a smaller young bird catch up in growth is to place it under another pair, as long as the pair has only one and it is the same size. As mentioned before, once the pin feathers have started to bloom, exposing the color, you should refrain from the switch. Only switch young when they are still in the yellow downy stage. Don't forget to mark the foot with a marker to help keep track of the bird for your notes when you are banding. If it turns out to be a champion, you will surely want to know which pair the bird came from.

Weaning Young Birds

You can wean your young birds at 35 days old. Some breeders will wean them a few days earlier.

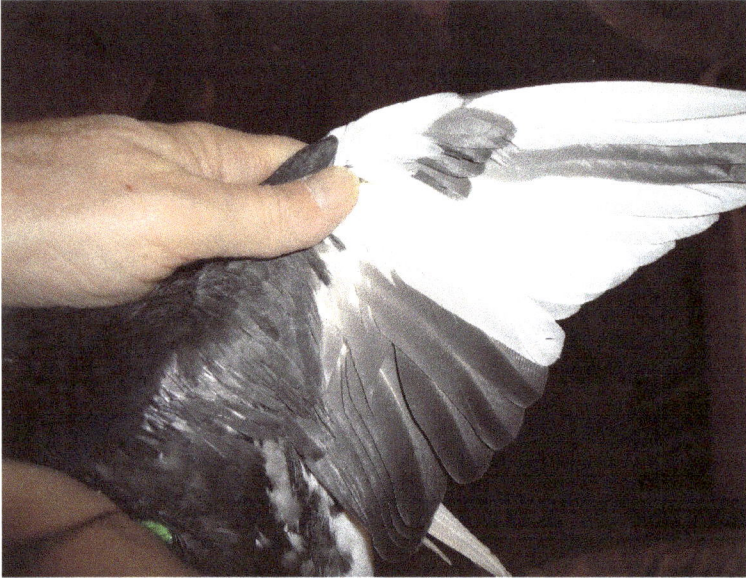

You can tell when to wean your young birds by looking under their wing at the feather growth, as in the previous photo. When the feather growth is almost complete, you can pull them from the nest. They will be able to fly. Training of birds at this stage to get accustomed to their surroundings and trapping would best be done with a training cage. This will allow you to keep the young contained while training and seeing their surroundings for a few days, without your young birds flying away.

You can pull the young from the nest before they are fully feathered to cut back on their ability to fly. Pulling birds out of the nest at this stage (photo above) is usually done if you are setting them out on the fly box roof to get used to their surroundings and not using a training cage. At this stage of growth, you will not have to be concerned about them flying off if they get spooked during training. Closer observation should be given to these young birds to make sure they are eating and drinking. They tend to catch on a little slower than the fuller feathered young in photo to the left.

When pulling out young birds, place them in an area with two or three old stock hens or foster hens if you have them to spare. If you only have one hen to spare, then she by herself will still be of help. Old hens normally will not hurt the young. Having the old hens with the young birds will aid in their learning to eat and drink on their own. Once in a while, one of the old hens might get rough with the young birds. If this happens, pull her out and replace her with another.

On your last round of young birds to be raised, you can pull all the mother hens and their young together and place them in a training box. You would want to do this right before the hens lay again. All the hens will treat the other young just fine, and some may even feed young that are not their own. Be sure to keep enough feed with them so as to have some left when you go to feed them again the next day. As soon as the young are eating and drinking on their own, you can put them in a fly box without the mother hens.

While weaned young on their own (without old hens with them) are learning to eat and drink, they should be checked every day for slow blinking. Slow eye blinking indicates the young bird is not getting enough water. It would be advisable to dunk young birds' beaks in the water container each day for three or four days to allow them to get a good drink and learn where the water is, especially when separated from both parents. Pigeons drink water differently than other birds. They do not tip their heads back to swallow. They drink like horses do. One long deep drink. When dunking their beaks, you will know when they are drinking and when they are not.

One good drink a day will keep them healthy. Sometimes, one or two young birds will not drink by dunking the first or second time. The ones who don't drink right away are the birds that will show the slow blinking, which is because of a lack of water to moisten the eyes. You can take a syringe and squirt some water down the young bird's throat if you think it's necessary. Give them enough to be able to see it in the crop. Make sure to keep water and feed in front of them at all times while they're learning to eat and drink on their own.

Also, be sure to observe the young to confirm they are all eating and drinking on their own before the trapping-in training. Prior to trap training, be sure to keep plenty of feed in front of them. If you do not have a separate box for weaning, you can do all the above in the fly box before you train them to trap. If your young birds have not set on a perch yet, place each one on a perch to help them understand what the perches are for. If you do not do this when you first wean them, it might take a couple of days of sitting on the floor of the fly box before they figure it out.

At this point we are getting ready to start training the young birds to be accustomed to the outside and learn to trap into the fly box. There are a couple of ways to go about training the young birds to trap because of weaning ages: flying age and non flying age, as mentioned earlier. We will cover both.

While in the trap training sessions, always put in more than enough feed at feeding time. They are not going to be eating it all anyway. After they all trap, eat, and go to drink, remove the tray. Take back your remaining feed and place it in a container to be reused. This will assure that the birds will not be overfed but get enough feed for the day.

If you overfeed the young birds by leaving the feed in the fly box, they will not respond to trapping in very quickly the next day. Try to do your training and feeding around the same time every day. This will give them the necessary time to get hungry. If you start the next day's training and feeding earlier than when you fed them the day before, they will be slow to trap in the fly box. If you do have slow trapping on one day, for instance, 2 p.m., and then wait until 3pm or 4pm the next day, they should trap in a lot quicker because they are hungrier. Less feed will also make a big difference.

Using a Training Cage for Fully Feathered Young (That Can Fly)
Having the training cage over your trap door entrance with your
trapping bobs up will allow the young birds to go in and out
whenever they want. This will allow them to become accustomed to
their surroundings and to go in to feed without the chance of losing
any birds because they get frightened and fly away. After three to
four days of this approach, place all the young birds out into the
training cage and drop the bobs on the trap door. Place the feed tray
inside and leave them to work it out. If they seem to need a little
encouragement, place a couple of old hens into the fly box to eat.
Watching the old hens will encourage the young birds to push on
the bobs to come on in to feed.

You should be using your whistle when you feed your young
birds in the fly box, or, if you are using a dropper, place her in during
feeding time. If you are using the orange triangle, be sure to have it
turned around for them to see the orange side. After all of the birds
have fed, turn the triangle back to the unpainted side. If you are
using a dropper, pull her out after they have eaten. (For more
information on droppers and orange triangles, go to **Visual Aids for
Pigeon Housing and Training** further on in the book).

Some pigeon trainers will shake a little feed in a tin can and whistle at feeding time to stimulate them to trap. Whichever method you use, always be consistent with it, and you will have better control of your pigeons. Two to three times of placing the young birds in the training cage and dropping the trapping bobs before placing the feed in the fly box is usually sufficient. When you see that all the young birds are pushing through the trap and coming in to eat, you will be ready to take off the training cage.

The first time you take off the training cage you may want to give your birds just one spoon of feed the day before. When you're ready to call them in, they will be more responsive because of hunger. Always remember that the feed amount is your control of pigeons. On the day you remove the training cage, pull the bobs up on the trap door and leave the birds to come out on their own. Try not to make them fly unless they do it on their own. It's always better if you do not frighten them. Hopefully there are no loud noises like lawn mowers, your neighbor shooting a gun, kids or dogs getting around the fly box, or a strike from a hawk. With the first couple of releases, the calmer your birds, the better.

When the birds will come out and notice the cage is gone, some may fly to the ground and back up to the fly box. Others will go up on their own for a couple of circles and then crash land either on the fly box, your house, or the nearest tree. I once had one try to land on the chimney of my house and fall in. If they do go up for a little flying, it can sometimes get pretty crazy for a few minutes. Eventually, things will calm down and they will make their way back to the fly box.

After 30 to 60 minutes, try calling them in. Now and then you will lose one or two for a while, but they will usually return before dark. So it's best on the first release to do it early in the day to allow yourself time to retrieve birds that may have ventured a little farther than you had expected.

After you have released and trapped in your birds in this manner for three or four days, you can begin to flag them. More on flagging ahead in the book, after trapping and training young birds that cannot fly yet.

Homing Instinct of Rollers
Scientists have confirmed that pigeons have their own biological

compass, which is called the "magneto receptor." The magneto receptor works off of naturally occurring magnetic fields created by the earth. The homing instinct of racing homers is quite remarkable. If released early in the morning, the best bird can fly a 600-mile race and get home before dark. Our rollers, on the other hand, do not have the racing homer's outstanding homing abilities. Most generally, they are lost within only a few miles from home. I and others have had them return from 20 miles, but it is not a common thing. So take special care with your rollers not to fly them into a strong wind. If you fly while it is snowing or dark, they will be easily lost because of not being able to see any landmarks. If they fly too far from their normal flying area, there is a good chance they will not return.

Trapping and Training Young Birds (That Cannot Fly Yet)
Without a training cage, it works best to wean the young birds before they are fully feathered under the wings. This way, they cannot fly. Place them on top of the fly box to get used to their new surroundings. If you plan to put your young birds out in this manner, always place the birds out hungry before feeding time. Give them about half an hour to set out and get a good look around.

After some time out on the roof, place them by the trap door and push them in with feed and fresh water waiting inside. (Along with dropper or turning triangle to the orange side if using them). Neither droppers nor orange triangles are necessary for training pigeons. They are just training options. It is always good, however, to either whistle or use a whistle when calling your birds in to eat. After a few days of encouraging them through the trap door, they will go in on their own as soon as you put them by the trap door. As soon as you see these young have good feather growth under the wing and can fly well, they will be ready to flag.

Flagging and Flying Young Birds

When starting your young flying and returning to your loft or fly box, keep in mind not to put them in the air too soon. If they can fly the first time you put them out, it will be important that they just hang around for a half hour or so and return back inside. If you startle them on the first time out, you may lose some of them. Go slow and easy at first; you are not wanting to fly them. Just get the routine of liberating them and being called back in and fed. You should do this for three to four days before you flag them. When you do flag them, they will scatter in every direction. Be sure to allow them to return to the fly box or loft. You want them to feel safe when they return. Once they have all come back, call them in and feed them. You should repeat this process for a couple more days. If you over-flag your birds in training, you can cause them to not want to land on the fly box, or they may just leave.

In the beginning when trying to get them back to the fly box for trapping, some may go and hang around your birds that are not being flown and are in their flight cages. When they do, they tend to stay around them for comfort and may not trap in when you call them. They may sit there until dark. So it is always helpful in the beginning of your training to block the access to the cages of the birds you are not flying. On the other hand, it will be helpful if you're missing a bird or two to have pigeons in their flight cages. Seeing them will aid in attracting a lost pigeon back to your loft.

Once you do flagging for a few days, you can flag them a couple of times or more on the same release. Make them fly off the fly box, but that's all. When they come back to the fly box, give them 20 to 30 minutes and then flag them again. After the second flagging and about ten minutes of rest after they've landed, call them in. Do this every day until they get strong enough to stay up for a good flight. Once they are flying well, pigeons will trap in more easily if they have a little time to clear their heads. Give them five to ten minutes before calling them in after they land.

You will want to get 45 minutes to one hour out of them. If you have the time, fly your pigeons two to three times a day, which will help them come into the roll faster. If you do fly them three times a day, give them one spoon (per bird) shaken (not heaping) of feed after each fly. Expect each release flight time to be shorter than the previous. In the beginning, your birds will not kit very well; they will be all over the sky. Within two weeks of flying every day, they will group together very nicely.

Any roller pigeon that lands too early, tree sits, or out-flies from the kit should be culled. You may have a bird or two that does not stay with the others in the kit. If this happens with one of your birds, give it some time to become a team player. If it is the same age as (or older than) the rest of the birds yet persists in not kitting, cull it out of your flock. Try to give any bird with a problem the benefit of the doubt. Sometimes pigeon trainers are too quick to cull a bird.

Some problem birds will end up being a keeper if you give them a chance. If you have a bird that goes and sits in a tree and does not fly with the others, chase it from the tree. If the bird tree sits after you have chased it out on a few releases, that is when you should consider culling it out before other birds start following it into the trees. If one of the pigeons lands earlier than the others, most of the time for no apparent reason, it should be taken out. If the bird is "outworking" the others, which means it is out-rolling all of the others by depth or velocity, then you would have a reason to overlook the early landings. This roller is just using more energy, so there's a good reason its flying time would be shorter. If there is no apparent reason for the bird to be landing early, then culling is called for.

As previously mentioned, you can fly your roller two to three times a day if you have the time. But, once they start rolling, you must pull them from the flock and put them in with other workers. Once you have a group of workers together that are spinning (not just flipping over or tumbling), you will want to fly them every other day. Now and then you can fly them a couple of days in a row, but not consistently. The same with rest days. If you fly spinners every day, you can fly the roll out of them or cause them to become sloppy in the roll from not getting enough rest. The muscles used to fly and perform their aerial feats need to recoup with the right amount of feed and rest.

Now, let's discuss rolling age. Any young bird that comes into the roll earlier than four months old is usually too soon for the bird to end up being a keeper. They usually become roll-downs. However, some do make it once in a while. It may take up to a year for all of the birds you just raised to roll. I would recommend any birds that do not roll within one year of regular flying to be culled. For me, a pigeon needs to show good rolling by one year. If not, I need the room for the ones that do. Fly them for years if you want to, but only breed from birds that roll in their first year.

Considerations for Time of Day to Release Your Pigeons
When you are flying your rollers, try to fly them early to avoid the heat of the day. The best time to fly rollers is early in the morning.

You can also fly them well in the evenings before dark if you think it's best for your needs. Sometimes this is done because of your work schedule or to give the hawks time to eat before you fly. But it does not always work out the way you may hope. You can still get hit by hawks in the evenings.

It is very important that you know your birds' flying time if you fly in the evenings. If your birds have been flying for two hours and it gets dark at 8 p.m., you don't want to release them at 7 p.m. If you do, they will fly the extra hour in the dark. This can cause you to lose most, if not all, of your birds. Rollers do not know where they are in the dark and will continue to fly until they run out of energy. This can put them many miles away from the loft when this happens.

To be safe during evening flying, consider your birds' average flying time and add extra time as a safety margin. For example, if your rollers have two hours of energy, fly them with an added minimum of a one-hour safety margin. You now have three hours of allowance before dark. This will give you the time you need to safely fly them and call them in for feeding. Always give yourself a safety margin. The time of sunset changes every day. Make sure you keep track of when it gets dark if you fly rollers in the evening.

Measuring Daylight
Here is a quick way to check to see how much daylight is left for the day if you're wanting to fly your rollers in the evening. Placing your hand at eye level, block the sun out with one hand. Place the bottom of your top hand at the bottom of the sun. For every hand you can get under the hand blocking the sun to the ground, you will have approximately one hour of sunlight left in the day. Each finger will represent 15 minutes. Work your hands down to the horizon. In the next picture, you will see that I only had room for one hand (four fingers) down to the horizon, which means that I only have one hour before dark. This would be cutting it too close for safety, leaving no room for the safety margin if my birds have been giving me 45 minutes to one hour of flying.

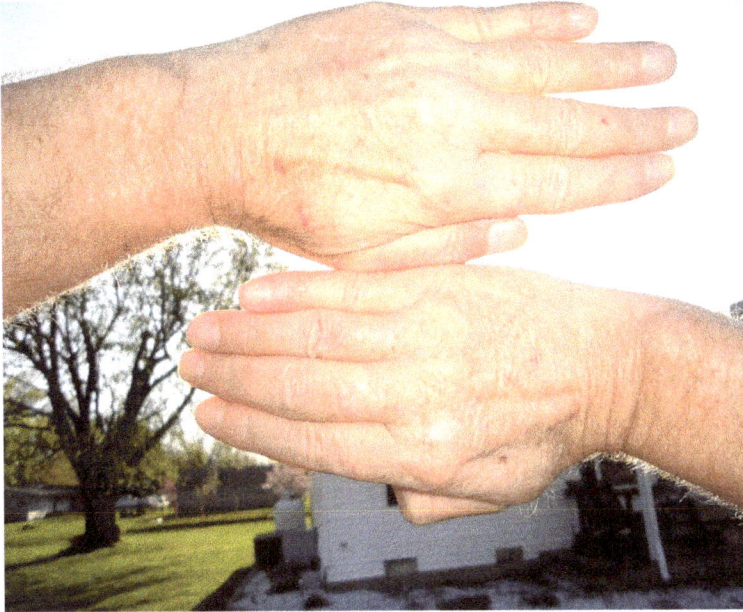

Another problem that can occur is a predatory strike from a hawk or owl just before dark as your birds are landing. This can send them back up into the air with adrenaline-filled energy, which can cause an overfly into the dark. Other things that can cause issues, which I call air traffic, include crows, buzzards, or any other large bird. These can affect your pigeon's flying time by flying longer than normal, especially if they have been chased around by a hawk earlier. Sometimes they will also circle the loft way longer than they should due to being leery of a possible hawk strike while landing. Try to whistle, shake the feed can, set a tray of feed on top of the fly box, whatever you can do to entice them to land. The longer they circle, the more chance your deep rollers may hit the ground or another hawk strike may occur, sending them right back up into the air. If it's close to dark, all the more reason to get them down as soon as possible.

Recovering an Escaped Pigeon

Pigeons do have a way of getting loose from time to time. This is a big deal, especially if you have borrowed the bird from a friend or bought a nice one to use in your program. A pigeon that hasn't been flown in a while will usually go up and fly some before either leaving your sight or landing somewhere close. If you have birds that you can release, they will give you some help in getting the lost bird back. If the bird is still flying, flag your kit. A lot of the times, the lost pigeon will land with them when they come down, or at least land close by.

If the lost bird has already landed by the time you get to your flyers, release them but do not flag them to fly. Some might still go up without flagging. That is okay. The remaining birds can help you get the lost bird to come over and land on the fly box. They will sometimes trap in with your kit when you call them in, or at least land on the box for you to catch in the dark with a flashlight.

If you lose a valuable pigeon and cannot release any birds to help you get it back, make sure your pigeons are not blocked to go out into their flight pens. A lost pigeon will be attracted to the birds in the pens and will many times be caught on top of one of them. If you have lost sight of the bird, be sure to fly your kit the next day. You may pick it back up with the kit. After about three days, there is a good chance you will never see the lost pigeon again. If the bird was borrowed or recently bought it would be a good idea to call the person you acquired it from. If not too far away, you may get lucky and it will have returned to their loft.

PART FOUR

— *Pigeon Housing* —

In this section, I'll explain how I work with my housing. For those of you not new to raising pigeons, some of my designs might seem a little different to you. Most roller flyers will have a few differences in their way of housing their pigeons. Over the years, I have always enjoyed looking at a flyer's pigeon housing. I've based my designs for both mine and the birds' needs to get what works out well for us both.

As we move forward, a key point to keep in mind is that whatever type of pigeon housing you have, never overcrowd your pigeons. If you do, some will die from these circumstances, and it will probably be some of the ones you like the best. A good rule of thumb is to have a perch per bird. If you do, then you will not be overcrowded. It also helps to have any outside cages facing the sunrise in the mornings, because the sun is very beneficial to the health of your pigeons. You will also want to keep your housing setup dry and well ventilated.

If you're going to own pigeons, you're going to need housing that will suit you and your birds' needs. I have seen housing for pigeons in just about every design one can imagine. Everything from orange crates to lofts better than some people's homes. The pigeon housing (pictured on previous page) setup is mine and consists of an individual breeding loft, open breeding foster loft, and two fly boxes. Moving around like I have has made these types of housing setups best suited for me. I have everything I need for breeding and flying, and they are fairly easy to move with a rollback truck. This saves me the time and money of rebuilding if I move to a new location.

Far left (in the picture) is the individual breeding loft. It has 12 individual breeding sections in the far end that are 2x2x2-feet square. Windows have been cut and put on hinges, with wire in place when they are open for ventilation along with an exhaust fan. The 8x16-foot loft is the largest of the group and has had an attached box on the outside back of the building. The attached box is divided into two sections that are accessed from the inside. These are used for weaning the young and can also be used for flying out of during competition.

Being able to feed and observe your A and B teams from inside is a real convenience. Especially with lighting inside when you may have to feed at night. Occasionally a pigeon will fly out of a box while feeding for competition. Being inside the loft, the escaped pigeon is easy to catch and put back with the team to get its fair share of feed during competition prep work. The 8x16 also functions as the feed storage area, with two show cages and plenty of room for me and a few others to look at some birds on bad weather days.

The 8x8 loft next to the individual loft is for foster breeding in an open loft situation. Eggs from the individual pairings are transferred to it for raising. This loft has 24 dowel rod military style nests for the job and is very convenient. (They can be seen in the open-loft breeding section of this book.) The loft also has a flight (or what some call a sun cage) for getting sun and taking baths. The loft is not flown from but has a trap door above the flight cage for the occasional escaped pigeon. The birds in the flight cage will attract a loose pigeon to the cage. Once the pigeon is on the cage it does not take long for the bird to trap in. This loft has windows cut out and hinges on them for easy closing during bad weather. The smaller boxes are called fly boxes. Between the two of them, they will house 120 pigeons for flying. Each box contains three sections that will hold 20 pigeons a section.

Each box has the roofs slanted forward to be able to see the pigeons well when they land. The roof being slanted opposite the feeding and handling doors also cuts down on water running into the feed trays and you while feeding on a rainy day.

This is an inside look at one of the compartments of the fly boxes.

On the outside rear of the 8x8 loft is another attached box for any extra stock birds that are not being bred from. This box is also divided into two sections for keeping hens and cocks separate.

The training cage on the fly box is used for familiarizing the young rollers to the area before being released. I also use this cage to acclimate a new bird I have brought home. The training cage can be moved to each section as needed. Once all birds are ready to be released, the training cage can be removed and stored until the next breeding season. During lockdown, it can be rotated so that all the birds in each section can get some time outside. For those unfamiliar with this term, lockdown is when you have to stop all flying activities due to bad weather or predators for an extended period of time.

It also comes in handy when you want to scrape your perches during lockdown. Just run all the pigeons into the training cage and close them out by closing the trap door. This will allow you to clean the perches without having to release the birds.

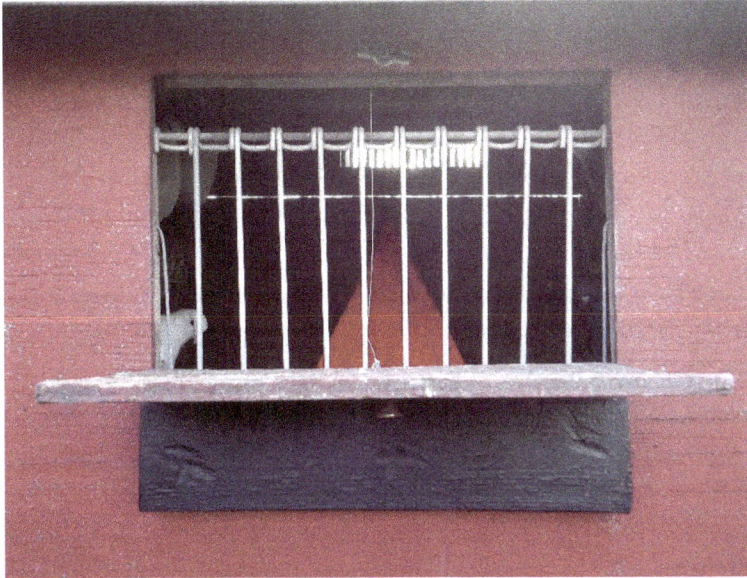

When pigeons enter back into their fly box, different methods are used. Some trainers throw just a little feed in the box to get them in while the door is open. If they have wire bottoms, some trainers only put a limited amount of grain in a feed tray, to get them in and feed when ready. Others cut a hole slightly bigger than the pigeon and block it up after the birds come in. I have used regulation trap doors like in the picture above for my pigeons since I started raising pigeons as a young boy. This allows me more control over my pigeons.

One of the problems with using one of the other methods is that if one of your birds gets full of feed, he will come right back outside and not come in until dark. The regulation trap will not allow birds out, only in, though once in a while you might run into a Houdini. That would be a bird that is able to manipulate the bobs in a way that will allow him to escape from the box. His escape usually happens before feeding when you may open the trap door cover to allow a little more light in the fly box for feeding. This bird normally will do the Houdini escape when hungry and will quickly trap back in if not scared into flight when you place the feed in the fly box.

Some days, one or two birds might not have trapped in right away with the others. By the time it does trap, the feed is usually gone. If you're not training for a competition, it will not be too great a concern. The late-trapping pigeon or two will be the first to trap in tomorrow. You can usually get them in faster by leaving the bobs up until they are all in. Once they are all in, but for a problem bird or two, drop the bobs. Make sure to close the trap door cover as soon as it is no longer necessary to be open. This will keep your pigeons safe so predators can't get to them.

Some pigeon keepers (not trainers) will keep and allow flight of their pigeons by what is called open loft flying. Open loft flying is when pigeons have access to the outside of their loft at will; whenever they want, they can go outside. The only control you would have in this way of keeping pigeons is knowing they would be back in by dark; at least the ones that have not been captured by a predator that day. Open loft flying would never be recommended by an experienced roller flyer. Always control your releases for best results.

The trap doors I use have 50-lb test fishing line attached to them so they can be pulled up for easy opening on the release. The pigeons are released from the trap door side always. This way, they do not fly out of the box when you open the door to feed them. If they are not used to going out that way, they won't. You can stand with a friend and look at the birds with the door open and not have to worry about them flying out. The doors on the feeding side of the fly box are cut out higher than the floor level so as to leave a lip higher than a pigeon is tall.

This helps keep them inside the fly box. The pigeon will not be able to walk over to the edge looking out when the door is open. Each section has a wire floor, allowing the droppings to fall through to the ground. Wire floors in your fly box not only allow droppings to fall through but also help with air circulation. With flooring other than wire, the extra heat, waste, and lack of air circulation will promote germ growth that can cause sickness in your pigeons.

The surrounding bottom of my fly boxes are enclosed with small holed black lattice to keep the pigeons and other animals from going underneath. You will want to keep young birds from eating any old feed that may be lying under the boxes. Try to keep your young birds off the ground as much as possible. It is fairly easy for young birds to get sick from eating bad feed on the ground. As they get older it is not as much of a problem.

When building your roller breeding and flying setup, be sure to not only place it in a position that will allow you good access for your daily routine but also consider your rollers. Trees, power lines, and other obstacles can cause problems when releasing your pigeons. Depending on your situation, you may just have to deal with it. But if you have options, consider the best for both you and your pigeons.

Your roller setup should be visually appealing. Nice paint and cutting your grass goes a long way with people who think the worst of pigeons. The last thing you want is the neighbors talking about those old dirty buildings and nasty pigeons the guy has in his yard. If your loft setup is easy on the eyes, it helps give the impression you're a pigeon trainer, not just a keeper of pigeons.

Security

Don't forget about security for your birds. Predators and humans alike will want your pigeons. For anything you build with wire on the bottom, consider adding more wire a few inches below the first floor, especially if the initial wire floor is a little on the big side and you're not using lattice. Hawks, cats, and dogs will get under your fly boxes. Predators will definitely try to get through your wire bottoms if they take notice of the birds. This will have to be considered by you. With the commotion of a predator trying to get in, some of your birds' feet can be grabbed if the wire is too big. If you go with too small a wire, the pigeons droppings will add up quickly.

If you are not using lattice, use two floor levels of 2-inch x 1-inch wire with six inches between the two. The bottom layer of wire will need more cleaning attention than the top one. You may want the lower level to slide out rather than be nailed in place. Two wire floor levels are a little inconvenient as far as the extra cleaning, but it's well worth not finding one of your birds dead or seriously injured when you open the door.

Locks on all your setup doors will be of help. For convenience, try to buy locks that all work off of one key, and don't forget to have a spare. If you're like me, you will lose your keys from time to time. Locks will not ensure your pigeons will not get stolen. If a person really wants them, that little lock will not keep them out. Just about every pigeon fancier I have known has had one or more pigeons stolen. A pigeon trainer once told me the lock just keeps an honest man honest.

Placing rubber or some water-resistant material over the lock to cover it will increase its longevity. If you have ever had to deal with unlocking an ice-covered lock, you will appreciate the lock cover. Putting oil on the locks once a year helps keep them working smoothly. Also, it never hurts to take one last look at locks and doors before you go back into the house, especially if something has interrupted your normal routine with your birds for the day.

Another good security measure for your pigeon setup area is a motion-sensor-triggered light. Ideally you want it to come on when anything comes into the area. If a cat, raccoon, fox, or weasel is around your birds at night, you will want to know about it.

Line of sight is important too. If there is any way you can place your setup so that you can see your entire pigeon training area by looking out of one of your home windows, you will be glad you did. Being able to see your loft and fly boxes will come in handy for a multitude of reasons. You may experience things like I have, such as a snake hanging on the fly cage trying to get in to eat a pigeon, pigeon visitors you didn't know were in the yard looking at your birds, a hawk sitting on the loft or hanging from your fly cage, a cat under your fly box, or a dog trying to bite the feet off your birds under the fly box through the wire. You might also see the two young boys your friend told to play outside, both with a long stick poking your young pigeons in the training cage.

Looking out towards your loft at times, you will see late pigeons you thought you lost sitting on the fly box wanting in. Other times it may be one that was hiding in the woods after a dive from a hawk, finally getting the courage to come home. Now and then birds will return to your loft that someone may have bought from you. So it's always a good idea to place your loft where you can take a quick glance to see what's going on out there. Especially if you look out and none of your birds are taking advantage of the flight cages. This is usually a good indicator of a hawk sitting somewhere close to the loft.

Now that we've discussed the basics of your loft setup, let's move on to how to build your perches.

Removable Perches
Over the years, I've used almost every type of perch mounted to the

wall. All perches need to be scraped periodically, and you'll usually find yourself standing in an awkward position while cleaning them. Many times the weather will work against you, too. If it's hot outside, you'll have sweat dripping off the tip of your nose with another 100 perches to go. Other times, when you're ready to scrape the perches, it starts raining or it's so cold you can't get much off the perch because everything is frozen to it.

I got tired of all these scenarios, so I thought I would try something easier and less time consuming, removable inverted **V** perches. This is one of the best things I've ever done for myself. They are so much more convenient than a flat surface perch, which has to be scraped almost every day to help keep your birds' feet clean. Inverted **V** perches will also allow more time in between cleaning as opposed to flat perches.

A removable perch allows the option of taking them anywhere you want to clean them. Another reason a removable inverted **V** perch is so handy is that you can make twice the perches you need. Whenever you get an unexpected call from roller guys who are stopping, you can quickly switch out your perches so that your birds are looking their best while sitting on a clean perch.

Removable inverted **V** perches are easy to take down in a hurry by grabbing the bottom one and raising it up to the next one, so that you can take down a row quickly. When taking them back to hang up, start at the top nail and place the hanger over the nails as you lower the stack with your hand. You will love how fast you can take down, clean, and rehang them.

Every so often, you may need to tighten or replace a picture frame hanger or give a loose perch a tap to tighten it while you're cleaning them. They will last for years with very little maintenance. To make your own removable inverted **V** perches, refer to the pictures following as you follow the construction directions:

1. Cut your first 1-inch x 4-inch board (A) to 6 inches long.
2. Cut a second 1x4 board (B) to 5 inches (deduct 1 inch or the thickness of the board you're using.)
3. Place board A on board B. Attach with two 1-1/2-inch finishing nails (C).
4. Attach picture frame hanger (D) at the top of the perch with a ¾-inch nail as seen in the photo.
5. Hang the perch on the wall of your fly box or loft by anchoring a small nail (E) at a 45-degree angle. Nails are safer when they're not protruding out enough to allow a pigeon band to get caught on it. When spacing your nails for your perches above each perch, a 10-inch spacing is recommended in the fly box, with 12 inches apart between the rows. Spacing of 12 inches is recommended between nail hangers for the stock loft.
6. The S hook (F) is used for hanging perches on wire. Close one end on the wire and leave the other end open to hold and be able to remove the perch when needed.

You can cut down on cleaning your perches by using only the number needed. If your fly box is set up for 20 perches and you only have 11 pigeons in it, pull out the remaining nine until you need them. This is especially important when you are competing with an

11-bird fly. The fewer perches the better for saving energy in your competition birds. As long as each pigeon has a perch, they will do fine and actually better in competition by not jumping from one perch to another, thus allowing more rest.

If your birds are accustomed to another style of perch they may not get on the inverted **V** perch right away. To speed up the process, set each bird on a perch. After that, they will have no more problems. I also like to pull unnecessary perches during open-loft breeding, only leaving the perch that is used to land on to go into the nest. They seem to take care of their breeding business better that way. Now, let's move on to fly boxes and ventilation.

Fly Box and Ventilation

Each of the three compartments in the fly box (picture below) has a vent at the highest point to release heat in the summer. The vents can also be closed for cold weather when you want to keep in the heat. Along with wire floors they get good air circulation. The more ventilation your birds have, the healthier they will be.

I like to keep the fly boxes semi-dark for my flyers, enough light to see to eat and drink, but dark enough to rest and be still. When feeding in the fly box you can leave open the trap door cover, which will allow more light in. I also do this on lockdowns and days off of their flying schedule. Don't forget to close the trap door covers when you're done with your pigeon chores.

On any fly box that you build, make sure it is easy for you to reach any part of the fly box inside. Do not build your fly box in a way that puts your birds beyond reach. There will be times you will want to handle a particular bird. If you can't reach to the other side, you will not be able to catch one of your pigeons with ease if it's sitting there. You can bet where you can't reach is where they will go.

Flying Tools

Having the proper tools when flying and training rollers is a must, just as in any sport or hobby when trying to get a good end result. Refer to the picture above as you read below:

1. A flag on a pole will be needed when starting off the young that you will be raising, or any time a bird does not go up

when the birds are released. The flag is used to scare them off the roof at the same time with the others. After they are flying well, you'll use it less often. Your stick or pole can be any length that suits your needs. Some use metal poles, fishing rods, or cane poles. Flags or any type of cloth on the pole will suffice.

2. A hat will help block sun on your head and in your eyes. Holding your hat up to block the sun works great when your birds get too close to it. I sometimes throw my hat into the fly box to get them out a little quicker.

3. Sunglasses or prescription glasses that are tinted will help to enhance your observations of their aerial progress.

4. A coach's whistle will help remind your rollers that they are hungry. The whistle can be heard when your birds are high. Use the whistle at feeding time so that your birds associate the whistle with the feed, which will give you a little added control when trying to get your pigeons down.

5. A tossing stick is used to toss upwards to your kit or team to climb higher. The tossing stick should be the length you can swing without catching the ground when you swing to throw it up. If your team is allowed to circle low too long on the release it can create a situation for some of your deeper rollers to hit the ground. When landing after being flown, they can stay low longer than you like and won't land, resulting in a possible mishap. When this occurs, toss the stick up to the team. They will climb after a couple of tosses. In some places I have flown rollers, I have had power lines over the loft. This cuts down on deep birds hitting the ground on their attempt to land after being flown. With power lines, some of your rollers may at times land on the lines first when released and not go up with the other birds. The tossing stick is a great tool for getting them off the power lines and into the air right away. The same tossing stick method can be used by the trainer to get them off landing poles. Landing poles are used in the same way the power lines help in saving birds that may go into a performance during landing. They

are T in shape and are placed high above one's loft or in close proximity to it. You should practice with your tossing stick before you need it. When you can throw it straight up with good height and get it to land where you want, you will be ready to use it without killing one of your rollers or having to go over to the neighbor's house and retrieve it from their yard. I have seen pigeon trainers use other things for tossing, but with some practice the stick works best. Use one with some weight to it and you will be able to achieve considerable height with ease on a toss.

6. Tennis balls work very well for getting birds off rooftops that you cannot reach with the flag or the tossing stick. Remember, if they are not in the air flying, they should be sitting on your fly box. If you allow a pigeon to sit in a tree or someplace other than your kit box, others may follow.

7. Having a cloth rag comes in handy when handling birds. They also help in keeping your feed trays clean and dry. Keeping one on each fly box and inside your lofts saves time that can be spent on the task at the moment instead of looking for a rag. Wash them as needed or throw them away and replace.

8. Another good tool is a long-handled fishing net. It will come in handy for the occasional accidentally released, injured, or problem bird when you cannot reach it.

Visual Aids for Pigeon Housing and Training

Research says that a pigeon can see red and orange better than any other color. This setup is red because of that. I have also found orange-colored triangles to be a very useful tool.

The triangles hanging on the side of my fly boxes are for letting the team know it's feeding time. They are painted orange on one side and the fly box color on the other side. They are laid on top of the fly box with the orange side up when it is feeding time. This is for my flyers when I need to encourage them to come down. In each of the flying sections on the inside of the doors are also triangles painted orange on one side and the natural wood color on the other side.

These are turned over to the orange side during feeding. After the birds are fed, they are turned back to the unpainted side. You can turn them over with ease by drilling a hole at the top of the triangle and attaching some fishing line to the screw eye. To make sure it does not move around as you open and close the door, insert two shoulder hooks under each corner for the triangle to sit on.

The triangle can be lifted up and turned around but does not move much when you are opening the door. Your pigeons will associate the color orange with feeding, and that will help give you a little more control. One of the things the triangle will help you with is if your birds are circling low too long trying to land. If you have deep birds in the team, you will not want them circling low more than necessary. By putting one of the triangles on top of the fly box, you will help them to come down. Another use for the orange triangle is with overflys. An overfly would be when your birds fly on longer than you had planned, into the dark.

Tossing one of these triangles down on the ground with the orange side up and a light shining on it will help get your birds back into the yard before they are lost in the dark. There will be some crash landings since rollers do not see well in the dark. If you use a light to help your birds land in the dark, try to use more of a focused light, like a light beam down towards the triangle or whatever you are using to direct them to land on.

A funneled light, more like a flashlight beam, is a better choice than a light bulb, which will throw light up. Birds looking down on a bulb light in the night will be somewhat blinded and have a difficult time seeing where to land. Some may fly off into the night.

I have saved a few teams in the dark with orange triangles using this method. I had once lost a team in a flyaway, which is when you lose them during day flying. At the place I was flying my birds, they would land on power lines in my yard before coming down to the loft. A couple of days after I lost them, I saw them setting on some power lines a few miles from my house.

I left for home and returned with one of the triangles and some feed. When they saw the orange triangle on the ground next to the feed tray they flew right down to it. While they were eating from the tray I was able to grab 19 of the 20 birds to take home. For best results, use the orange triangle as soon as the young birds are weaned. Anytime feed is in front of them, show the orange side.

Droppers

A dropper is a bird used as a visual aid when you want your flying pigeons to come down sooner. Most use a fantail pigeon to help with this. Putting a fantail in with your birds during feeding time, then pulling it out when they are done feeding, is the proper method of training them to respond to it.

The fantail is a signal that it is time to eat. Always keep the fantail out of sight from your rollers until it is feeding time. You can set the fantail on top of your fly box when you want your rollers to come down. Set the fantail out hungry so it will trap in right away with your birds. However, there is a drawback: if you are in a competition with your rollers and anything else gets out that may resemble your fantail, they could land earlier than you wanted. That is why I personally do not use them.

Carrying Boxes

If you're going to get into the roller fancy/hobby/sport, you will need a large carrying box for moving birds around to different sections of the loft, especially when moving young birds to the fly box. It is also useful when taking your birds to a show or down the street for a release to get them up flying again if they've gotten lazy. If you're buying several birds, it also comes in handy for bringing them home. In the meantime, a cardboard box will suffice. Be sure to cut air holes in the top and sides for good ventilation until you get to where you are going. I like to keep a small carrying box in the car with enough room for one or two birds. Most fanciers do not have a carrying box with them because it takes up space in the car. Still, it is a lot better than being without something to carry a bird and having to pick up your new bird on the next visit, because that bird might not be there on your next visit. Remember, it's always better to be prepared. In a pinch, you can also use a paper sack or small cardboard box. The small carrying box on the right is for a bantam chicken. They work out great for one to two rollers. When closed they have an opening at the top both for your fingers to carry the box and air for the birds to breathe.

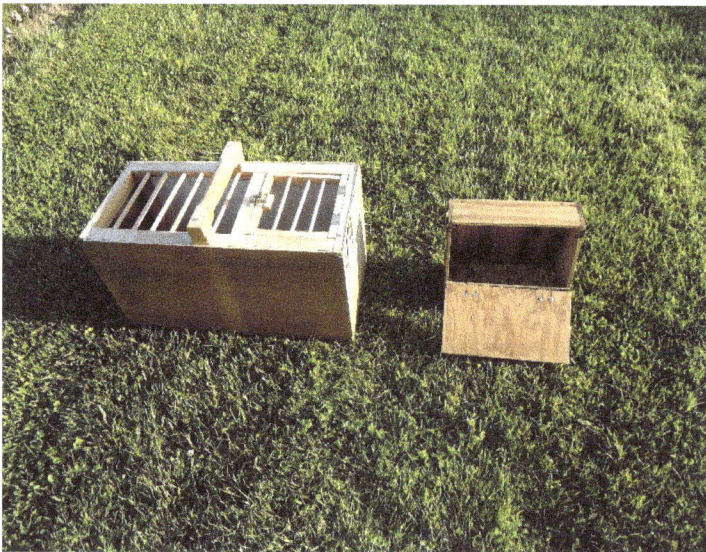

Considerations for Purchasing Birds

I suggest before buying your first rollers that you watch an experienced flyer's birds. If you see performing birds that you like, make a deal on a kit of young birds. Take them home, train them to trap, and fly them out. This is normally the most inexpensive way.

The very best way to acquire good birds is to pick old birds from the sky. It may cost a little more per bird than buying young birds, but at least you have a better idea of what you're breeding from. Go to as many roller flyers as you can to watch them fly their pigeons. Ask questions about the age of the birds. Most flyers keep good notes and can tell you all about the bird you're interested in. If they cannot answer your questions, it would be wiser to move on to another flyer for purchasing your birds.

I also suggest watching a flyer's birds as many times as you can before dismissing or purchasing them. A flyer may have good birds, but they may be fed up, meaning the flyer has been giving the birds all they want to eat. If there are good birds to be seen, they will be seldom rolling and long flying caused by overfeeding. If they fly but do not roll, or the style is lacking in the performance, they may be too young, so be sure to ask about their age. From four months old and up, you should be seeing some kind of work from the flyer's birds. If they do not fly at all and the weather is good (the heat and humidity is not too high), consider contacting another roller flyer to purchase your rollers.

Some pigeon keepers will tell you just about anything you want to hear to sell you a bird. They are most commonly known as feather merchants. Beware of feather merchants. Normally, their birds will be unbanded and not look their best. They will either tell you they have the best rollers or say that they just got them from some credible flyer. Try to acquire birds from a true roller trainer, someone you know has had some success in roller flying competition and will fly them for you. Anything less, you will be taking a chance and may have to start over, wasting time and money in the process.

Purchasing a good roller might not come cheap. Occasionally, a credible roller flyer will give you a good start for free with roller pigeons if he thinks you can handle them with the knowledge you have. If not, you might pay on average of fifty dollars for a young bird straight out of the nest. If the bird is a proven flyer, you could pay up to five hundred dollars. A proven flyer is a roller that excels in the air with all good habits and traits. If you are after a guy's proven breeder, which is a breeder that reproduces a high percentage of good birds, you could pay up to one thousand dollars or more. Most flyers will never sell their best at any price. Still, if you consider all the time and effort in producing good birds, it's not too much to pay if you're really serious about raising rollers and entering competitions.

Go in with as much knowledge as you can when trying to purchase roller pigeons. Never purchase rollers that do not fit the flying standard. Knowledge is your best ally, and nothing beats watching them first. If you see one or two pigeons you like, and the flyer will let you acquire them, ask about purchasing the parents of the birds, too, because you know that the parents of the birds can produce good performers. If your purchase of a bird comes down to picking between a cock and hen of the same caliber, always pick the cock. Good cocks are harder to come by than good hens. They can also be used in a bull cock breeding program that can save you a lot of time.

When watching rollers perform, watch for the most impressive bird in the team. You will need to keep a close eye on the bird as it makes its way down to land. The guy flying them may have many of the same color. Once you're sure of the bird of interest, ask particular questions about the bird. How long has he been flying the bird? How old is it? How old was the bird when it started rolling? Has it ever rolled down before?

If the roller pigeon you're interested in is over a year old and has been flown hard and never bumped or rolled to the ground, he would be worthy of consideration. Try to find them with a good amount of air time; around a year and a half of flying would be best. I have used birds that have spent one year in the air of hard flying before being selected to breed from and have done well with them, but more air time is always better to help ensure stability.

It works out well if the bird you're interested in started rolling from four months old and up, but no earlier. These tend to be more stable. At four months old, they would be called early developers to the performance. Most that start rolling any earlier than four months old usually do not make it a year in the air. Most will die in the performance before they are a year old. There are exceptions, but those are rare.

Some flyers will breed an early developer to a late developer, which would be rollers that start rolling closer to a year old. This is a common practice to help balance your offspring and is what I recommend. Birds that start rolling after one year of flying should not be considered for breeding. Using these types of late-rolling performers would reinforce this trait. Who wants to wait more than a year for their birds to start performing when it isn't necessary? Breeding late developers to late developers tend to reproduce the same. This also goes for breeding early developers to early developers. Consider these things when picking birds to take home for your breeders.

It's always wise to know when your breeders started rolling, so balance your breeding pairs' starting time late to early if possible. With that said, don't pass up a good roller pigeon if you cannot get the age that it started rolling from the trainer. If it is a high-quality roller you can find that out by keeping breeding notes on the offspring. By studying these notes, you can tell whether or not the young birds of this performer tend to be early or late developers.

If the flyer's birds are fed up and he wants to impress you with his rollers, he will try to get an advance notice that you will be coming by so that he can cut back the feed on his flyers. Hopefully, he will have a week or two to get them ready for you. If they are good birds and he has the feed right, there will be plenty of performing to watch. When the birds roll over, watch for the best-performing roller in the group, not the deepest-performing roller. The deepest rollers are not always the best. Watch flying rollers for high wing placement and good velocity first and depth second. Depth is easy to breed into rollers, while velocity and wing placement are not. I would suggest that you do not purchase birds rolling shorter than one second or deeper than three seconds.

In closing, keep in mind that if you cannot get all your breeders from one flyer, do not be too concerned. As long as you ask many questions and choose birds that fit your needs, it will not hurt you. Don't worry about ruining the birds because they are not the same line or family. As long as you are selecting them for their aerial traits, you will be fine. Nothing beats breeding best to best from the air. I've noticed many new roller flyers still ask the question, "What is best to best?" While it seems simple, others seem to want either to complicate the question or might simply need a little more information. I would hope after you read this book you will not have to ask the same.

When breeding best to best I would say air first, ground second. For example, let's say you buy a team of birds and fly them for a year or more. By that time you should have learned what to look for when viewing a quality performance. Some of your team will perform better than others. For example, you may notice that all are scorable but six of them stand out when performing above all others.

Now let's say you are going to breed your birds, and the team you are flying are all that you have. To make this hypothetical scenario easier, the six top birds are three hens and three cocks. Get as much offspring from these six and use all the others as foster parents. This is what is meant by "best to best from the air."

When choosing "best to best on the ground," in my mind this refers to breeding from the same six birds by the body type when pairing them together. You may breed like to like if you feel the two birds you're putting together are the body type you are striving for. You may also have one larger than you prefer and want to try to bring the size down in the offspring. You may want to breed it to the smallest of the six birds you are working with in your breeding program, while all along considering the performance depth of the birds you are pairing. I personally call this "best to best from the air to best to best on the ground." Go with your higher percentages from your breeding pairs after that. If percentages are low with some of the pairings, try a different mate for these pairs.

Settling New Birds to Your Loft
When you acquire new birds from another flyer and want to fly them

from your loft, you will need to settle them into your new loft first. A training cage would be the easiest (if you have one). Use the cage attached to the fly box you're going to be liberating them from for about a week. When you're ready for their first release, skip feeding them the day before you are going to release them. When you do, try not to make them fly. You will want them to feel at ease at their new home.

After an hour or so, call them into feed. If a couple of the new pigeons went up and are still flying around, give them as much time as you can to land back on the flying box before calling the rest in to feed. If you happen to have birds that are already settled, let your new ones out when your settled birds land after flying. Have your new birds marked or their bands noted so that you can separate them after they trap in. A couple of days of this and you can start chasing them up.

Most of the time, the birds will have all gone up on their own by the time you decide to flag them, especially if they have been flown on a regular basis at their last home. If you lose a bird or two trying to settle them to your loft, contact the trainer you purchased the birds from, so that he can keep an eye out for the missing birds coming back to his loft. Some roller flyers do not count their pigeons after flying them and may not notice that one or two of your birds have returned to him. Anything less than twenty miles between your loft and the flyer you purchased your birds from increases the chance that the bird will return to him.

If you do not have a training cage, tape can be used to keep the birds from flying until they get accustomed to their new surroundings. When taping a pigeon's wing, electrical tape seems to work best. It is easier to get off when you're done settling them. Taping only one wing will work best for you. Starting with the tenth primary, count back seven to eight feathers and tape them together as shown in the picture on the previous page. While their wing is still taped, prop your trap door bobs open for a couple hours every day so they can go in and out. Then call them in to feed. Do this for a few days. Then take the tape off.

Another way to train your taped birds is to place them on the fly box for an hour and then open the trap to call them in to eat. After a few days, remove the tape and let them do what they want for a couple of releases before calling them in. Then start flagging them on the next fly.

For further evaluation of a new single pigeon brought home to fly with yours, tape the wing and set it on top of the loft after you have flagged your flyers. Allow it to trap with your flyers when they come in for a few days, but not more than a week. At times I have brought home a new pigeon and tossed it up with my group of flyers the next day. This works most of the time, especially if the new bird has been a regular flyer at the last place he flew and his flying time is about the same as mine. If you lose the bird, let some of your flyers out early the next morning. Most of the time you can get the bird back then.

PART FIVE

— *General Care* —

With proper care, a pigeon can live 15 years or more. I recently had one pass away I have had for 20 years. General care consists of clean feed, grit, and water; keeping the housing area dry and well ventilated; and guarding against direct draughts in the winter.

The following products are what I use for general care of my rollers:

1. Just like worming your dog or cat, your pigeons need to be wormed, too. You especially need to worm your birds before and after your breeding program is finished and before training starts for a competition. If your birds have worms, it will affect how well they absorb nutrients from their feed. The last thing you need is for something to affect how your

birds should react to your feeding methods during training for a competition.

Pigeons can live with a slight infestation of worms, but they will eventually kill your pigeons if left untreated. It is recommended not to worm your pigeons while raising young or when your pigeons are in the molt.

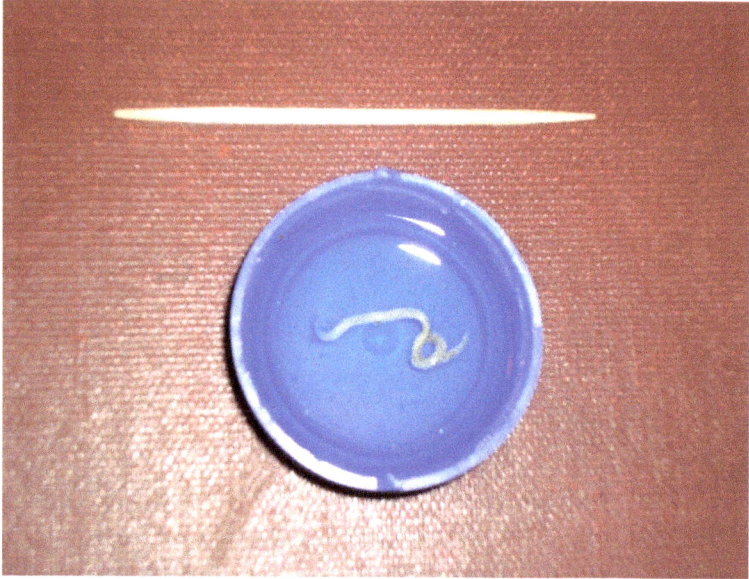

In the previous photo is the roundworm, one of the most common internal parasites that will inflict damage to your pigeons. Other common internal parasites include hairworms, stomach wall worms, gape worms, strongly lids, and tapeworms.

I've known roller pigeon guys to accidentally kill most of their flock by not getting the directions right when deworming their pigeons. Always follow directions so that you do not overdo it with the worm medication. When deworming, the water should be pulled prior to feeding. You will want your birds thirsty so they drink when they are finished eating. Wait until all of the birds have eaten, and then put the treated water in. I always treat my birds for two days just to be certain they all went to drink. The amount of

Wazine wormer medication (the medication that I use, shown two pages back) recommended is two ounces per gallon. In 30 days, a follow-up treatment is also recommended to break up the large roundworm life cycle. It is recommended to alternate your worm medication so your pigeons will not build up a resistance to it. Regardless of what type of worm medication you use, be sure to scrape your perches and floor the next day. This will help prevent reinfestation.

2. Apple cider vinegar will restore gut bacteria lost from deworming. A couple of days of a tablespoon per gallon in the water will help with getting your birds back to digesting their feed properly. Aside from this, my birds seem to stay healthier by putting one tablespoon per gallon in their water twice a week. Regular use will help guard against paratyphoid/Salmonella and E. coli.

3. A couple of days of cod liver oil will help a light pigeon get back its weight and stamina. The vitamin D in the oil will also aid birds that do not get enough sunlight. I like to use cod liver oil on the birds' feed for a couple of days after the worming and apple cider vinegar treatments. Remember, when mixing cod liver oil, do not use so much that the feed sticks together. You want the feed to be shiny, not sticky. I suggest adding a little at a time to the feed. Shaking the feed in the coffee can to blend the oil with the feed mix works best. If the feed sticks together, add more feed.

4. Poultry dust helps in controlling a variety of external feather parasites that will get on your birds. There are three main groups of external parasites: lice, mites, and flies. In the mite category there are six different types: red mites, feather mites, depluming mites, quill mites, nasal mites, and scaly leg mites.

It's always a good idea to dust any new birds brought home. This could keep you from having to dust your whole flock. Just sprinkling a little around the neck, under the wings, and around the vent area will do fine. After you sprinkle a little on the pigeon, rub it into the feathers slightly. Considering all the precautions you are taking to assure your birds are in good health, it is wise to also guard against wild birds gaining access to your loft. Wild birds getting into your loft can infect your rollers with a number of external feather parasites. They range from blood sucking to feather eating parasites.

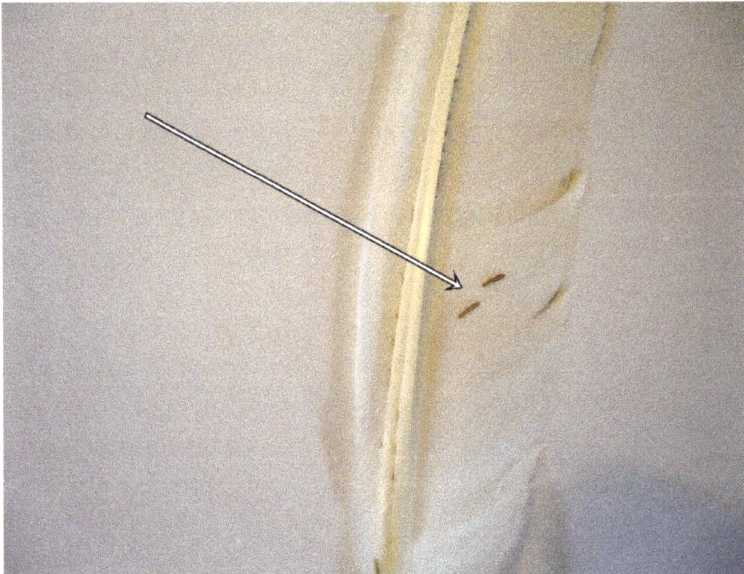

Our goal is to prevent any and all parasitic infestations to assure our birds' health. For example, the red feather lice pictured above will cause weak feathers and irritation. Damage from red feather lice will look like needle punctures and thinning streaks in the feather. The mites tend to look locked in place but will move around if disturbed.

The pigeon fly pictured, which is around the same size as the common house fly, survives by feasting on your birds' blood. They tend to be slow flyers, but quick with the legs. If you think you saw one run across your hand while you were holding a feral bird, you probably did. They are very fast movers.

5. Calcium is a necessity, especially when one of your hens loses too much calcium from laying eggs. If you notice one of your hens can't walk after laying her eggs, lack of calcium will normally be the problem. A couple days of calcium will fix her. This is an uncommon occurrence, but it is nice to have some calcium on hand when you need it. Crushed chicken shells will also help with calcium deficiencies during breeding. Adding crushed chicken shells with the feed during breeding will keep the hen's calcium levels up. The eggs laid will also be of better quality, with nice strong healthy shells. I suggest drying the eggshells in the oven at 250 degrees for fifteen to twenty minutes before crushing them.

6. Anytime you have a young or old bird that is not looking healthy, always check its throat and, with young birds, the

navel, because you might need canker medication. From my experience, the navel canker will only show up in the young who are still in the nest. They can still have it show in the throat or navel at the same time. Canker will look like a cheesy substance. Old birds will normally show it in the mouth and throat areas only. It is said that all pigeons carry canker and it can express itself when a pigeon is under too much stress. Keeping a clean, dry nest will help prevent navel canker showing up in the young birds.

In regard to medicating pigeons, some think that the less one gives medication to his birds the stronger they will be in the long run. I tend to agree with that way of thinking and try not to medicate my birds unless absolutely necessary. If you feel you need some medications and don't know where to buy them, I recommend Foy's Pet Supplies. They have been my supplier when I've needed anything from trap doors to medications. You can order by phone, fax, or email. They have a very wide selection of pigeon supplies. You can find them at FoysPetSupplies.com

Bathing Birds
Giving your pigeons access to a pan of water for bathing will help cut back on natural pigeon dust that pigeons accumulate. You can occasionally set out a pan of fresh water roughly four inches deep for your pigeons to bathe in when landing after a release. They will all pile in together and splash around and then go to the ground or the rooftop and lie on their sides, spreading their wings to dry out. Dump the remaining water from your bathing pan when all the birds are finished to keep the birds from drinking from it when they land after the next day's release.

When bathing young birds, keep them off the ground so they don't pick up and eat something that can make them sick. They are more susceptible when younger. Older birds have better resistance and can probe around on the ground.

Most of the time, your rollers will get enough bathing from getting caught in the rain during flights or in the flight cages for your stock. If it rains during flight, your rollers will be slow to trap because of the chance to take a shower after landing. Normally, after the rain has stopped, they will trap in.

Cleaning Toes

Occasionally, especially during breeding in individual pens, you will notice a breeder with manure collecting on its toenails. It may be removed fairly easily by using a pair of pliers. Adjust the pliers to where they will not close all the way. Go slow and give the soiled toe in question a couple small squeezes. The manure will usually come right off. With large pieces of manure, use the larger opening inside part of the pliers first.

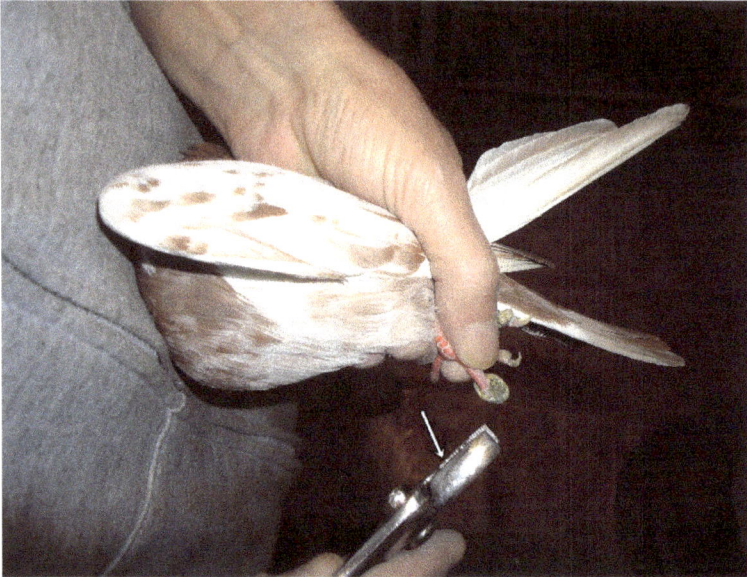

Feeding

Feeding your pigeons has to be done once daily. Most roller trainers feed a mix of grains. Some flyers mix it the way they prefer, while others purchase commercial pigeon feed already mixed. A full pigeon will eat all he wants and then go to the perch. The amount of feed per flying pigeon will be two to three coffee spoons. I don't use a measuring spoon when I train rollers. I use my morning coffee spoon. Depending on whether you're taking them up or down in condition, you will be going back and forth between two or three spoons per bird. This can go from three full spoons down to two spoons shaken.

The main thing on feeding flying rollers is to not let them have all they want to eat. If you do, you will not have any control. You do not want them to fly for hours, if they do fly at all; they may just get too fat and lazy to fly.

If you're not getting ready for competition and not using the spoon, the best way to know if a pigeon has had enough feed for the day is to wait until the birds go to drink. You can pull the feed tray at this time. Once they've moved to drinking, they have had enough feed to keep them strong, healthy, and flying well. You can place the water in the fly box before they eat so that you can observe the first two or three go to drink. Then pull the tray. But, when using a precise limited amount of feed during training for a competition, place the water in after they eat. This way they all get their fair share of feed before drinking and don't miss out if they went to drink first.

If they eat and have feed left in the tray and you do not pull the feed tray, it will cause your pigeons to be on the heavy side and not fit for good flying. But it's okay for maintaining your stock.

If you're not sure how much feed to give, you can also control the amount of feed by measuring and monitoring the results in the air. Measuring their time spent flying will determine the amount of feed given. Food is fuel, therefore the more feed you give your pigeons, the more time they will spend in the air, or on the loft after flying. If your flyers are slow to trap in, it's a sign that you should give them a little less grain. If their flying time is short and they are trapping in extremely fast, then the feed needs to be increased.

If your pigeons are being fed grain, make sure to supply them with pigeon grit to keep them healthy. The grit helps them digest the grain properly. Make sure it's pigeon grit and not poultry grit. Flyers only need grit a minimum of every two weeks. For your breeders, keep a bowl of grit in the corner of their breeding pen for continual access.

Feed can also be purchased in pellet form, both in breeding grade and flying grade. I've used breeding pellets, and while youngsters do very well on pellets, they are twice the mess to clean up. When feeding your birds pellets, grit isn't necessary.

Medicated large chicken starter crumbles is an alternative to give to your breeders to feed their young. Grit is not needed while on chicken starter. You can switch to grain when you wean them from their parents.

Mixed Feed Grains

Grit

Coffee or Tea Spoon

Peas   Wheat   Milo

Refer to the picture. This spoon, a mixed feed grain (consisting of wheat, milo, and yellow peas), and grit will get you by just fine as a flyer. If you feed just these three grains, you can be very successful at peaking rollers out for competition or for visitors.

Some flyers train their rollers on these three grains and feed them separate to the birds after they land—milo first, then wheat, and the peas last. This ensures that the pigeons do not get more of one grain than another. You can still do well by leaving the three grains mixed when you feed them. Some roller flyers fly their birds just on wheat and will add peas at certain times, while others will use the three mixed grains all the time.

If you like to feed a wider range of grain to your stock and your flyers, that is your choice. It is more expensive to the roller breeder but not necessary for your flying pigeons. Some roller breeders do feed a wide mix of grains, especially when breeding pigeons, and again during molting time. For raising young during breeding I would recommend it. Adding black sunflower seeds to your feed during the molt will aid in producing nice feathers in your pigeons. Some breeders also like to use popcorn in their mix in the winter for heat.

Protect your birds' health by using a feed storage bin for your grain. A metal barrel with a lid that can be fastened down tight works well. You can pour the feed into the barrel, but it is easier to just set the bag down in it. By leaving your feed sitting out in the bag instead of a good storage container, you risk mice or something else contaminating your feed. So always check your feed to make sure it's clean and dry. If mice or other rodents get into the feed container and contaminate the feed, you can lose a large number of birds before you figure out what has happened.

When feeding and watering your flying birds, you'll only need a tray and water container. Plastic milk jugs work very well for watering your birds. Cut a hole in the side of it big enough for a pigeon's head to get in to drink. If you make the hole too large, they will get inside and take a bath. Replace the milk jugs periodically to help cut down on germs and bacteria that can develop in water containers. The sun is a great germ killer. Laying feed trays out in the sun from time to time will help kill germs that may have gathered.

There are many different types of feeding trays and other methods of feeding, from throwing feed on the floor to eating out of just about anything that will hold pigeon feed. I prefer trays with spinners in the middle of them for feeding my young weaned birds and flyers.

The spinners in the center of the tray help keep the birds from getting all the way in the tray, allowing the others to get their fair share of feed. The center spinners rotate when a pigeon tries to stand on one, which causes the bird to be uncomfortable and fly off the tray.

As a side note, you'll notice from the picture on the previous page that I use wood shavings as flooring. It is an absorbent material to help keep the floor dry to combat disease. It is easily disposable and doesn't hurt the environment. Other options include sand and ground-up corn cobs. Back to feed trays.

If the trays get dirty, the center spinner will pull out for easy cleaning. You can find them in multiple lengths at most feed stores. A good rule of thumb is to use a slightly longer tray than needed when you feed your birds. This assures that if one bird gets pushed out of the way, it can find a place to continue eating. This is especially important when feeding your flyers for competition or when trying to peak them out. Using a short, overcrowded tray can cause a flying bird to not be in the same physical shape as the others. The slightly weaker or smaller birds will continue to go down in condition as the others grow stronger in condition.

If you are training your birds and do not have a large enough tray to feed them all, use two trays. When feeding, pour the feed the entire length of the tray and level it out with a little shake. Take care not to set a tray on top of one of the birds when you put it into the fly box. If one of your pigeons gets trapped under the tray, its weight plus the weight of the other birds can injure or kill it.

If you are on lockdown and giving them all they want before you pull the tray, a longer tray won't be of too much concern as long as some feed was left in the tray when they were done eating. It's always best to pull your trays after feeding. This will allow them to stay nice and clean. Save any feed that is left and put it in another container to be reused during the next day's feeding. By doing this you will save a lot of wasted feed and money. In addition, it is not a good idea to let feed sit around in the trays, because feed can be soiled before the pigeons eat it all and can also attract rodents and feral birds.

When feeding your flying pigeons, it is always better to have the feed ready to place in the fly box as soon as the last bird has exited.

This way you can keep an eye out for predators while they are liberated. Many good pigeons have been lost during flying while the trainer is getting the feed ready before they land.

Another type of tray is the open loft feeding tray pictured above. These types of feeders work well in the open loft and are very durable. I use this one. The top will need to be scraped from time to time. Measure your feed so there will be some left after feeding. When breeding pigeons in an open loft, you will want a little feed left in the tray by feeding time again the next day. This way, no young will go hungry. Be sure that your loft is secure so that rodents and wild birds do not have access to the feed. These and many other types of water and feeder designs can be ordered from pigeon supply catalogs.

These feeding and watering containers work well for holding stock or open-loft breeding pigeons. Again, I prefer these. You may like another method. The water container pictured above will hold up to one gallon of water. It is ideal for watering a large flock of pigeons. Do not use any medications or vinegar in this type of water container because it will rust the tin. If you use water only, it will last you for many years.

Most pigeon breeders will keep a good amount of grit in a separate container in the corner of the loft. The grit holder pictured above works for both held stock and open-loft breeding. It is a nice convenience for the birds to get grit as they need it. In the summer, you may find your grit getting damp because of high humidity. In this case you can sprinkle dry grit on the birds' feed when you feed them until the humidity drops.

Watch with these types of feeders that you do not set the wire cover on one of the pigeon's necks when feeding. When the pigeons are hungry they will get in your way when you try to place the cover over the pan.

Catching a Pigeon
Catching a pigeon does take a little practice if you are new to it.

Unless you're best friends with a rollerman, one should never attempt to catch another man's birds without permission while in the loft. Consider this "pigeon etiquette." Always ask to handle a bird, but never ask to handle a bird if you're not good at snatching up a bird without much effort. The more feathers that fly when you try to catch one, the less pigeon trainers will allow you to handle their birds.

Many roller pigeon trainers like to handle birds that are seen performing well or said to be great performers to examine the physical makeup of the valued pigeon. Normally when you ask if you can handle a bird, the owner will either grab it and hand it to you or give you consent to grab the bird. So, remember, if you would like to handle a roller flyer's best pigeons, you should be fairly proficient at it.

One should practice catching their own birds first. The best way to practice is to pick out one bird and see how close you can get to it before it flies, which depends on the speed that you approach the bird. Slow but steady works best. Keep your grabbing hand in towards the center of your chest when approaching the bird. If you extend your hand to the bird on the way in, the bird will be more inclined to fly before you get close enough. When you get as close as you can, right before you think it will fly off, grab forward and down as quickly as possible onto the back of the bird. Hold the bird firmly, but not so firm as to hurt it. The hand positioned over the back will keep the wings from rising. The grab, or, as I call it, "the snatch," will come in handy if you're working with a lot of birds.

As a breeder/flyer you're always moving birds from one loft to another and from one section to another, which means that being proficient at snatching up a bird will be a great time saver. If you find yourself in a loft that has a ceiling higher than you can reach, you can spend a lot of time trying to catch a bird. A handheld fishing net will come in handy in this case. One of our local fanciers built a very nice but large loft. He mentioned to me once he wished he had given the ceiling height a little more thought prior to building. He used a handheld fishing net for the rest of his life because of it.

Catching Pigeons in the Dark

Sometimes, one or two birds will not trap with the others and stay out after dark. For example, after the release of young birds for the first time, one or two will not trap in with the rest of the birds. Occasionally, a new bird may be released by accident and come back that day or the next and not know how to get back in with the others. If this happens, you will have a good chance to catch the bird when night arrives.

Other times, a team will not trap into the fly box if it is raining or starts to rain as they are landing. They normally will not trap in until the rain stops. If this happens close to dark and the rain persists into the night, the birds will still be out sitting in the dark in the rain. If the rain stops after dark, they still will not trap for lack of being able to see. You will need to retrieve them before daylight so that an owl, cat, or another predator doesn't get to them before you can. This is when a flashlight and a long-handled fishing net become helpful.

If you plan on catching a pigeon in the dark, keep in mind the darker the better for the best results. Take a good look around to make sure to turn off any lights in the area that may enable the bird or birds to see you come towards them. You may have lights on in your loft or motion detectors that may turn on when you approach the bird or birds to be caught. If so, turn them off before you return later in the night to retrieve your birds. If they see you trying to catch them, they will fly off into the night out of fear and will probably be in a worse predicament than they were setting on your fly box or loft. Their night vision is very poor, but good enough to spot you if they have enough light when you are close.

Once you feel it is dark enough and you have turned off any unnecessary lights in the area, grab your flashlight and net. Head to the last place you saw the pigeon. Flash your light in that direction to make sure the bird is still there. Once in a while they will have moved to another spot. When the location is confirmed, turn your light off and move in towards the bird. As you move in, turn the light on, shine the light directly into the bird's eyes, quickly turn it off, and then move forward as soon as you switch the light off.

If the moon is full, you will not want to move forward at all until you switch off the light because the birds can see you from the light of the moon. Still, blinding them does detract from seeing you in full moonlight. If you wait too long in between turning the light on and off, the bird's vision will adjust to the moonlight in enough time to see you and fly away when you get close. The same thing can happen if you leave your flashlight on too long from a distance. The light will illuminate a large area, and the birds will be able to see as they might under a full moon. Then they are more apt to move or fly to a more comfortable spot, which may be more disadvantageous.

The key to catching a pigeon in the dark with a flashlight is to keep the bird at an optical disadvantage by only quick, necessary flashes into the bird's eye to allow you to see the bird and give you the necessary time to grab the bird while its eyes are trying to readjust to the dark. Be sure not to hold your hand in front of the light and in between your pigeon in preparation for catching it. If the bird sees your hand too close, it may startle the bird. If something goes wrong and the bird does fly off, try to watch and listen for it to land. Sometimes they will crash land in a spot close enough that you can still retrieve it.

If you have many birds out setting on the fly box, using a long-handled fishing net instead of catching them one at a time by hand will save a lot of time. In this case, it always goes a little smoother if you have someone with you to flash the light in the bird's eyes, right before you come down with the net. Remember, don't move until the instant the light is turned off. In time, this method will become easy and will help to save many birds in the long run.

In preparation for a successful night capture, I suggest practicing in your loft at night, catching a dozen or so birds, using the flashlight and putting them in a carrying box. This will help improve your timing of the light and catching the pigeon. The key is not leaving the light on too long and grabbing the bird as soon as the light goes out.

Holding a Pigeon

The next picture shows the best way to hold a pigeon and keep control of the bird, by holding it against you with light but firm pressure. The pigeon will not escape if you keep the wings held down. Notice the wing flights are above the tail. This is a normal position and will help keep the bird calm. Also notice that the feet are straight back. This will keep the bird from pushing down on your hands for leverage to get away.

Once you have control, you can remove one hand and pull away from your body. If the bird tries to get away, bring it back to this position until you have control again. The more you handle them, the easier they are to handle.

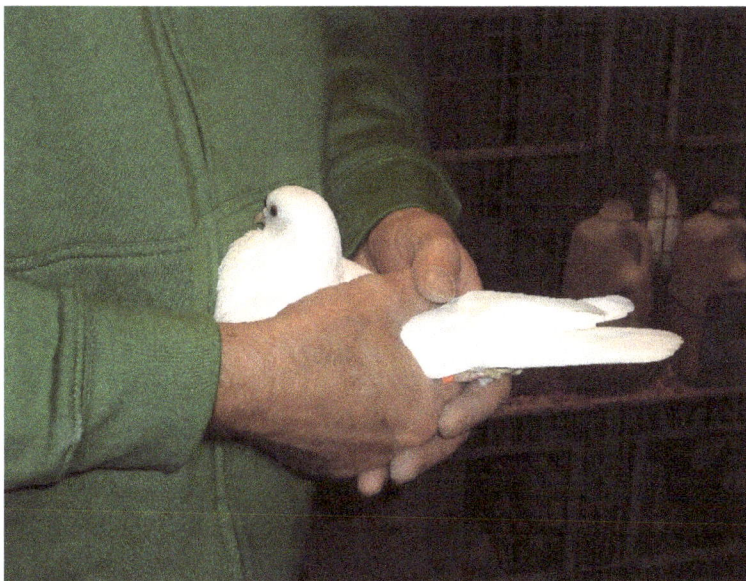

Realigning Feathers

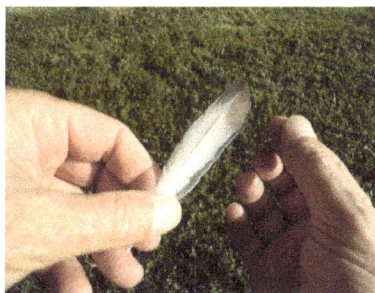

Occasionally when handling a pigeon, you will notice a split or tear in the tail or flight feathers. This can be easily repaired. This area on either side of the shaft, which some call the quill, is the vane and has many small hooks and barbs in the structure that hold them together. By placing your thumb and finger in the center of the feather with slight pressure and an outward pull, you can zip it back together, just like the zipper on your clothing. This is something you may want to do before your bird is evaluated or shown. However, a pigeon will correct each feather when it preens itself.

I personally handle my birds as little as possible. This seems to cause pigeons to be more alert and hard to catch. I like that in my rollers. Some do not. The ones who do not tend to show their pigeons. A wild-acting pigeon could cost you a win in the show cage at a pigeon show. If you show your flyers in the winter with your club or for a fundraising event or for camaraderie, place your birds in a show cage and handle them before the event. This will help them acclimate to things to come at the show. A calmer bird will get a better evaluation.

In fairness to you as a serious roller flyer, be sure the show judge is also a serious flyer. If you are a serious roller flyer—known as a hardcore roller flyer—and understand that showing your rollers doesn't do a thing to help you in the sky, you probably won't participate in them.

However, pigeon shows do have their good points. They give club members a chance to visit and talk birds with each other. They can also raise money for the club, if it is an advertised show open to the public. Members can take this time to help educate visitors about rollers and our great hobby. If you are a serious flyer, don't get caught up in who wins or loses at a pigeon show. Your show is in the air.

Pros and Cons of Showing Rollers
There is a big difference between a true show roller and showing a flying roller. The physical traits are different in both. The typical show roller is twice the size of a flying roller and does not exhibit the aerial qualities of the flying standard. This is because show traits do nothing for the true roller. The show roller and flying roller are now two distinct breeds. Showing a roller has led to this. Putting too much into showing a roller has caused it to be another pigeon altogether.

Another reason for not getting too involved in showing true rollers is that there is no way to tell if a flying roller is a good one just by looking at it. All we can do is assume a bird is a good roller and judge it according to what we know about our best performers' physical makeup and look for that in the hand. It is possible for a flying roller to win a flying roller show and not be worthy in the sky.

For this reason, most roller flyers have no desire to show their birds unless, as I stated, there is a beneficial purpose or if there's nothing to do and it's winter and the hawks are hitting you too hard to fly, or you want to do some PR for the club and birds, or for raising funds, or for the camaraderie, etc.

Just keep things in perspective. Our performing rollers are not show birds. If an odd-eyed bird keeps you from placing high in the finals at a show, just remember that it won't stop it from being a champion in the sky. Not having enough back skull or acting wild in the cage won't, either.

— *Champion Performers* —

As I wrote this book, it occurred to me that it would be nice to have a few pictures of some truly great working rollers, or "Real Champions."

With as many great roller flyers as there are, I thought I would ask a select few to submit a picture of a champion roller. So I contacted some of the best roller flyers there are, the elite, the "Master Flyers."

The following images are a collection of roller champion pictures that have been presented by these elite individuals who are well known and knowledgeable in the roller pigeon fancy. All have been recognized by the National Birmingham Roller Club as "Master Flyers." These individuals know what a champion performing roller looks like in the air when they see one.

I would like to express my extreme thanks to these five roller flyers for their contribution to this book: Thank you to Ken Easley, Rick Mee, Rick Schoening, Jay Starley, and George Mason. I appreciate you gentlemen getting the pictures to me on such short notice.

I will start off with one of my champions. This performer's mother was a gift from Bobby Bradley, who was a great roller flyer and good friend of mine.

John Bender - Portsmouth, Ohio - My Champion

4509-11 Blue T check with bronze Cock, multi depth 1.5 to 3.0 second performer. This bird has tight H wing placement, good velocity, and does everything right.

Ken Easley - Cedar Crest, New Mexico - Master Flyer

623 06 Easley red check Hen is probably the best performing roller Ken has ever raised. This bird is a true champion, fast and deep.

Rick Mee - Yakima, Washington - Master Flyer

038 RLM 95 Grizzle Cock is a multiple-depth frequent performer flown for 5 years. This bird performs with tighter than H wing position - bowed in. This is Rick's foundation cock.

Rick Schoening - Polson, Montana - Master Flyer - Hall of Fame

833 Pure Ollie Harris red check cock. Not only a great bird in the air but also has produced many high-velocity spinners.

Jay Starley - Eagle Mountain, Utah - Master Flyer - Hall of Fame
Known as BBE (Best Bird Ever). Utah 322 spins 50 ft. Dark check
cock. This is the best bird ever raised by Jay Starley. Jay says this
one can spin as fast as a bird can possibly spin and has been
witnessed by many who agree.

George Mason - Derby, England - Master Flyer - Hall of Fame
Tort. 8 2010. A top-quality cock. Now in George's stock loft.

— *Pondering Possible Rollers in The Future* —

I think back on how William Hyla Pensom's book of collected writings inspired me. I felt very excited and lucky to have had a chance to read the information he conveyed. It gave me more knowledge to work with to improve my birds. For me, it made all the difference in the world. Understanding what you are trying to do and having an abundance of knowledge handed to you is a big plus.

When I first read Pensom's writings, I highlighted with a yellow marker all the things I felt I needed to remember. One of them was the comment Pensom made about his belief that the ability to roll was the action of multiple genes. I had never thought of it that way before. This caused me to think about breeding rollers in a different way. I understood a little more about why you don't get good performers from good performers every time, or sometimes not at all. It's because the genes I was hoping for didn't transfer the way I thought. It was not just one gene from each parent, but multiple genes from the parents.

Until then I had assumed one gene from each parent created the offspring. I now realized that the parents were carrying genes that weren't apparent through aerial observation. These genes that produce traits I could not evaluate in the air could be bad or good. So, all the more reason to keep breeding only the best that I can see from what they reveal to me in the sky, and then hope for a good understanding on the best body type. By doing these things, I was hoping to purge out all the possible bad genes in time, in an effort to get higher percentages of good ones.

The entire comment Pensom made was,

> "Of course, the ability to roll is the result of the action of multiple genes, but nobody knows how to separate them."

This comment was made over half a century ago. A lot of things have changed since that statement was made. With today's advancements in technology we actually can do just that. With genome editing tools such as Talen and Crispr, scientists can add, subtract, or edit genes. Scientist Ben Novak with Project Revive & Restore began the first experiments to genetically engineer pigeons in the fall of 2017.

I ponder the possibilities and wonder if roller flyers will take advantage of this in the future—putting only the genes we want in the birds and removing the ones we feel are unworthy for our cause. Imagine finding the genes responsible for control of the roll—no more roll-downs. Or duration of roll for setting depth. Maybe locking in the maximum velocity that can be achieved by a roller pigeon and the perfect body type to do it. Now that would be a pigeon to breed from. A super roller pigeon that has a long lifespan. Genes that were tweaked to be resistant to common pigeon diseases.

Having gene editing knowledge, as scientists do today, we could biologically reset rollers as we know them. Perfect them for breeding in very high percentages. Of course, it would take some collaboration from top rollermen in the sport to agree on the finished product. But in time it could be done. With the propagation of these superior rollers through cloning, competition scores and backyard entertainment would definitely improve.

This brings me to cloning as an alternative way, other than genetically creating super performers. We may decide not to get involved with gene alteration or manipulation; we could just clone the best bird you own, cloning the best of the best. This would mean that if your best pair of breeders died, the dead birds could be saved for later reproduction.

Scientists now can take genetic material from one creature and insert it into an egg cell that has had its own genetic material removed. They then make copies of this and can reproduce as many clones of the donor as they need. Scientists have already cloned many animals over the years, horse, pig, sheep, goat, fish, and monkeys, just to name a few. My understanding is that the clone will be 98% the same as the donor. I could go with those types of percentages.

Film star and singer Barbra Streisand is said to have two clones of her dog that passed away. Korea says they can clone any dog of any size or shape for one hundred thousand dollars. I saw on TV not long ago where a guy had his Labrador cloned for eight thousand dollars. Texas Digital made a watch that came out in the '70s that sold for $1,500, which you can now buy for around two dollars. In time, the financial aspect of this type of gene technology should also come down.

Can you imagine if our cloning laboratories had the genetic material on hand of the famous Pensom roller - black self 514 or the genetic material from all the Master Flyers' best pigeons?

The laboratories that do these things would have a thriving business as long as they could keep the price range reasonable. Imagine calling them and ordering great champion pigeons to work with.

"Yes, I would like to order five copies of Ken Easley Red check 623, 5 Jay Starley Blue - T Utah 322, 5 George Mason Lt. Tort. 8 2010, 5 Rick Schoening 833, 5 Rick Mee Light Grizzle 038. Oh! While I have you on the phone, could you please send me copies of the last two World Cup champion teams?"

Taking the best rollers you have and getting exact copies of them—or 98% of a copy of them—wow! What a time saver that would be.

Yes, the future development of the Birmingham Roller has great possibilities with our advancing technology. I see roller flyers having these opportunities in the future. One might ask himself if this is something to be pursued, or would it take all the fun out of doing it the old-fashioned way, the hard work and your own wits? What say you?

— *A History of Pigeons* —

In ending, I hope you've enjoyed *The Pigeon Trainer & The Birmingham Roller*. I wish you the best of luck, whether your goal is focused on simply raising birds for backyard flying or training a champion team for flying in competition. It is my sincerest hope that this book is a help to you in your roller pigeon endeavors.

But before ending, I would like to touch upon the history of the roller pigeon. I'm not much of a history buff when it comes to rollers or pigeons in general. My knowledge of our flying rollers history is limited. My main concern over the years has been flying and breeding good ones. I do, however, understand there are many who desire as much as can be absorbed when it comes to pigeon history. With that in mind, I submit to you two very knowledgeable pigeon men who can satisfy anyone's interest in pigeons and roller pigeon history, Ben Novak and Tom Monson. Both are world renowned for their abundance of pigeon knowledge.

Ben Novak, a young scientist from Santa Cruz, California, has worked with ancient DNA and is in charge of bringing back the extinct passenger pigeon. Ben has offered to write on the subject of the pigeon's history from a prehistoric evolutionary aspect. Following that, Tom Monson, an attorney, roller flyer, and historian from Salt Lake City, Utah, will continue with the history of the Birmingham Roller pigeon. Tom also has top-quality performing rollers. Some of the best rollers I have flown were raised by Tom Monson. I would like to take this moment to thank both men for their knowledge and time to help make this book a better one.

— On the Relationship of Pigeons and Primates —
A Journey in Science and History by Ben J Novak

Picture taken by Ryan Phelan of Revive & Restore
at the Smithsonian National Museum of Natural History

Ben J. Novak.
8/17/2017

When we think of Charles Darwin and the theory of evolution through natural selection, an almost folkloric level of rhetoric that comes to mind will be a tale of "a stroke of genius" inspired by the many species of Galapagos Island finches. But Darwin's notion of how species evolve from one form to the next, as nature selects among the variation of a species to yield adaptation over generations, was not an idea arrived upon in a quick moment nor inspired by a single form of life. For more than 20 years after collecting countless specimens from the Galapagos Islands and around the world, Darwin found key inspiration not stemming just from finches, but from Galapagos mockingbirds and tortoises, South Americas flightless rheas and fossil giant sloths, meticulous studies of barnacles, the life cycle of bees, and inheritance through domestic breeding. If one subject among the many can stand out as more important than the others in his great abstract "On the Origin of Species," it is Darwin's comparison of artificial selection, or domestic breeding, to that of natural selection. And if we care to decide that Darwin's immersive studies of animal husbandry and domestic breeding are the true foundations of evolutionary science, then the species we have most to thank for all modern evolutionary biology is not a finch or a barnacle, but *Columba livia*, the rock pigeon.

It was the vast diversity of pigeon breeds that allowed Darwin to extrapolate the science of selection from the domestic pigeon. The drastic differences in traits, down to the very structure of the skeleton, between pigeon breeds had led many fanciers at the time of Darwin to believe that pigeon breeds stemmed from different stock species—or possibly even different genera. Darwin himself when summarizing his studies wrote:

> *"... it is impossible to conceive a more perfect gradation than I have now lying before me, from the rock-pigeon, through Persian, Lotan, and Common Tumblers, up to the marvellous short-faced birds; which latter, no ornithologist, judging from mere external structure, would place in the same genus with the rock-pigeon.[1]"*

To the untrained naturalist the Barb, Scandaroon, and Runt may seem like distant relatives, but Darwin provided the first thorough scientific treatment to argue that the hundreds of different pigeon breeds indeed descend from a single origin: the wild rock pigeon [2].

The First Few Hundred Million Years ...

While deciphering the single origin of all pigeon breeds, Darwin couldn't possibly at the time have fathomed the true evolutionary origins of the pigeon, which today we can finally piece together from paleontology, archaeology, and genetics. The story of the relationship between humans and pigeons runs parallel for hundreds of millions of years before colliding intimately together on Mediterranean cliffs of the Stone Age.

This journey through evolution begins in the Carboniferous period, more than 300 million years ago at the dawn of reptiles. The simplest way of seeing the evolution of vertebrates—animals with backbones—is that from 550 million years ago up to 350 million years ago, soft translucent organisms of the Cambrian period, similar to today's lancets, gave rise to jawless fish, which eventually formed jaws and later, during the Devonian, evolved strong fleshy fins and lungs, and 375 million years ago took the first steps on dry land. It was one small step for fish and a damn giant leap for every land-dwelling vertebrate to come.

From that momentous experiment, amphibians were born and adopted a transitional land-dwelling lifestyle bound to the water's edge owing to their soft jelly-like eggs. Some amphibians finally freed themselves from the water's chains, laying watertight eggs with a leathery shell, giving rise the first scaly skinned reptiles in the Carboniferous period. While there was nothing truly so simple about that progression that gave rise to reptiles, until that point the ancestors of pigeons and humans were one and the same—a single lineage from fish, to amphibians, to early reptiles—and at this point there is absolutely no way to consolidate the story of evolution afterwards in a simple fashion.

The dawn of reptiles is a complex bush of diversification, which in a short geological time span sent the very earliest ancestors of pigeons and humans on their independent trajectories. The ancestors of humans began with mammal-like reptiles, which dominated the landscape for more than 50 million years, including iconic extinct species like *Dimetrodon*, *Gorgonops*, and *Lystrosaurus*. The ancestors of birds occupied much more humble spaces in the primordial ecosystems of the Carboniferous and Permian periods, slowly and steadily diversifying while continents slammed together to form Pangea, leading to the world's most devastating mass extinction—the end of the Permian period, a time when over 90% of biodiversity on earth died out.

The Permian extinction was the key event that reshuffled the ecological playing field. This extinction marks the start of the Mesozoic Era, made up of the Triassic, Jurassic, and Cretaceous periods. Mammal-like reptiles continued on but shared dominance with new groups of reptiles, the archosaurs. By the end of the Triassic, the ancestors of pigeons and humans finally began to take their more familiar shape: ~200 million years ago the first protomammals appeared, covered in fur, looking very much like shrews, like the tiny four-inch-long *Megazostradon*.

Alongside them, the first bird-like traits took shape when two-legged dinosaurs like *Coelophysis* debuted the classic familiar dinosaurian form, covered in yet another new skin coat—primitive feathers. These meat-eating dinosaurs, the theropods, would eventually give rise to birds, which to modern scientists are no longer considered distinct from dinosaurs at all, but simply the avian branch of the dinosaur family, giving rise to the terms "avian dinosaurs," or all birds, and "non-avian dinosaurs," those types we commonly think of from our childhood fascinations with dinosaurs from *Tyrannosaurs rex* to the plant-eating *Triceratops*.

Our childhood book illustrations of *Tyrannosaurus* and *Triceratops* showed lumbering, fat, stupid brutes covered in scaly skin. This image could not have been further from the truth, unless scientists had drawn them breathing fire as well! In the 1980s, paleontologists finally began to bother considering dinosaur fossils realistically, revealing that dinosaurs were warm-blooded dynamic creatures, just like today's birds. But the notion of scaly skin remained.

For over 150 years scientists contended that the feather was the unique adaptation of birds, developed exclusively for flight. But at the turn of the 21st century a flood of discoveries from China showed that meat-eating theropods had feathers—and not exclusively for flight. These flightless theropods, like *Sinosauropteryx*, were covered in simple downy feathers that served the same purpose as mammalian fur—to aid the control of body temperature. Even finely preserved tyrannosaurids have been discovered showing a coat of downy feathers surrounding their skeletons.

Other more elaborate species, like *Caudipteryx*, possessed tail and arm fans for displaying to mates. Today paleontologists have discovered inarguable proof that theropod dinosaurs of all types were covered in feathers. More surprisingly, feather-like structures have been found among some plant-eating dinosaurs as well, meaning that the origins of feathers begin 230 million years ago with the early dawn of dinosaurs [3], before dinosaurs began to look remotely bird-like at all. Feathers were an adaptation to control body temperature and a superb way to attract mates in the beginning, but soon enough, sometime in the late Jurassic 160 million years ago, feathers would take to the air.

The Pigeon's Ancestors Take Flight ...
Just as feathers are not unique to living birds, neither is the innovation of flight. In fact, it's hard today to find many traits that are wholly unique to living birds; even extremely exaggerated traits—prized abnormalities of domestic breeding, like the extremely feathered feet of the Saxon fairy swallow, giving it the appearance of having four wings—are not new traits.

The theropod dinosaur *Microraptor*, discovered in 2000, was gliding through early Cretaceous forests on its well-developed wings and feathered hindlimbs. In fact, so many traits of modern birds have now been found in theropod dinosaurs that the line between the two is blurred to the point that it is almost impossible to decide which fossil is the true first bird (or avian dinosaur) and not a non-avian theropod.

At the time of Darwin, the late Jurassic *Archaeopteryx* was regarded as the first bird, given its asymmetrical flight feathers, but *Archaeopteryx* was discovered 135 years before any other feathered dinosaurs. Perhaps *Archaeopteryx* is considered the first bird merely because it was the first bird-like animal discovered that preserved fine feather impressions in the stone surrounding its fossilized bones.

Some modern paleontologists have suggested that *Archaeopteryx* is actually simply a theropod non-avian dinosaur experimenting with flight, which many types of other Mesozoic theropods also experimented with. The only thing we can be certain of is that sometime in the late Jurassic to early Cretaceous, the first magpie-sized avian-dinosaurs took to the skies to fly among pterosaurs the size of small planes, while the small mammalian ancestors of humans scurried among the forest floor under the footsteps of giant dinosaurs. While the age of dinosaurs reigned, birds and mammals had that one theme in common: they were small.

The Rise of Pigeons …
Small size, according to many scientists, is likely the trait that let mammals and birds survive the extinction of non-avian dinosaurs 65 million years ago. The world without giant dinosaurs was open for the taking, and both birds and mammals radiated in forms diverse, both familiar and alien to what we observe today. As the first primates began a life among the trees in China 55 million years ago[4], the very first proto-pigeons were hatching, likely from a nest in Australia. And since that primitive pigeon first pipped from its egg, the pigeon has been an evolutionary winner, diversifying across the globe to inhabit every landscape between the Arctic and Antarctic circles.

The exceptional broad diversity of pigeon breeds attracted Darwin to study the bird for his early ideas of selection; but, while the domestic pigeon exhibits more diversity among its breeds than any other domestic species in history, the diversity of domestic pigeons barely compares to the diversity of wild pigeons. The order Columbiformes is the sixth-most speciose order of birds in the world—an amazing statistic when one considers that Earth's 10,965 living species of birds are grouped into 36 orders, of which 6,592 species (60%) belong to a single order—the Passeriformes (sparrows, finches, and other perching and songbirds)[5].

Of the remaining 4,373 species, 351 of those are pigeons and doves, outnumbered only by Charadriiformes (seabirds and shorebirds broadly), Psittaciformes (parrots), Piciformes (toucans and relatives), and Caprimulgiformes (hummingbirds, swifts, and relatives).

Table 1. Total numbers of living bird species ranked from most to least speciose order.

Order	Total Species	Representatives
Passeriformes	6,592	Songbirds & relatives
Caprimulgiformes	593	Hummingbirds, Swifts, Nightfars, Frogmouths, Potoos
Piciformes	484	Jacamars, Puffbirds, Toucans, Barbets, Honeyguides, Woodpeckers
Psittaciformes	398	Parrots & Cockatoos
Charadriiformes	377	Plovers, Gulls, Terns, Auks, Snipes, Buttonquails, Jacanas, & relatives
Columbiformes	351	Pigeons & Doves
Galliformes	307	Chickens, Turkey, Grouse & relatives
Accipitriformes	250	Eagles, Hawks, Kites, Old World Vultures, Buzzards
Strigiformes	236	Owls
Coraciiformes	188	Bee-eaters, Rollers, Ground-rollers, Todies, Motmots, Kingfishers

Anseriformes	169	Ducks, Geese, & Screamers
Gruiformes	168	Rails, Coots, Gallinules, Cranes, Trumpeters, Finfoots & Limpkin
Cuculioformes	149	Cuckoos
Procellariiformes	140	Albatross, Petrels, Shearwaters
Pelicaniformes	109	Pelicans, Ibises, Bitterns, Herons, & relatives
Bucerotiformes	72	Hornbills, Hoopoes, Woodhoopoes
Falconiformes	64	Falcons & Caracaras
Struthioniformes	62	Ostriches, Emus, Cassowaries, Rheas, Kiwis, Tinamous
Suliformes	53	Cormorants, Frigatebirds, Gannets, Boobies, Darters
Trogoniformes	43	Trogons
Otidiformes	26	Bustards
Musophagiformes	24	Turacos
Ciconiiformes	20	Storks
Podicipediformes	20	Grebes
Spheniciformes	18	Penguins

Pterocliformes	16	Sandgrouse
Cathartiformes	7	New World Vultures
Coliiformes	6	Mousebirds
Phoenicopteriformes	6	Flamingos
Gaviiformes	5	Loons
Mesitornithiformes	3	Mesites
Phaethontiformes	3	Tropicbirds
Cariamiformes	2	Seriemas
Eurypygiformes	2	Kagu & Sunbittern
Leptosomiformes	1	Cuckoo Roller
Opisthocomiformes	1	Hoatzin

The world's modern lineages of pigeons likely arose in Australia. The world's oldest pigeon fossils are found in Australia [6], dating to 26-24 million years ago. It's very difficult to trace the evolution of pigeons from fossils, as very few pigeon fossils survived the eons—small bones are easily destroyed and eroded, even in short time spans, let alone millions of years. To discover when each lineage of pigeon first arose we rely on genetic data to form a more comprehensive picture. I've had the personal experience of working on deciphering the evolutionary origins of pigeons from the DNA of several genera of Columbiformes [7], including genetic samples of extinct species from museum drawers and archaeological sites. The genetic analyses stemming from my and my colleagues' lab work and computational data crunching yielded results that align well with the fossil record, placing the origins of all modern pigeons at the end of the Oligocene epoch—a time which appears to have yielded an explosion of pigeon diversity.

The sheer diversity of pigeons and doves of Australia and the rest of Oceania, if no other data existed, would identify the region as the birthplace of modern pigeons and doves. More than 50% of all Columbiform species are natives of the Oceanic/Southeast Asian regions and exhibit the most unique forms, including the top-knot pigeon, the knob-billed pigeon, nicobar Pigeon, pheasant pigeon, thick-billed species, crested species, and arguably the oddest of them all, the tooth-billed pigeon.

Oceanic pigeons and doves range from some of the smallest species in the world (1.1 oz) to the world's largest living species, which can be more than 5 pounds. Even the species that would seem in every sizeable and shapely respect to be a familiar pigeon are painted with the most vivid coloration, rivaling even the most spectacular birds of paradise, such as the bronzewings, bleeding hearts, and various fruit doves all patched, striped, and speckled with bright greens, pinks, purples, yellows, oranges, blues, and every metallic hue. It is all the result of nearly 30 million years of evolution.

Among an Oligocene world dominated by flowering rainforests, when one could still walk from Australia to South America by way of Antarctica's glaciating landscapes—the joined continents forming the continent of Gondwana—the pigeons flourished. Flying above strange and wondrous marsupials, early pigeons and doves spread across Oceania, island hopping to Southeast Asia, where they finally met the ancestors of humans.

Undoubtedly the first encounter between our ancestors was that of an ape picking ripened fruits off a tropical tree branch abruptly startled, surprised eyes gazing at the fruit dove alighting on the same branch and enticed by the same fruits. The pair may have fed upon the fruits side-by-side, ignorant of care. To each, neither would be cause for alarm—to the eyes of the primate the pigeon's small slender bill, talon-less toes, and stalky proportions were clearly not the signs of a dangerous raptor looking to seize a meal of our distant relative.

To the fruit dove, the monkey-like animal, with its gangly proportions and strange thumbs, would have been entirely foreign in every way to the predators it had become accustomed to avoiding, like snakes, lizards, birds of prey, and marsupial quolls and thylacines. And so the relationship between primates and pigeons would go on in such a docile way for millions of years—mostly harmless competition for the same fruits, nuts, and figs among prehistoric forests.

As pigeons spread to Asia, the *Columba* genus was born. The first predecessors of the living rock pigeon inhabited a Miocene world of lumbering giants quite different from those we know today[7]. The genus Columba appeared at the same time as the *Deinotheres*, elephant-like behemoths with downward pointing tusks from the lower jaw. The odd pair of species would meet as the two quickly spread across similar distributions overlapping Eurasia and Africa, coming into contact with other oddities of the past including the *Chalicothere*—a horse relative lumbering like a panda-sloth hybrid.

Columba pigeons spread over Eurasia as three-toed horses and antelope-like giraffes herded under wing. As the genus Columba began to diversify to its eventual 32 living species[5], the Mid-Miocene was the heyday of our ancestors, the great apes. Dozens, possibly more than 50 genera, of apes thrived across Africa and Eurasia [8], ready to greet the newly evolving Columba species.

The Rock Pigeon and the Cave Men ...
As wood pigeons cohabited the forests with apes, some members of the Columba lineage embraced the challenges of a more rugged ecology among highlands and cliffsides, giving rise to the true rock pigeons. And just as the rock pigeons were leaving their lifestyle in the trees, so too did our hominid ancestors, giving rise to an eerily familiar world in which apelike human ancestors walked upright, erect on two legs alongside cliffs and gorge walls smattered with

nesting colonies of greyish pigeons.

As homonids diversified, growing larger and crafting ever more sophisticated tools, the rock pigeons would take on their modern shapes. The progenitor of all fancy, homing, and racing pigeons, the main character of our story—*Columba livia*—finally arrived on the scene ~1 million years ago [7].

The rock pigeon evolved in a world characterized by constant change—amidst the Pleistocene epoch's warming and cooling world of glaciating ice ages and changing coastlines. Dozens of ice ages have come and gone over the past two million years. The rock pigeon clung to the Mediterranean cliffs, a stout and robust bird withstanding every change in climate. When countless other species came and went, the rock pigeon survived, superbly adaptable to changing conditions.

Among the cliffs the rock pigeon met its nemesis—the peregrine falcon. The two species have been locked in a battle of predator and prey since before either species existed. The peregrine falcon is practically a pigeon-hunting specialist, preferring pigeons throughout the world over other prey[9]. Even when other prey is available, peregrine falcons will favor hunting pigeons.

A seven-year study observing hunting success of peregrines at Cape Peninsula, South Africa, found that peregrines attacked pigeons ten times more often than small passerines, despite having six-fold higher success taking down smaller birds[10]. Apparently the reward for taking down pigeons warrants the extra effort in hunting over other birds—in Spain, breeding success of peregrines was notably highest on a diet composed mainly of pigeons, based on observations and analyses spanning twenty years[11].

The seemingly relentless persecution of the pigeons by falcons has shaped them to be such difficult birds to capture. Pigeons and doves, as any handler will know, shed feathers excessively when stressed—making them hard for a predator to grasp. The tumbling acrobatics of domestic breeds, exaggerated by selective breeding, may stem from behaviors to avoid peregrine falcons. Every trait of the wild-type rock pigeon is adapted to evading falcons. Wild-type pigeons possessing a white rump are captured by peregrines ten times less than feral pigeons of solid coloration lacking white rumps—this may be because the white rump disrupts the visual target for the falcons when pigeons roll to evade attack[12].

More-recent studies have found that the diversity of rock pigeon individual personalities, many behaviors that are inheritable, are directly responsible for successfully evading or unsuccessfully succumbing to raptor attacks[13]. While dodging attacks by falcons, the rock pigeons finally experienced their first encounters with humans. The pigeon fanciers of Charles Darwin's era were far from the first people to exploit pigeons—by contrast, modern Homo sapiens cannot claim the pigeon as their own exploit. New discoveries show that Neanderthals hunted pigeons 67,000 years ago[14], possibly even cooking them (I like to think for a refined flavor to go alongside ice age herbs, berries, and tubers, a meal fit for a cave-king). For nearly 40,000 years at Gorham's Cave, Gibraltar, Neanderthals hunted pigeons.

By the time modern Homo sapiens moved into the cave, pigeons were certainly quite familiar with the human-figure as a predator—a sinister change for the pigeon's relationship with primates from millions of years of docile competition for fruits and seeds. Modern human relationships with pigeons would only become ever more intricate with time.

Domestication ...

After tens of thousands of years of being hunted for food, the rock pigeon was domesticated and bred for a multitude of utilitarian purposes, including couriering written messages, for which the pigeon is perhaps most famous. Though the first two uses of the pigeon are most certainly as a food item and secondarily to obtain guano for fertilizing grain crops. The domestication of the pigeon is likely intimately tied to the development of modern agriculture.

Though the exact date of domestication is unknown, the pigeon was the first domesticated bird species of eastern Eurasia, sometime between 8,000 to 10,000 years ago. The pigeon is represented in ancient Middle Eastern cultures prominently—Johnston and Janiga's 1995 book "Feral Pigeons" chronicles Mesopotamian,

Babylonian, Sumerian, and Egyptian references to pigeons that date as far back as 6,500 years, with clear evidence that Egyptians were breeding pigeons en masse around 3,200 years ago[15].

Around the same time, the oldest indications of falconry are recorded in China[16], which may indicate the Chinese were also already breeding pigeons—pigeons are commonly used to train falcons for hunting and retrieving prey. In fact, the aforementioned intimate co-evolution of pigeons and falcons is a key element to the art of falconry, and therefore the domestication of the pigeon was perhaps the necessary precursor to making falconry possible.

The dovecote (also known as doocot) was the tool of pigeon domestication—early dovecotes were constructed of mud and clay, shaped like beehives, and lined with perches and nesting platforms. Grains were used to attract breeding pigeons, and the beehive shape concentrated guano droppings in a fashion easy to collect for fertilizer.

As the uses of domestic pigeon breeds became more elaborate, the dovecote changed little—only modified by the architectural design preferences of the times in which it was built. The keeping of pigeons proliferated throughout the Middle East and Mediterranean. The Romans spread pigeons throughout Europe, and consequently by medieval times dovecotes were everywhere in Europe. The pigeon occupied a position as the preferred food of nobility—chickens brought from Asia were seen as a "dirty" bird, a bird for peasants (my how the times have changed!).

My first exposure to the history of dovecotes was on a guided tour through Urquhart Castle, on the shores of Loch Ness, Scotland. The worn remains of the base and four breeding boxes remain from its early 1500s construction. A pigeon fancier can't help but feel a curious excitement when having the chance to inspect the stony surface and realize it housed a brooding pigeon atop its straw and twig nest over 500 years ago. Anyone wishing to tour archaic sites, castles, and manors throughout Europe will see a plethora of dovecotes built over the millennia.

The Fancy and the Feral: Globalization of the Pigeon ...
The domestic pigeon perhaps reached its peak in vogue during the

European colonization of the world. Europeans brought pigeons with them to every reach of the globe as a food and military communications resource. Domestic pigeons quickly escaped and established successful feral populations across the globe. One cannot visit a single urban center anywhere between the Arctic and Antarctic circles without seeing feral pigeons. The feral pigeons' success in urban settings is not simply due to their roots in domestic stock living in dovecotes and extensive handling by people.

The pigeon's long history with urban architecture, stemming back to the very formation of cities in Mesopotamia over 6,500 years ago, conditioned the birds to human-made environments. But not only does the pigeon have this long history living among temples and buildings, its natural ecology as a cliff dweller predisposed the species to breeding among the nooks and crannies of urban construction. The millions of years spent evolving to harsh ice age Mediterranean environments made the birds robust and adaptable, as mentioned earlier, making the birds excellent colonizers of mild and agreeable equatorial climes of the world. The pigeon may become quite pampered living alongside an island beach resort paradise, but the species is truly a super-bird, showing its ice age–borne resiliency worldwide.

The Mediterranean landscape of the wild rock pigeon is quite temperate and pleasant in modern times, but do not ever let that fool you into believing the pigeon unable to weather the severest of conditions. In my early twenties, when walking during winter in my birth-town of Williston, North Dakota, I came upon a juvenile pigeon separated from its colony perched on a third-story ledge of a brick building. The bird couldn't have been more than 40 days old given its lack of fully developed side feathers under the wings and upon its bill. That day I witnessed it in -10°F chill in late winter. Its parents had bred, nested, brooded, and raised a chick nearly to fledging, all in below-freezing conditions! A stark contrast to the cliffs and buildings of Italy, Greece, Turkey, or Egypt; yet, the birds thrive, nonetheless.

But upon closer observation, the feral pigeon has not been restricted to city limits. Touring across the rural areas of the world, one will find feral pigeons in every agricultural community, and where the natural conditions are right, the birds will fully separate from human attachment. When hiking near Jordan, Montana, I witnessed a breeding pair of feral pigeons occupying a rock cavity about 40 feet up the wall of a gorge cutting into the rock layers below the Hell Creek Formation. This breeding pair in the autumn sunlight, secluded from any nearby human structures, looked every bit as natural an element of their habitat as rock pigeons would appear in their native Eurasian ranges. The pair wasn't simply a confused couple of birds, nor has the experience been a rarity.

Anyone visiting Pictograph Cave State Park, near Billings, Montana, will observe cliff dwelling rock pigeons—in a seemingly alien environment to their Mediterranean origins—when one peers past the rock walls to the panorama of the Montana plains. These birds are breeding and thriving in a world of drastic winters and different fauna and flora to their evolutionary roots, yet the feral invaders are quite at home.

The pigeon was not brought on board ships to colonize the world simply for utilitarian motives, however. The keeping of fancy pigeons was not only increasingly trendy at the time but also signified a certain social status, which was deeply entrenched in high society by the time of Darwin, when all manner of domestic breeding was in fashion. I came to discover my own somewhat eccentric account of keeping pigeons quite by a tangent to my focal research on the extinct passenger pigeon.

My maternal grandmother witnessed a display of zooarchaeological remains identified as passenger pigeons at Fort Union Trading Post National Historic Site near my childhood hometown in North Dakota and promptly made sure I was aware of my favorite species' presence at the historic site. At the time I was quite entrenched in seeking out samples for DNA sequencing, and the Montana/North Dakota border was on the western fringe of the passenger pigeon's former range, making them potentially valuable to study (but even more so, I was excited to learn of ties between my favorite bird and my hometown area!).

Before grinding small chunks of pigeon bone in the laboratory to sequence their DNA, I first perused the Fort's archives for references to passenger pigeons. Among accounts of the extinct passenger pigeon in the surrounding Missouri river bottom woodlands, I came across a passage pertaining to domestic pigeons kept at the fur trading post in the journal of Edward Harris, an ornithologist that accompanied the famous naturalist John James Audubon on his 1843 expedition up the Missouri River. Harris described the hypocritical mannerisms of Fort Union trading post's resident clerk of the American Fur Company, Edwin T. Denig. He described him as constantly complaining about shortages of stores and begrudging the accommodation of guests using up the finer amenities such as sugar and milk, making it difficult to undertake cordial proceedings with First Nation's traders, only to secretly dine upon fine meals and even worse—show favoritism to the Fort's birds:

> *"He [Denig] stood before me an idle braggart. He supplies all the corn needed for chickens and pigeons that are laying no eggs and, besides, will most likely be frozen to death before winter is over, but none to preserve the strength of horses, cows, and draught oxen in daily service.*[17]*"*

I'd think that Harris is overly harsh on his treatment of Denig's care for the Fort's pigeons over hooved livestock, as Harris may have had a biased fondness for horses; he did introduce the Percheron draft horse to America[18]. But when I analyzed the DNA of several pigeon bones found at Fort Union trading post, which were identified as the extinct wild passenger pigeon, they turned out to be the bones of domestic pigeons (much to my disappointment for my research, but quite exciting from a historic perspective!). Not only were the remains from domestic pigeons, but the breed in keeping was likely the English Trumpeter—not exactly a poultry breed for food or a utilitarian breed for carrying messages. It would seem that Denig was fondly fostering a bit of ornamental accouterment to his otherwise pioneering lifestyle at the trading post.

The true success of the pigeon, both in conquering new habitats and also in its intertwined intimacy with humans, lies not only in the adaptability or allure of its physical traits, but in its intelligence. Commonly regarded in ignorance as a dumb pest in modern times, the pigeon is among the smartest birds in the world, second perhaps only to parrots and corvids. Not only can domestic pigeons be trained to recognize letters of the alphabet, derive simple mathematics, cooperate together for complex tasks and even play pingpong[19], pigeons also exhibit a high degree of innate untrained intelligence.

Feral pigeons have been discovered to not only discriminate between human faces but also remember their treatment at the hands of humans and respond in kind to negative or positive interactions even long after the initial meeting[20]. Most amusing and striking was the report of three pigeons cooperatively using a drinking fountain to bathe and drink in Brisbane, Australia's Post Office Square[21]. One bird would weigh down the lever to allow the second bird to drink and bathe, with the third bird standing watch. The three birds alternated roles until all three had quenched their thirst and attended to personal hygiene!

A Bird of Science ...

The pigeon, with its natural adaptability, utility, beauty, and intelligence, has been a constant ally and companion to humans for thousands of years. Entire books are written about the subject, going into deep detail of the heroic deeds of war pigeons and entreating the bird's cultural history far better than can be given justice in a story of the species' evolutionary journey and significance to science. Culturally in the United States, the pigeon has gone from historic icon of high society to a perceived pest, which is quite disheartening, as the bird continues to provide important discoveries and services to society.

Today the story of our scientific discoveries relating to and stemming from the rock pigeon comes full circle back to Darwin, as the species becomes a major source for genetic discovery in the age of modern genomics. The same diversity of traits that brought Darwin to study pigeon breeds for his experiments on selection and inheritance is the foundation for discovering how genes and mutations produce and modify shape, form, and function of body and behavior. The rock pigeon genome was sequenced from a Danish Tumbler in 2013 and since has been used to compare the genomes of nearly 60 breeds of pigeon, from fantails to owls, pouters, swallows, and more, yielding discoveries of mutations involved in forming head crests, color patterns, and even feathered feet[22].

The discoveries that stand to be gained from correlating genetics to the development of the diverse traits in pigeons solidly mark the species as one of, if not *the* most important animals to evolutionary science in the world. And though Darwin could not have known or traced the evolutionary journey of the pigeon over hundreds of millions of years, let alone appreciate an understanding of genomics, his assessment of pigeons stands the test of time. The historically assumed relationships of species, especially birds, has been completely reorganized by genetics, and rightly so. Genes are the only uncompromised measurable information passed from parent to offspring, and the comparison of whole genomes illuminates the relationships of organisms to an exactitude that no other means can provide.

Yet, in an age of correcting historic research, a 2012 genetic study found that Darwin's original classification of fancy pigeon breeds, in which he grouped breeds based upon their physical—the only true evolutionary tree of relationships he constructed in his career[2]—was right[23].

Bibliography
1. Darwin, C. R. Variation of animals and plants under domestication. (John Murray, 1868).
2. Secord, J. A. Nature's Fancy: Charles Darwin and the Breeding of Pigeons. Hist. Sci. **72,** 162–186 (1981).
3. Baron, M. G., Norman, D. B. & Barrett, P. M. A new hypothesis of dinosaur relationships and early dinosaur evolution. Nature **543,** 501–506 (2017).
4. Ni, X. et al. The oldest known primate skeleton and early

haplorhine evolution. Nature **498,** 60–64 (2013).

5. Birdlife International. Handbook of the Birds of the World and Birdlife International digital checklist of the birds of the world version 9.1. (2017). at <http://datazone.birdlife.org/species/taxonomy>

6. Worthy, T. H. & Worthy, T. H. A phabine pigeon (Aves : Columbidae) from Oligo- Miocene Australia. Emu - Austral Ornithol. **112,** 22–31 (2012).

7. Soares, A. E. R. et al. Complete mitochondrial genomes of living and extinct pigeons revise the timing of the columbiform radiation. BMC Evol. Biol. **16,** (2016).

8. McNulty, K. P. Apes and Tricksters: The Evolution and Diversification of Humans' Closest Relatives. Evol. Educ. Outreach **3,** 322–332 (2010).

9. White, C. M., Cade, T. J. & Enderson, J. H. Peregrine Falcons of the World. (Lynx Edicions, 2013).

10. Jenkins, A. R. Hunting mode and success of African Peregrines Falco peregrinus minor: does nesting habitat quality affect foraging efficiency? Ibis (Lond. 1859). **142,** 235–246 (2000).

11. López-López, P., Verdejo, J. & Barba, E. The role of pigeon consumption in the population dynamics and breeding performance of a peregrine falcon (Falco peregrinus) population: conservation implications. Eur. J. Wildl. Res. **55,** 125–132 (2009).

12. Palleroni, A., Miller, C. T., Hauser, M. & Marler, P. Predation: Prey plumage adaptation against falcon attack. Nature **434,** 973–974 (2005).

13. Santos, C. D. et al. Personality and morphological traits affect pigeon survival from raptor attacks. Sci. Rep. **5,** 15490 (2015).

14. Blasco, R. et al. The earliest pigeon fanciers. Sci. Rep. **4,** 5971 (2014).

15. Johnston, R. F. & Janiga, M. Feral Pigeons. (Oxford University Press, 1995).

16. Stewart, H. & Stewart, A. Historical Falconry: An Illustrated Guide. (Amberley Publishing Limited, 2015).

17. McDermott, J. F. Up the Missouri with Audubon: The Journal of Edward Harris. (University of Oklahoma Press, 1951).

18. Mischka, J. The Percheron horse in America. (Heart Prairie Press, 1991).

19. Skinner, B. F. Two "synthetic social relations." J. Exp. Anal. Behav. **5**, 531–533 (1962).

20. Belguermi, A. et al. Pigeons discriminate between human feeders. Anim. Cogn. **14**, 909–914 (2011).

21. Birds of a feather drink together: The pigeons who help each other sup from a water fountain | Daily Mail Online. at <http://www.dailymail.co.uk/news/article-1206608/Birds-feather-drink-The-pigeons-help-sup-water-fountain.html>

22. Domyan, E. T. & Shapiro, M. D. Pigeonetics takes flight: Evolution, development, and genetics of intraspecific variation. Dev. Biol. **427**, 241–250 (2017).

23. Stringham, S. A. et al. Divergence, Convergence, and the Ancestry of Feral Populations in the Domestic Rock Pigeon. Curr. Biol. **22**, 302–308 (2012).

— *Birmingham Roller Origins by Tom Monson* —

Tom Monson and his rollers

Tom Monson
Salt Lake City, Utah
© 2002[1], 2017

The origins of the roller pigeon are shrouded in mystery and conjecture. The roller performs as it does because it has inherited a gene for rolling (the *ro* gene). No, this gene doesn't make these pigeons roll perfectly. It causes them to exhibit a tumbling reflex. Certain "additive" genes enhance the roller pigeon's aerial performances. Some speculate that additional, unidentified Mendelian gene mutations also may be present. Accordingly, we might more properly refer to the "*ro* gene complex." Additionally, proper type, physique, and a unique mental endowment are required before a pigeon can utilize the *ro* gene complex to perform like a true

Birmingham Roller.

No one knows just when the germinal *ro* gene mutated to become a part of the pigeon genetic compendium, or whether it might have mutated in more than one pigeon on more than one originating occasion. There are many breeds of tumbler pigeons around the world, most of which no longer tumble—or even fly— because they were later cultivated for their unique show characteristics of type, feathering, feather coloration, and handling qualities.

Man has kept pigeons for millennia. Many of the mutations that led to our different pigeon breeds originated in the swath of ancient Middle Eastern countries running from Turkey down through Syria, over to Persia (now Iran), and beyond. Wendell M. Levi wrote:

[T]his we do know: that the domestic pigeon accompanied civilization, and that the Eastern countries cradled its domestication. There is no record of fancy domestic pigeons indigenous to the soil of Germany, France, Great Britain, or of America. Most breeds of domestic pigeons of these countries can be traced back to importations from countries of ancient civilizations—Persia, India, and Asia Minor. The present-day Occidental breeds are not creations from wild species but from races previously introduced from the East.[2]

Levi calls tumblers "one of the oldest of the known varieties of pigeons."[3] He cites a 12th century Persian manuscript which mentions tumbling in pigeons.[4] Because it is known to be a much older breed than the Birmingham Roller, writers have theorized that all roller pigeons may have originated from the Oriental Roller, which is known to have been cultivated in ancient Turkey and Persia. However, certain marked differences exist between the Oriental Roller and other varieties of tumblers and rollers. For example, unlike the Birmingham Roller and most other pigeon breeds, the Oriental has no oil gland and possesses more than the standard twelve tail feathers. These differences have persuaded other authorities that the *ro* gene complex may have also mutated among pigeons other than the Oriental Roller. In 1881, James C. Lyell asserted that the first Oriental Rollers (he called them "Turkish

Rollers") were introduced into England from Smyrna, Turkey, shortly before 1874 by one H.P. Caridia, the same pigeon fancier who introduced the Oriental Frill to England.[5] Flying tumblers were to be found throughout England at least two centuries prior to Caridia's importations of Oriental Rollers from Turkey.

Recent scientific studies provide additional insight. In two studies reported in 2012 and 2013, University of Utah geneticist Michael D. Shapiro, Ph.D., and his team of geneticists collected DNA from 735 pigeons, including ferals from Utah and Virginia as well some 70 domestic pigeon breeds. The DNA was derived from blood and feather samples donated by the members of the Utah Pigeon Club and the National Pigeon Association, two organizations which revolve around the showing of multiple pigeon breeds.

After processing the DNA and loading the enormous amounts of DNA-derived data on their computers, the team settled upon tracking 32 DNA repeat structures known as "microsatellites." These are strings of non-coding[6] DNA that tend to be relatively constant and mutation resistant. These microsatellites are basically inherited microscopic strings of chemicals which tend to grow slightly longer with each passing generation. As such, they are suggestive of the number of generations that have passed since they commenced in individuals hundreds of generations ago. Similarities in these repeat chemical strings from one breed to the next are believed to provide clues to the degree of relationship between breeds of the same species, even suggesting that one breed evolved from another, or that two breeds evolved from some now-extinct precursor breed, anywhere from a few hundred to a few thousand generations ago.

The University of Utah geneticists applied complex statistical analysis to selected microsatellites extracted from the DNA of the 70 pigeon breeds. The results were reported in separate papers submitted to the science community in 2012 and 2013.[7] Among other things, the two studies concluded:

> Confirming Charles Darwin's 1859 theory, the 70 domestic pigeon breeds included in the studies all derived from

Columba livia, the wild rock pigeon believed to have originally nested on cliffs around the Mediterranean Sea;
The 70 domestic pigeon breeds from which DNA was extracted can be grouped genetically into five broad breed clusters within the pigeon species, based largely upon similarity of characteristics; and
The initial genetic mutations which led to the current five breed clusters may have begun as early as 5,000 years ago, calculated through estimating the number of pigeon generations that appear to have passed.

Although the Shapiro studies were focused initially upon investigating the evolution of the show pigeon breeds that bear head crests, the studies also postulated that the Birmingham Roller may have evolved from one family cluster that includes a variety of tumbler breeds. Under this theory, over a period encompassing potentially thousands of generations, some long-ago tumbler variety mutated and evolved so as to eventually produce multiple family branches. These family branches include, from earliest to latest, the Budapest Short-faced Tumbler, the Cumulet, the Oriental Roller, the Flying Tippler, the West of England Tumbler, the Birmingham Roller, the Portuguese Tumbler, and the Parlor Roller. Because no feather samples from the rare Dutch Tumbler were provided for DNA testing, the breed was not included in the study. Multiple additional tumbler breeds were likewise not examined.

These University of Utah studies would appear definitive; however, like most fresh scientific assertions, they rest in part upon assumptions which are subject to modification as the science in question (here, DNA genetics) becomes further refined and expanded in coming years. For example, Shapiro's 2012 study appears to identify the Oriental Roller as a probable distant *cousin* of the Birmingham Roller. By contrast, the 2013 study suggests that the Oriental may have been an *ancestor* of the Birmingham.

The conclusions are also subject to some question because the DNA sampling of Birmingham Rollers appears to have derived largely from show rollers—which are notable for a history of having received genetic infusions by way of outcrosses from other show breeds to enhance their physical "show" features. From reading the studies, it is difficult to know the effect of outcrossing on these determinant microsatellites. The Birmingham Roller as bred by most flying roller enthusiasts has been cultivated solely for its performing qualities over at least the last 130 years. Outcrossing upon other pigeon breeds is frowned upon by most experienced rollermen who are devoted to perpetuating the Birmingham Roller breed as it was handed down from its founders in Birmingham, England, and surrounding towns and villages. They view outcrossing for show features of thick, broad feathering, squatty stance, and overlarge heads as a departure from the elite athleticism of the breed.

Moreover, neither study was directly aimed at determining the direct ancestry of the Birmingham Roller. The roller ancestry observations of these studies are insightful but peripheral to the studies' principal conclusions. Future studies may clarify and refine these general conclusions of the Shapiro group with respect to Birmingham Rollers.

The type of the Birmingham Roller is dissimilar to either the long-faced or short-faced English Show Tumbler or even the versions of those tumblers from 150 years ago, artistically depicted in old English pigeon treatises. Instead, because the Birmingham Roller so closely resembles the Dutch Tumbler and the West of England Tumbler, some have speculated that the Birmingham Roller and the West of England Tumbler may have originated from some infusion of Dutch Tumbler blood, crossed upon the old English Flying Tumbler pigeon. In the earliest known western pigeon treatise, John Moore suggested in 1735:

A Tumbler is a very small Pigeon, short bodied, full breasted, thin neckt, spindle beakt, and a short button Head; and the *Irides* [irises] of the Eyes ought to be of a bright pearl Colour.

The Dutch Tumbler is much of the same make, but larger, often feather leg'd, and more jowlter-headed with a thin Flesh or Skin round the Eye, not unlike a very sheer Dragoon; some People don't esteem them on this Account, tho' I have known very good ones of the Dutch breed, not any Ways inferior to what they call the English.

Others have remarkt that they are apt to tumble too much, and lose Ground, that is, sink beneath the rest of the Flight [the kit], which is a very great Fault, but I have observ'd the same by the English, and am apt to believe that most of the extraordinary Feathers have been produc'd by mixing with the Dutch breed; for it is generally observ'd that the English Tumblers are chiefly black, blue, or white.[8]

Moore's suggestion that the English Flying Tumbler of his era likely benefitted from an infusion of Dutch Tumbler genes is somewhat strengthened by the known history of the English "Midlands" where the English Flying Tumbler and the Birmingham Roller originated. (The West of England tumbler originated around Bristol, England, 100 miles southwest of Birmingham.) During the 17th century, scores of Dutchmen and their families immigrated to Birmingham and the surrounding Midlands villages to establish breweries for a new Dutch beer which had become more popular than the traditional local ale. Could some of these Dutch brewers have immigrated with some of their favored livestock, including the Dutch Tumbler?

British Development

In any event, it is known and accepted that flying tumbler pigeons were common in England, particularly in the West Midland counties of Staffordshire and Worcestershire, for at least 200 years prior to 1900. Some of these were the slightly short-faced varieties pictured in the old treatises by John Moore (1735), J.C. Lyell (1887), Robert Fulton (1876), and Lewis Wright (1879). These English flying tumblers were usually described as single flippers and short workers, though descriptions of deeper workers increasingly appeared, particularly in the later 19th century. Similarly, it was not until the opening of the 20th century that "West of England" tumblers were even referred to by that name.

What is less commonly appreciated is that the term "roller" was generally reserved as a description of a pigeon's *performance*; until about 1900, "roller" was rarely used to describe a *breed* of pigeon distinct from the English flying tumbler. Although references to "Birmingham rollers" began appearing as early as 1870, those references were to pigeons that were known to *roll,* as distinguished from other varieties of performance. This usage could be compared to referring to a horse as a "jumper," irrespective of the breed of the horse. For example, "Of John's nine Arabian horses, two are good jumpers." In Birmingham and its surrounding Midland hamlets, all performing pigeons continued to be referred to as "flying tumblers" until the 1920s, when the Birmingham Roller finally became recognized as a breed distinct from the English flying tumbler.

The performances of the flying tumbler breed were distinguished by sometimes flowery descriptions. *Common tumblers* flipped and tumbled several somersaults. *Tipplers* did little more than flip over. Another performer, the *twizzler,* was described as a pigeon horizontally chasing its tail without actually turning over, so as to resemble a spinning plate. *Platers* or *plate rollers* were those that descended a considerable distance while twizzling. *Rollers* were those which turned rapid backward somersaults, head-over-tail, revolving so rapidly as to give the appearance of a closed-up, spinning ball, while descending several yards from the flock or "kit" of pigeons flying high over their home lofts.

While flying tumblers were bred in profusion throughout Britain in the 19th century, deep-spinning *rollers* appear to have been relatively unique to the districts surrounding Birmingham and Newcastle. So it was that in 1879, Lewis Wright wrote:

Of actual *tumbling* pigeons there are several varieties, even in performance, which are well understood and specially cultivated in some neighborhoods, particularly those of Newcastle and Birmingham. It is first to be understood that the "tumble" is a complete backward somersault in the air. *Tipplers* throw only one such at a time, but repeat such detached performances frequently during their flight. *Tumblers* often make two, three, or more backward revolutions without stopping; and lastly, there is the true Birmingham *Roller,* which turns over backwards with inconceivable rapidity through a considerable distance like a spinning ball.[9]

With the birth of the Industrial Revolution around 1760 in the West Midlands of England, thousands of Englishmen began to leave their employ as peasant farmers and animal keepers on the manorial estates of England. They moved to the "Black Country" to work in the burgeoning coal and iron ore mines, iron foundries, steel mills, and factories. The Black Country lay just west of Birmingham. It was so named because of the density of smoke and soot which belched from the district's smelters and industrial smokestacks. From 1800 to 1900, the population of Birmingham grew from 71,000 to more than 500,000 souls.

Nevertheless, the adage, "You can take the boy out of the farm, but you cannot take the farm out of the boy," held true. These miners and iron workers may have given up farming, but they didn't give up their love of livestock breeding. Numerous breeds of terrier dogs were founded by the rough men of the Black Country during this period, including most prominently the Staffordshire Pit Bull Terrier.

Other men bred flying tumbler pigeons; many were wont to wager their best pigeon's performing prowess against the quality of other men's tumblers in competitions. These competitions were hatched in each district's local public house, where industrial workers and miners resorted after work of an evening. In these pubs they consumed pints of the local ale and bragged about their champion tumbler and roller pigeons as they sat at tables, legs stretched out, feet resting on the floors strewn with sawdust to catch the spilled ale and any stray chewing tobacco which missed the spittoons.

Although many tumbler fanciers flew kits of pigeons that tumbled, twizzled, and plated, the "champion" of any kit was the pigeon which could perform an array of tumbling, twizzling, and plating, according to the actions of the other birds in the kit. But it was essential that the champion also be one found to roll deep and solid for many yards. The most highly prized pigeons were those whose velocity of roll or "spin" was the greatest and which had the capacity to roll varying distances, from one to ten yards or more, depending upon the height at which the kit was flying. Competitions were held frequently in the districts in and around Birmingham. A neutral judge was chosen to determine which fancier's champion could put up the best performance on the day. The competitor's champion would be flown with a small kit of tumblers, but only the champion was judged. Both the owners of these pigeons and their friends engaged in friendly wagering on the outcome of these contests.

In general, the best rollers were to be found in the less densely populated Midlands neighborhoods, particularly in the open, semi-industrial, semi-rural districts of the Black Country. Within the built-up neighborhoods of the city of Birmingham, the shorter-working tumblers came to be preferred, since they were less likely to meet with casualties when flying low over the tiled roofs of the tens of thousands of closely built row houses with small backyards shared in common by multiple dwellings. Stories have been told of fanciers who, having no proper loft in which to house their pigeons, kept kits of tumblers which trapped into wicker baskets for their food and water after flying. The birds in their baskets would then be stored in the owner's attic or cellar until the pigeons' next daily exercise.

Competitions among the best *individual* rollers of every district of the Midlands had been common during the 19th century. In 1921, the first organized flying tumbler society, the Perry Barr Club of Birmingham, initiated *kit* competitions. Each club member flew his kit of pigeons—20 for young birds, 25 for old birds—to be judged for twenty minutes. Scoring was based solely on "turns" or "breaks," without regard to quality, depth, or velocity of performance. Turns or breaks are when more than five of the kit members perform simultaneously. Well-trained kits can perform together each time they turn or change direction. The more birds tumbling, twizzling, or rolling together on each turn, the greater the number of points was awarded. One "full turn" in which all twenty of the kit members perform simultaneously, with no holdouts, would beat any number of quarter-turns, half-turns, or three-quarter turns. Flipping, twizzling, tumbling, plating, and rolling all were scored equally.

High-quality, deep-spinning rollers were at a disadvantage in these competitions because they performed less frequently and, when they did perform, they required more time to return to the kit than did the common tumblers and flippers. Any bird flying out of the kit prevented the kit from being scored until the errant bird returned. So the pigeons cultivated for these early kit competitions were short workers with a range of tumbling, twizzling, and plating contortions that would qualify for "turns" under these rules. Many fanciers of first class, deep-rolling pigeons gave them up for the short-working "competition tumblers" which were bred specially for these competitions.

By the 1930s, numerous clubs in the Birmingham area staged their own local flying kit competitions. The largest of these was the Harborne Roller Club, of Harborne, now a Birmingham suburb, some seven miles east from the borders of the Black Country. Harborne was residential in nature and not so densely populated as was Birmingham. About the same time, the Midland Roller Society was formed, which was an amalgamation of the various local clubs. The MRS staged annual competitions in which the best three kits of each local club were entered in a competition to declare which kit was the "Best of the Midlands."

Rollers in North America

The *ro* gene complex made its way to North America in the 1870s, on board the first flying tumblers/rollers exported from Birmingham and its surrounding Midland counties. It is believed that the first rollers arrived in Ontario, Canada, though because no records were kept of the first imports, no one knows for certain. These pigeons' popularity soon spread to the United States, particularly in New England and Ohio.

Many of the rollers found in Canada and the United States up until 1930 were referred to as of the "Whittingham" strain, a family of rollers cultivated by a fancier of that name in Wolverhampton, England, some 12 miles northwest of Birmingham. The Whittingham pigeons arrived in multiple shipments to Canada between about 1890 and 1915. J.V. McAree, a Toronto newspaper reporter and feature writer, imported many pigeons from Whittingham, beginning about 1901.

Whittingham himself sent the early exports to North America. When he passed away, his son took over and exported more pigeons. The Whittinghams were said to be proprietors of a

Wolverhampton pet shop, or "cage," where pigeon fanciers sold their surplus pigeons or pigeons they had strayed or lured in by catching them from neighboring flocks. The Whittingham family business was based on acquiring pigeons and reselling them to customers who wished to purchase them. The Whittinghams probably maintained a separate loft and flew their own tumblers and rollers for their personal enjoyment.

It is unknown today whether the Whittingham pigeons exported to McAree were a closely bred strain or whether they represented the diverse types of rollers and tumblers which the Whittinghams sold in their pet shop. It is likely that most of these pigeons were of reasonably high quality and genetically equipped to produce a percentage of acceptable rollers. The pigeons arriving on Canadian and United States shores appeared not to constitute a particularly uniform strain; pigeons from the Whittingham strain could be expected to breed a variety of performing types. To produce a uniform family of rollers from these, McAree and others selected the offspring exhibiting their standards of acceptable performance and bred these individuals together to produce more of their kind, selecting the best from each succeeding generation.

Most North Americans of this era selected their rollers for longtime high flying, with deep rolling repeated every three to five minutes. Accordingly, up until about 1930, virtually all rollers found in North America were bred to fly high and long, sometimes up to three or four hours at over 1,000 feet in height. They rolled exceptionally deep, 40 to 150 feet and more. By the 1920s, such rollers were to be found across North America. Roller shows also became popular by this time, and rollers began being bred for certain standards of type, conformation, and markings, in addition to performance qualities. The United Roller Club of America was founded in 1935 to promote both the flying and showing of rollers.

Mention should be made of the Rev. James E. Graham. Originally of Ontario, Canada, Graham became interested in McAree's Whittinghams during the late 1920s or early 1930s. He later purchased and imported other rollers on a visit to England. Based upon McAree's Whittinghams, Graham founded his own

strain of roller pigeon, which he called the "Fireball Strain."
Initially, they were mostly bull-eyed or odd-eyed badge- and saddle-
marked pigeons. Many were recessive red in plumage color. Over
the decades, Graham was posted to several church congregations
across the USA. At each new assignment, he brought his pigeons
with him. The "Fireballs" became increasingly popular in North
America until about 1950, when their popularity began to decline.

The Rise of the "Pensoms"

In 1932 a Catholic priest who loved pigeons imported Birmingham
Rollers from William H. Pensom, a 27-year-old roller fancier in
Harborne, England. Father Schlattmann, of St. Louis, imported
eight Birmingham Rollers from Pensom and began breeding and
flying kits of rollers that were the envy of all who saw them. Other
importations followed, and the good father shared his stock with
others.

The "Pensoms" ignited a craze among the American pigeon
fraternity. These new English imports represented the best of the
bloodlines of the most respected ten to twenty rollermen Pensom
had become acquainted with in his search for quality rollers
throughout Birmingham, Harborne, and the Black Country. The
Whittinghams and other preexisting Birmingham Rollers soon came
to be called "American" rollers to distinguish them from the new
English imports, which were called "Pensom rollers." These Black
Country rollers distinguished themselves from the traditional
American rollers by flying lower, usually 200 to 500 feet; by rolling
shorter, from five to ten yards; by rolling with impressive velocity;
and, when trained "English style," by staying aloft during their
flights for only 30 to 60 minutes.[10]

Little did Father Schlattman know that he had dropped a
snowball that would trigger an avalanche of change across the North
American roller pigeon hobby.

Despite the notoriety in America of the Whittingham strain that
originated in Wolverhampton—only 12 miles northwest from
Birmingham—Pensom claimed never to have heard of the
Whittingham family flying a noteworthy kit of rollers. Pensom

repeatedly declared that the highest-velocity spinning rollers all originated in the more southerly reaches of the Black Country some ten miles south of Wolverhampton and were developed to their impressive standard mostly after World War I. Pensom himself reported in 1968:

I am familiar with what went on in the flying tumbler fancy in and around Birmingham since 1900. With the exception of Bert Goode of Harborne, who is the last of the old rollermen to be alive, I am the last one left who can authenticate the situation. Whoever imported flying tumblers from England prior to the First World War from any source must have got all they wanted for three pence apiece. This is all they were worth.[11]

Soon after Schlattmann's first importations, other American fanciers imported additional pigeons from Pensom. These importers included two men, named Riches and Teesdale; J. Leroy Smith and Francis Buckley of New York; Raymond Perkins of Connecticut; Chandler Grover of New Jersey; Ciro Valenti of Missouri; and Al Walker of Michigan. Scores of other fanciers obtained Black Country stock from these original importers.

So taken were they with this new roller that these and many other fanciers combined to form the "Pensom Roller Club," devoted to retaining the family "purity" of this new strain of roller. This purity fad was ironic, since the pigeons Pensom exported, though mostly from his or Jim Skidmore's lofts, claimed parentage from a dozen different Midland roller strains. PRC rules forbade crossing the Pensoms onto any other strain of roller or housing the Pensoms together with any other strain. Pensom himself objected to the club's name; he recommended the designation "Black Country Roller Club." Pensom's wishes were ignored and he was made an honorary lifetime member of the PRC.

Pensom himself immigrated to the United States from England in 1950, taking up residence near Los Angeles, California. The "English style" of roller became so popular that, over a period of some thirty years, it overtook the old "American" rollers all across North America, with a few isolated exceptions. Showing of these Pensom rollers became common in the PRC and the United Roller

Club of America. By the early 1960s, some were breeding more for show qualities than for performance. Bob Evans, of San Mateo, California, always a staunch leader of the PRC, frequently preached that only proven, quality performers should be entered in shows. His pronouncements fell largely upon deaf ears; by 1970 the PRC became known more for showing rollers than for flying rollers.

A rift arose between Evans and Pensom in the early 1960s. When Pensom imported two pairs of Competition Flying Tumblers from his friend Ken Payne, of Harborne, Evans feigned outrage and demanded that Pensom dispose of these pigeons, insisting that Pensom's keeping them violated the PRC's "purity" credo. Pensom had no intention of crossing these "comps" with his real rollers; moreover, everyone knew that Pensom had long been breeding Show Tippler and Modena pigeons at his home, in addition to his rollers. Rather than bow to Evans's demands, around 1963 Pensom resigned his honorary lifetime membership in the roller club that bore his name.

Pensom immediately organized the National Birmingham Roller Club, which soon gained a strong following among the scores of rollermen more dedicated to the performing type than the show type of roller. Over time, the NBRC gradually discouraged the showing of rollers and promoted roller kit flying competitions. In time, new kit competition rules were crafted by two Boise, Idaho, roller fanciers, Brent Martindale and physics professor Richard Reimann, Ph.D. These new rules graded the "turns" against multipliers based on depth and quality of rolling. This encouraged the flying in competition of quality, high-velocity rollers, a quantum improvement over the old English rules of the 1920s.

Pensom died of a heart attack at his home in Canoga Park, California, on June 5, 1968. Today, some fifty years after his death, it is no exaggeration to suggest that virtually every first-class Birmingham Roller pigeon in existence in Europe, North America, Australia, and South Africa can trace some fraction of its pedigree back to pigeons originally hatched in Pensom's lofts. This remarkable achievement never will be duplicated.

The origins of the roller pigeon are shrouded in mystery and conjecture. We cannot know conclusively when or where the precious little *ro* gene complex that is the hallmark of the Birmingham Roller pigeon first mutated. What we do know is that this microscopic bundle of chemical genes is being preserved today by thousands of roller fanciers in Europe and on four continents throughout the English-speaking world. It is being preserved in pigeons which are selected and bred for their aerial athletic excellence, without regard to color or show standards. The club Pensom founded to promote the breed, the National Birmingham Roller Club, has boasted as many as 1,750 members in the United States and Canada. A great number of the club's members actively compete in flying competitions, scores of which are being held across North America on any given weekend, particularly in the fall of the year. An international roller competition organization, *The World Cup Roller Fly*, conducts similar competitions from March through June in North America, Europe, South Africa, and Australia.

There is probably a competition scheduled not far from where you live, in the coming weeks.

[1] Original version of this article was written upon request for the PIGEON DEBUT magazine in 2002. This material is used by the express written permission of Tom Monson. This material may not be copied or published elsewhere without the express written permission of the author.

[2] WENDELL M. LEVI, THE PIGEON, §47 (1941, 1963).

[3] *Id.,* §218.

[4] *Id.,* §231.

[5] JAMES C. LYELL, FANCY PIGEONS, 324 (1881).

[6] "Non-coding" means that, although this was indeed DNA from the chromosomes within the cells of the pigeons in question, it was not DNA containing genes that create new individuals through the joining of chromosomes in *meiosis*, leading to fertilized eggs and eventual embryos, nor could it lead to replicating new daughter cells through multiplication by *mitosis*, which is what a pigeon's body does as it grows, loses

feathers, skin cells, and the like, to be replaced by identical feathers, skin cells, and so on. Non-coding DNA is sometimes referred to as "junk DNA."

[7] Michael D. Shapiro, et al., *Divergence, Convergence, and the Ancestry of Feral Populations in the Domestic Rock Pigeon,* CURRENT BIOLOGY Vol. 22, No. 4, 302 (February 21, 2012). Michael D. Shapiro, et al., *Genomic Diversity and Evolution of the Head Crest in The Rock Pigeon,* SCIENCE Vol. 339, Issue 6123, 1063 (March 1, 2013).

[8] JOHN MOORE, *COLUMBARIUM:* OR, THE PIGEON-HOUSE, BEING AN INTRODUCTION TO A NATURAL HISTORY OF TAME PIGEONS, 39 (1735).

[9] LEWIS WRIGHT, THE PRACTICAL PIGEON KEEPER, 128 (1879).

[10] As described by FRANCIS J. BUCKLEY, *The Pensom Rollers—Why I Prefer Them to Other Types,* AMERICAN PIGEON JOURNAL, March-April, 1941.

[11] WILLIAM H. PENSOM, *Breeding the Birmingham Roller Pigeon,* AMERICAN PIGEON JOURNAL, May, 1968.

Last, I would like to thank my friends Roy Thayer, Mike Harris, Jack Shaw, and George Abner for loaning me birds to photograph; Josiah Whitley, Denise Conrad, Monya Gambill for some of their time-saving assistance; Gina Gilliland, Jamie Gilliland, and Judy Riggs for assisting in taking pictures; Tom Monson, Ben Novack, and Ken Easley for their written contributions; Gabe Glenn and Rebecca Hall for their review feedback; the Portsmouth Public Library and the librarians who assisted in the taking of the passenger pigeon picture for the book; and last but not least, my friend and publisher Jaime Vendera, for without his assistance this book would not have been possible.

This book is dedicated to Bill Berry, Dave Staebler, and Joe Roe for providing me with the knowledge and inspiration to excel with my great love, the Birmingham Roller pigeon.

Always remember to keep looking up.

—John W. Bender
Roller World Cup World Champion 1994

ABOUT THE AUTHOR

JOHN BENDER has been involved with pigeons for 50 years, having won several titles, including 2nd place in the 1992 All Ohio State Fly, 10th in the world cup finals and a first in the regionals in 1993, and the rolling pigeon world champion title in 1994 along with a second place in the regionals the same year. He also took 1st place for eight years in a row in his local Portsmouth, Ohio, flying competitions from 1987 to 1994, then again in 1996.

John is a seventh-degree black belt in martial arts, who has run his own martial arts school, Bender Karate Academy, for over 30 years. He has trained students for international karate competition and trained fighters for toughman competitions. He is also an Eastern USA International Black Belt Hall of Fame inductee.

In addition, John worked as a professional dog trainer for ten years, training dogs for obedience and guard work. He is currently writing a unique approach to his dog training methods.

Prior to writing *The Pigeon Trainer & The Birmingham Roller*, John became a collaborator with Ben Novak, the lead scientist for the Revive and Restore Project, which is dedicated to bringing back the extinct passenger pigeon.

John has also released various pigeon ledgers for record keeping. He will be writing a new book pertaining to the passenger pigeon project.

Learn more about John at JohnBenderAuthor.com.

www.ingramcontent.com/pod-product-compliance
Lightning Source LLC
Chambersburg PA
CBHW050804270326
41926CB00025B/4531